# A
# Ghetto Grows
# in Brooklyn

The publication of this work
has been aided by a grant from
the Andrew W. Mellon Foundation

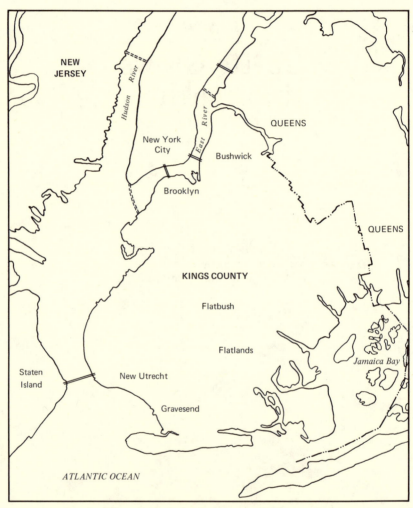

Map 1. The six original towns of Kings County.

# A
# Ghetto Grows
# in Brooklyn

*Harold X. Connolly*

New York • New York University Press • 1977

Library of Congress Cataloging in Publication Data

Connolly, Harold X
   A ghetto grows in Brooklyn.

   Includes bibliographical references and index.
   1.   Afro-Americans—New York (State)—Brooklyn—
History.  2. Brooklyn—History.  I. Title.
F129.B7C75        974.7′23′00496073        77-2471
ISBN 0-8147-1371-8

Manufactured in the United States of America

*To*
Barbara,
Keara,
Kristin,
Melissa,
Caitlin

# Contents

# Maps

# Acknowledgments

Just as no man is an island, no book is the product of a single person. Many individuals and institutions have contributed to the making of this book. Any book that requires extensive historical research involves libraries, their collections, and their librarians. Most especially I must extend my thanks to the Long Island Historical Society and its Executive Director, James Hurley; to the Schomburg Collection of the New York Public Library; and to the Brooklyn Public Library. Many persons have offered constructive suggestions, but I would like to single out Professor David Reimers of New York University who has encouraged me from the beginning of this lengthy research endeavor. Catherine P. Geary scrupulously proofread every word of the manuscript at least twice. Many fingers, including those of Ingrid Baccialon, Sandy Dyson, and Curtis Graves typed the various drafts of the manuscript as it wended its way toward publication. Finally, my family has been forced to endure occasional lost weekends, delayed home repairs, a dining room table piled high with books and papers, and other such aggravations.

# Introduction

Instead of *A Ghetto Grows in Brooklyn*, this book might with equal appropriateness have been entitled *The Anonymous Ghetto* or *New York's Other Ghetto*. In an historical sense, blacks in Brooklyn have long suffered from a triple disability, any element of which alone would have been sufficient to produce a certain obscurity, but which taken in conjunction rendered its victims almost invisible. First and obviously, there was their blackness: historically, blacks have never merited more than passing attention from the white world that, coincidentally, controlled the pathways of communication. Second, blacks were endemically poor, and lower-status persons, white or black, are unlikely to be written about or to write and preserve records themselves.

A final factor assured their invisibility—these poor black people resided in Brooklyn. Even before its integration into New York City in 1898, Brooklyn had been plagued by an undeserved anonymity relative to its more prestigious neighbor across the East River. After being stripped of its independent identity by the merger, Brooklyn seemed to exist in the popular mind only as the home of that peculiar (in fact nonexistent) Brooklynese dialect and of the Brooklyn Dodgers. Even the Negro press, which might have been expected to remedy the white press's neglect of blacks, was Manhattan-based and devoted but a page or two to news from "overseas."

This book is, therefore, about second-class citizens of the United States residing in a secondary borough of New York City. The classic studies about blacks in New York rarely recalled that blacks did live in Brooklyn and that Brooklyn was indeed a part of the city, at least since 1898. Such blacks might just as well have lived in Newark or Philadelphia or Buffalo for all the notice they received—at best a footnote or passing reference.

In recent years this neglect has been at least partially rectified. "Bedford-Stuyvesant" is probably now a generally recognized racial and geographic term west of the Hudson River, although it still lacks the connotative impact of "Harlem" or "Watts." The Bedford-Stuyvesant, Brownsville, and East New York sections of Brooklyn all experienced racial disturbances during the 1960s, but not remotely on the scale of the urban riots in Watts or Detroit or Newark or Washington. John Lindsay walked the streets of black Brooklyn as well as Harlem, but he is no longer mayor. The symbol of ultimate urban desolation is no longer Brownsville but the South Bronx. The nation's largest community development corporation and community action program are both Bedford-Stuyvesant institutions, but does anyone care anymore?

The current recognition accorded black Brooklyn is due, I believe, mainly to a single individual. It is not an exaggeration to suggest that the fiery, flamboyant, outspoken Shirley Chisholm made the nation aware of Bedford-Stuyvesant, not deliberately perhaps, but through the need for others to identify her. Virtually unknown beyond the borders of Bedford-Stuyvesant and the assembly corridors of Albany before her election to Congress in 1968, she became with stunning rapidity a national figure, even campaigning for the 1972 Democratic presidential nomination.

But she was elected to Congress less than a decade ago;

blacks have resided in Kings County for more than 300 years. The history of blacks in Brooklyn certainly deserves to be rescued from obscurity. A distinguished assortment of blacks have made Brooklyn their home, and they merit attention. More recently, black Brooklyn has evolved into the largest black community in New York City, far surpassing Manhattan in the 1970 census. Indeed, some have claimed that the Greater Bedford-Stuyvesant ghetto is the most populous black community in the country. Whether this honor belongs to South Side Chicago or Brooklyn is somewhat irrelevant; what is important is the emergence of Bedford-Stuyvesant and its environs as a major center of black population.

The story of blacks in Brooklyn is of course unique, but it is also generic. In 1950 Ralph Foster Weld authored a popular history entitled *Brooklyn Is America*. His basic premise can be extended to this present work: *Black Brooklyn Is Black America*, or certainly northern, urban black America, a place where some 10 million black people currently live. What can the history of Brooklyn teach us about the process of ghettoization? What, if anything, could have prevented the creation of some of these demographic and socioeconomic tragedies that litter America's urban landscape? In what directions can we expect the Brooklyns and Bedford-Stuyvesants of this country to evolve? The answers are still being determined.

While other histories of specific black ghetto communities have usually focused upon rather restricted time periods, I have extended the story of Brooklyn and Bedford-Stuyvesant into what Du Bois called the "present past." In traversing a broader time-frame, this work combines an essentially historical approach with a contemporary public-policy perspective, encompassing slavery and emancipation, migration and institution-building, the "war on poverty" and bitter school-desegregation confrontations. This book certainly does not exhaust the possible explorations of the history of black Brooklyn—it is impossible to encompass in one book some 300 years of black history. The story must begin somewhere, however, so let it be here and now.

# List of Acronyms

| | |
|---|---|
| ALP | American Labor Party |
| AME | African Methodist Episcopal |
| AT&T | American Telephone and Telegraph |
| AWME | African Wesleyan Methodist Episcopal |
| BLEDCO | Brooklyn Local Economic Development Corporation |
| CBCC | Central Brooklyn Coordinating Council |
| CDC | Community Development Corporation |
| CORE | Congress of Racial Equality |
| NAACP | National Association for the Advancement of Colored People |
| OEO | Office of Economic Opportunity |
| PAL | Police Athletic League |
| PR | Proportional Representation |

# PART I

# Background: 1640-1900

CHAPTER 1

# Slavery and Emancipation:
# 1640-1870

## COLONIAL BACKGROUND

Blacks have resided in that part of Long Island currently known as Brooklyn, or Kings County, since the area's early settlements in the seventeenth century. As Kings County evolved during the seventeenth century, it came to be composed of six towns—Brooklyn, Bushwick, Flatbush, Flatlands, Gravesend, and New Utrecht. On August 1, 1639 Anthony Jansen von Salee, "an African who had been a pirate," received from Director-General Willem Kieft of New Netherland a lease for 200 acres of land for ten years in the village of Gravesend. Jansen's (or Johnson's) precise racial character, however, seems debatable. References identify him as an "African" or a "Turk" but fail to mention his color—a feature, one suspects, that would have been noted had he been black. The maritime experience and piratical traditions of the North African littoral, moreover, add credence to the suspicion that

3

Jansen was from that part of the continent rather than from black Africa.[1]

More precise identification of the first known free black in Kings County is contained in a 1660 application for town privileges from twenty-three residents of Boswyck, or Bushwick. Among the petitioners and subsequent patentees of this town was one Francisco the Negro, undoubtedly a free man who owned property and was considered the peer of his fellow patentees. It seems likely that this Francisco was synonymous with another Francisco the Negro who was manumitted by the Dutch West India Company in 1643.[2] Whatever the historical truth concerning these individual cases, however, they seem almost irrelevant to the history of blacks in Kings County in colonial times. Jansen and Francisco may have been free and black, but that status was reserved for an exceptional few; most Negroes remained anonymous and enslaved. The first comprehensive census of the province of New York, taken in 1698, enumerated no free blacks in Kings County, but counted 296 slaves who constituted 15 percent of the county's 2,017 residents. Over 40 percent of the county's freeholders owned at least one slave. Most such families held only one or two slaves, although a few slaveholders did own five or more. These statistics indicate the existence of a pervasive system of slaveholding in Kings County in 1698, a system not of recent vintage.[3]

Throughout the New York province during the first half of the eighteenth century, slaves increased more rapidly than did the white population. Nowhere was this more evident than in the "Long Island townships of Flatbush, Flatlands, Gravesend, New Utrecht, Brookland and Bushwick" where "slavery made steady progress." By 1738 Kings County had become proportionately the heaviest slaveholding county in the province, a distinction it retained for most of the remaining lifespan of slavery in New York. By midcentury, one-third of the area's total population was black. This rising black population was due as much to white demographic stagnation as to steady black expansion during the eighteenth century. Not until after 1750 did whites permanently exceed their 1698 total and achieve a steady rate of increase. Such sluggish growth contrasted markedly with every other county in the province, including the other counties on Long Island. Even with the steady white growth after 1750, blacks maintained relative parity, increasing at approximately the same rate as whites. Thus in 1790, blacks still constituted more than one-third of the population of Kings County.[4]

Not only did Kings County in 1790 contain a greater proportion of blacks in its population than any other county in New York State; it was also the state's "slaveholding capital." Approximately one-fifth of the state's black population had achieved freedom by 1790, but only forty-six free blacks lived in Kings County, contrasted with 1,482 slaves. This represented the smallest percentage of free blacks (3 percent) in any county in New York State. Over 60 percent of the white families residing in the county were slaveholders, owning an average of 4.5 slaves per family, both figures being the highest in the state. In New York City, by contrast, 1,078 of the city's total of 3,262 blacks (33 percent) were free, and slaveholding extended to only 18 percent of freeholders, who owned an average of 2.0 slaves. Thus, in the near-century since the first census of 1698, slaveholding in Kings County had become both more broadly disseminated and more intensively utilized.[5]

Both the economic base and ethnic composition of Kings County seem to have contributed to this extensive reliance upon slave labor. Throughout the eighteenth century the area's economy depended primarily upon agricultural production. No local town of any consequence developed to attract excess labor or compete with agriculture for land use. As the comparative development of New York and Kings Counties indicates, slave labor and farming seemed somewhat more compatible than slavery and an urban life-style and economy. In other nearby agricultural counties, however, slavery was less prominent than in Kings County. In Queens and Suffolk Counties on Long Island, 26 percent and 51 percent of blacks respectively were free in 1790; on Staten Island 14 percent of blacks were free and in Westchester County 20 percent were.[6] Ethnically, Kings County remained more Dutch than any other county. To one observer who visited the area during the Revolution, the residents seemed to be "almost entirely Dutch," and continued "to make use of their customs and language in preference to English, which however they also understand." Members of this ethnic group constituted the most likely slaveholders in New York State. Linking the economic and ethnic factors was a distinct tendency toward more extensive landholding, which was more amenable to the utilization of slaves, where Dutch settlers predominated. It does not seem entirely coincidental that the other area of widespread slaveholding during the late eighteenth and early nineteenth centuries were some of the Hudson River counties, where the patroon system had been early established and still persisted.[7] A disproportionate degree of slaveholding remained the pattern in Kings County. In 1820, only seven years before mandatory emancipation in New York State, half of Kings County's blacks still remained slaves. Indeed, the number of slaves in Kings County actually exceeded that in Manhattan, although New York City blacks greatly outnumbered Kings County blacks.[8]

## NINETEENTH-CENTURY GROWTH

The history of Kings County in the nineteenth century is the story of Brooklyn's growth from a village of 2,378 in 1800 to the third largest city in the United States at the time of the Civil War. (Brooklyn held this rank until 1898 when it ceased to exist as an independent entity.) During this period Brooklyn came to dominate Kings County and to absorb the other communities that had originally formed the bulk of the county.[9]

No town of significance had emerged in Kings County during the eighteenth century; yet, in retrospect, one could glimpse in the small village sprouting near the ferry that linked Long Island with New York City in the 1790s the nucleus of a future population center. In 1794 a French traveler described a Brooklyn village of "about one hundred houses, most of them only one story high ... most are chiefly along the shore or scattered without regular plan." Yet even then, at least during the summer, Brooklyn served as a suburban residence for wealthy New Yorkers who lived there "during the hot season" and commuted "to New York in the morning, and returned to Brooklyn after the Stock Exchange closed." Furthermore, the convergence at the ferry of roads from the outlying towns of Kings County and Long Island placed the germinating village at a vital link in the local communication and transportation system. Between 1790 and 1810 Brooklyn's population increased impressively from 1,656 to 4,400. The introduction of steam ferries on the East River in 1814 tied Brooklyn's fate and future more closely to that of the most dynamic city in the country. New York had recently surpassed Philadelphia as the largest American city, and the opening of the Erie Canal in 1824 further cemented this primacy. The steam ferry, which made crossing the East River less hazardous and uncertain, accelerated Brooklyn's growth as bedroom and workshop.

Brooklyn's black population participated in this nineteenth-century growth, expanding steadily from 641 in 1800 to 1,253 in 1830 and approximately 5,000 in 1870. Spurred especially by immigration from Ireland and Germany, Brooklyn's total population simultaneously exploded from 2,378 to nearly 400,000. As a result of this enormous increase in whites, the actual proportion of blacks in the total Brooklyn population declined precipitously from 27 percent in 1800 to 4.6 percent in 1840 and to less than 2 percent in 1860. Not until 1930 did this percentage again exceed 2 percent.[10]

During this period no single black ghetto emerged to encompass the majority of blacks in Brooklyn, although concentrated settlements of Negroes certainly did exist. In 1830, Brooklyn's Fourth Ward housed approximately one-third of the total black population, but the other two-thirds were diffused throughout the other four wards and the outlying areas of Bedford, Gowanus, Red Hook, and Wallabout. In 1860 Brooklyn blacks still lived scattered about, with concentrations in the downtown and Fort Greene (Washington) Park areas and in a section of the recently annexed Williamsburg. Georgraphically, the most distinct, if not the largest, local black communities during this period developed in the semi-rural expanses of the Ninth Ward, far removed from the Negroes in downtown Brooklyn. Known as Weeksville and Carrsville and named for local blacks, they were situated in what is now a part of Bedford-Stuyvesant. They dated from about the 1830s and were publicly acknowledged neighborhoods by the 1840s at the latest. An 1841 Tax Roll for the City of Brooklyn identified these separate settlements by name, describing the forty black families living there as "Colored people." The area maintained its distinct identity for about another twenty years. Recalling the area as it had existed in 1850, one white observed, "Not a single white person [lived] among them except those who kept stores and got rich off them by selling them liquor." During the New York draft riot of 1863, many blacks, driven from downtown Brooklyn and New York City, fled to the Weeksville-Carrsville area for shelter. As Brooklyn expanded, however, "whites kept buying property and getting nearer and nearer to the darkies." Thus, although blacks continued to reside in Weeksville and other parts of the Ninth Ward in 1870, the area had lost its distinctive black character.[11]

Most blacks (and whites for that matter too) in antebellum Brooklyn earned their living by the sweat of their brows, engaged in various types of manual labor. Many blacks maintained a semisubstantial place in local economic life. According to the 1850 census, they performed skilled and semiskilled work as barbers, tailors, carpenters, painters, butchers, shoemakers, coopers, and ropemakers, as well as holding employment as domestic servants, waiters, and sailors. A smattering attained professional and white-collar positions as clergymen, clerks, teachers, and physicians. William Wilson, a militant and principal of the local "colored" school, noted the existence in 1854 of "polished colored circles" in Brooklyn. Samuel Scottron, a longtime black resident of Brooklyn, recalled a time of Negro economic opportunity during the 1860s when the Greenpoint and South Brooklyn sections "swarmed with colored craftsmen" employed in maritime trades. It was a "common thing" for blacks to engage in business without fear of intimidation or prejudice.[12]

The 1870 census confirmed the continued presence among Brooklyn blacks of a small group of white-collar workers as well as substantial numbers of waiters, coachmen, sailors, and various skilled tradesmen, especially barbers, carpenters, and masons. Most blacks, however, did not fit this more secure occupational mold but were concentrated in work of a "general meniality." The most common descriptive category for blacks in 1850 was that of laborer. Such menial, heavy, or dangerous occupations as laborer, porter, whitewasher, hostler, and cartman predominated in 1870. The spectrum of employment opportunities for black women was limited to such traditionally Negro, female, and menial positions as washerwoman, dressmaker, seamstress, and domestic servant. However, Brooklyn blacks at this time were probably better off relative to whites than in 1900; by that time many of the skilled and semiskilled positions were taken over by immigrants and their offspring. While a large black "upper-class" group might have emerged later, the economic fate of most blacks remained heavy, menial, and dangerous occupations.[13]

## BLACK INSTITUTIONAL BEGINNINGS

Slavery may have been extinguished in New York State in 1827, but prejudice survived. Even in integrated or black-oriented organizations, whites either excluded blacks or were unwilling to treat them as equals. As a consequence of such neglect and the frustrations thereby generated, blacks in Brooklyn and elsewhere erected a substantial network of separate, black-controlled institutions around which to focus their religious, social, and even educational existence. The first institution to undergo racial division in Brooklyn was the church. In 1798, the congregation of the Sands Street Methodist Church was interracial, consisting of fifty whites and twenty-six Negroes. By 1812 black parishioners were seriously discussing the possibility of forming their own church. The proslavery bias of Alexander McCaine, the church's pastor, added impetus to their determination. The first major step to independency was the formation in 1817 of a society to raise the necessary funds. Money was secured, property purchased on High Street in downtown Brooklyn, and a small building constructed. The incorporation of the new institution, the High Street African Wesleyan Methodist Episcopal (AWME) Church, was completed on February 7, 1818, with Peter Croger, Benjamin Croger, Israel Jamison, John E. Jackson, and Caesar Springfield constituting the board of trustees. Only a handful of blacks remained in the white parent church after this time.[14]

By midcentury, three additional permanent, black, religious institutions had been established. Rev. James A. Gloucester, a descendant of Rev. John Gloucester, the founder of Presbyterianism among Philadelphia Negroes, initiated a mission for blacks in 1847 on lower Fulton Street. This work prospered and achieved permanence with the establishment of Siloam Presbyterian Church in 1849 with William J. Wilson, John Still, and Henry Staughtenburg as the first elders. Subsequently, a permanent site and building were purchased at 160 Prince Street. In 1847 Elder Samuel White was called from the Abyssinian Baptist Church in New York City to organize the Concord Baptist Church. In the Weeksville area the Bethel African Methodist Episcopal (AME) Church was incorporated in 1849 with James Moody, Henry Wright, William Gray, Michael Ward, Samuel Bowman, John J. Brown, and Anderson Thompson as trustees. Meanwhile, the High Street AWME Church, having attained a membership of 292 by midcentury and outgrown its original structure, bought the white First Congregational Church on Bridge Street as a new house of worship.[15]

In addition to these religious institutions, blacks established social and mutual benefit organizations at least as early as the 1820s. The Brooklyn African Woolman Benevolent Society, named for the eighteenth-century Quaker abolitionist John Woolman, functioned as both a mutual aid society and as a benefactor of black education. The Brooklyn African Tompkins Association, which had been active since 1827, was officially incorporated in 1845 for the stated purposes of assisting "indigent widows and orphans of former members" and fostering the "improvement of the members in morals and literature, by forming a library and other appropriate means." Prominent blacks founded Widow's Son Lodge of the Prince Hall Masons in 1849 and held meetings in the downtown section at 178 Prince Street. One should also note the claim that the first black magazine produced in the United States—the *African Methodist Episcopal Church Magazine*—was published in Brooklyn in the 1840s under the editorship of George Hogarth, a prominent local black.[16]

Brooklyn blacks also showed a persistent regard for the education of their children. The earliest local black school dated from at least 1815 when Peter Croger advertised in the local press that he was conducting an "African school" at his house. Brooklyn early established a public school, and by 1817 blacks and whites attended the same school, although in separate rooms. Not only did black children attend the school but they were taught by a black teacher, William M. Read, a most unusual phenomenon in New York State at the time. Elsewhere, in New York City for example, this function was performed by a white person. During the 1820s the blacks were driven from the building, but their zeal for education persisted, and they had constructed their own building by 1827. While the school received some public monies and was considered a public school, it also relied upon tuition payments and black institutional support, especially that of the African Woolman Benevolent Society. The "managers" of this "African Public School" in 1831-32 were Henry C. Thompson, a manufacturer of boot blacking, and Abraham Brown and Michael Thompson, both laborers; all were black. This pattern of black management apparently continued through the early 1840s, at which time all the "trustees" of the "African Public School No. 1," who were elected by the all-white common council, remained black. They included George Hogarth, a former teacher and present official in the AME church; Henry

Brown, a laborer and former mustard manufacturer and activist in the Negro Convention movement; and Sylvanus Smith, a hog driver or pork merchant.[17]

After 1843 black management ceased, but between 1815 and 1843 Brooklyn blacks had the unique distinction in New York State, and perhaps in the North, of retaining direct responsibility for the education of their children through the selection of teachers, the maintenance of the building, and financial support. Why this arrangement ended is not entirely clear. Competent blacks certainly continued to reside in Brooklyn. Local racism, manifested for example in the rejection of an 1846 referendum to grant blacks equal voting rights in New York State, was certainly prevalent in Brooklyn in the 1840s, but racism and paternalism were common in the earlier period too. A clue may be found in the declining proportion of blacks in the total population. In 1815 blacks constituted some 15 percent of Brooklyn's population, but by the early 1840s this figure had declined to less than 5 percent. Even after control of the school passed from black hands, the roster of Brooklyn's black teachers included some of the leading local militants of the period. Among their ranks were George Hogarth, William J. Wilson, and Junius C. Morrell, all participants in the National Negro Convention movement. Probably the most outspoken was Wilson, who wrote for Frederick Douglass's paper and the *Anglo-African;* he defended John Brown and recommended black knowledge of military tactics as essential for self-defense. A fellow protester and Brooklynite, Dr. James McCune Smith, observed that Wilson "as a thinker and writer ... has few equals and no superiors among our people." [18]

Nor were Brooklyn blacks reticent to express their opposition to white indifference, hositility, or even paternalism. When the white and prestigious local branch of the American Colonization Society recommended in 1831 the transportation of free, consenting Negroes to Africa, a "numerous and respectable" group of blacks responded by condemning the aims of the society as "wholly gratuitous, not called for by us and not essential to the real welfare of our race." Spiritedly, they added, "we know of no other country that we can justly claim, or demand our rights as citizens ... but in these United States of America, our native soil," A local committee of blacks headed by Henry C. Thompson, James Pennington, and George Woods was formed to draft a reply. The resulting document maintained that the colonization movement actually increased prejudice against blacks and placed a stigma upon them. Rather caustically, these literate blacks asked their self-appointed white benefactors what they were doing in Brooklyn "to improve our condition?"

> In our village and its vicinity, how many of us have been educated in colleges, and advanced into different branches of business; or taken into merchant houses, manufacturing establishments, etc.? Are we not even prohibited from some of the common labor, and drudgery of the streets, such as cartmen, porters, etc.? It is a strange theory to us, how these gentlemen can promise to honor, and respect us in Africa, when they are using every effort to exclude us from all rights and privileges at home.

Eloquently they appealed to their own American citizenship, their enforced contribution to the country's economy, and especially the Christian God as the fundamental reasons why whites should abandon their prejudices.[19]

A later black organization, the Colored Political Association of the City of Brooklyn and Kings County, was described in 1855 as:

> An association of colored property holders in Kings County, formed for the purpose of consolidating their political power as voters, and bringing that power to bear on each political contest in such a way as shall best serve their interest in tending to bring them just and equal rights as *native born* Americans, and conduce to the cause of true democratic freedom, without partiality and without hypocrisy.

Among its officers were such prominent blacks as Rev. Amos N. Freeman of Siloam Presbyterian Church, who had been elected moderator of the Brooklyn Presbytery in 1854, a notable recognition, and Dr. Peter W. Ray, physician and pharmacist. Prior to each election this group examined the political views of the various candidates to ascertain who should receive their support. In 1855 it unsuccessfully petitioned the state legislature "to provide for an amendment . . ., which will place the Elective Franchise within the reach of all citizens, without regard to complexion." [20]

In addition to such local protest activities, Brooklyn blacks regularly attended most of the irregularly scheduled National Negro Conventions between 1830 and 1864. Rev. J. W. C. Pennington's association with these antislavery meetings spanned the entire period, although he was not always a Brooklyn delegate. Other prominent Brooklynites who supported the movement were businessman Henry C. Thompson; schoolteachers William J. Wilson and Junius C. Morrell; physicians James McCune Smith and Peter W. Ray; Rev. Amos N. Freeman; John Still, a conductor on the Underground Railroad, and J. Sella Martin.

In the political arena such protestations availed Brooklyn blacks but little. The New York State Constitution of 1821 had imposed a property qualification upon the black franchise while removing this limitation from white voters.[21] In 1846 and again in 1860, the white voters of Kings County, and New York State, overwhelmingly rejected referenda designed to remove the property stipulation for Negro suffrage. In urging rejection of the liberalization of the Negro franchise prior to the 1860 vote, State Assemblyman Theophilus C. Callicot of Brooklyn argued:

> Sir, the proposition to put negroes on a footing of political equality with white men is repugnant to the sense of the American people. They will never consent to share the proud title of "American citizen" with an inferior and abject race; nor will the people of New York consent that that race shall participate on equal terms in the sov-

ereignty of the Empire State. Many believe that our Constitution is even now too indulgent when it allows the few negroes possessed of freehold estate of the value of $250 to vote. That had, however, been the constitutional law of New York nearly forty years—it was designed to promote industry, economy and thriftiness among the colored race, and for that reason, although anomalous, it has been acquiesced in, if not universally approved,—but I venture to predict that this sweeping alteration which proposed at one blow to open the ballot box to the negro as freely as to the white man, will be rejected with indignation and scorn whenever submitted to the voice of the people.

Furthermore, warned Callicot, the granting of such freedom to Negroes would "invite hordes of blacks to pour into this state and compete with white labor." [22]

The early story of blacks in Kings County is sketchy and much research remains to be done. To the degree that there is clarity, the picture is mixed. Slavery was the predictable lot of blacks during the colonial period. During the antebellum period they lost their demographic prominence as Brooklyn, and many other cities, became distinctly foreign in character. Most blacks lived on the margin of poverty; racial prejudice persisted. But prominent local blacks did emerge to teach and protest and organize and create an institutional structure that was essentially separate from white life. Their presence was scarcely universally applauded by local whites, but blacks did form a permanent element in Brooklyn life.

## NOTES

1. E. A. Custer, *A Synoptical History of the Towns of Kings County from 1525 to Modern Times* (New York, 188?), pp. 11-12; Henry Onderdonk, Jr., *Suffolk and Kings Counties in Olden Times* (Jamaica, N.Y., 1866), unpaged; Rev. A. P. Stockwell, *A History of the Town of Gravesend, N.Y.* (Brooklyn, 1884), p. 3.

2. Henry R. Stiles, *A History of the Town of Bushwick, Kings*

*County, New York* (Brooklyn, 1884), pp. 8-9; Ralph Foster Weld, *Brooklyn Is America* (New York, 1950), p. 154; correspondence with Robert Swan.

3. E. B. O'Callaghan, arranger, *A Documentary History of the State of New York* (4 vols.; Albany, 1850), 3: 87-89. See Edgar J. McManus, *A History of Negro Slavery in New York* (Syracuse, 1966) for a complete study of this specific topic; Helen Wortis, "Blacks on Long Island; Population Growth in the Colonial Period," *The Journal of Long Island History* 11 (Autumn 1974): 35-46.

4. United States Census Bureau, *A Century of Population Growth from the First Census of the United States to the Twelfth, 1790-1900* (Washington, 1909), pp. 170-83; Henry R. Stiles, *A History of the City of Brooklyn, the Town of Bushwick, and the Village and City of Williamsburgh* (3 vols.; Brooklyn, 1867), 1: 232; O'Callaghan, *Documentary History*, 4: 120, McManus, *Negro Slavery*, p. 42.

The population of Kings County at the irregularly conducted censuses of this period was:

| Year | Total Population | White Population | Negro Population | Percentage Negro |
|------|------|------|------|------|
| 1698 | 2,017 | 1,721 | 296 | 15 |
| 1703 | 1,912 | 1,569 | 343 | 18 |
| 1723 | 2,218 | 1,774 | 444 | 20 |
| 1731 | 2,150 | 1,658 | 492 | 23 |
| 1737 | 2,348 | 1,784 | 564 | 24 |
| 1746 | 2,331 | 1,686 | 645 | 28 |
| 1749 | 2,283 | 1,500 | 783 | 34 |
| 1756 | 2,707 | 1,862 | 845 | 31 |
| 1771 | 3,623 | 2,461 | 1,162 | 32 |
| 1786 | 3,986 | 2,669 | 1,317 | 33 |
| 1790 | 4,549 | 3,021 | 1,528 | 34 |
| 1800 | 5,720 | 3,909 | 1,811 | 32 |

5. Census Bureau, *A Century of Population Growth*, pp. 194, 282; United States Census Bureau, *First Census, 1790* (manuscript). Microfilm copies of the federal census manuscripts for the censuses from 1790 to 1870 are available at the New York Public Library.

6. Census Bureau, *A Century of Population Growth*, pp. 194-95.

7. Ibid., pp. 272, 275; Weld, *Brooklyn Is America*, p. 157. The Dutch constituted 16 percent of New York State's white population in 1790 but 46 percent of the white residents of Kings County, the highest percentage of any county in the state. Thirty percent of the Dutch families in New York State in 1790 owned slaves contrasted to 11 percent of English and Welsh families and 9 percent of Scottish.

8. United States Census Bureau, *Fourth Census, 1820* (Man-

uscript). By 1820 there had developed a divergence in the status of blacks living in Brooklyn and those living in the outlying towns. Over three-fourths (657) of Brooklyn's total black population (847) was free. Conversely, three-quarters (689) of the Negroes (914) in the rest of Kings County were still slaves. The 879 slaves in relatively small (7,175) Kings County outnumbered the number of slaves (518) in populous (123,706) New York City. (Ira Rosenwaike, *Population History of New York City* [Syracuse, 1972], p. 18).

9. The addition of Williamsburg and Bushwick to Brooklyn in 1855 catapulated Brooklyn from seventh to third largest city in the country. The outlying towns of Kings County were absorbed toward the end of the century-New Lots in 1886; Flatbush, Gravesend, and New Utrecht in 1894; and Flatlands in 1896.

10. Population statistics for Brooklyn from 1790 to 1840 are derived from the manuscript census returns. Data for 1850 to 1870 are drawn from the United States Census Bureau, *Ninth Census, 1870, Population*, p. 211; Wortis, "Blacks on Long Island," pp. 41-42. The decennial population figures for Brooklyn between 1800 and 1870 were:

| Year | Total Population | Negro Population | Percentage Negro |
|------|------|------|------|
| 1800 | 2,378 | 641 | 27 |
| 1810 | 4,402 | 668 | 15 |
| 1820 | 7,175 | 847 | 12 |
| 1830 | 15,391 | 1,253 | 8 |
| 1840 | 36,233 | 1,772 | 5 |
| 1850 | 96,838 | 2,424 | 3 |
| 1860 | 266,661 | 4,313 | 1.5 |
| 1870 | 396,099 | 4,931 | 1.2 |

For Kings County the numbers were:

| Year | Total Population | Negro Population | Percentage Negro |
|------|------|------|------|
| 1800 | 5,720 | 1,811 | 32 |
| 1810 | 8,303 | 1,853 | 22 |
| 1820 | 11,187 | 1,761 | 16 |
| 1830 | 20,535 | 2,007 | 10 |
| 1840 | 47,613 | 2,846 | 6 |
| 1850 | 138,882 | 4,065 | 3 |
| 1860 | 279,122 | 4,999 | 1.8 |
| 1870 | 419,921 | 5,653 | 1.3 |

11. "Tax Roll for the Ninth Ward, 1841"; *Brooklyn Daily Eagle*, Aug. 14, 1875. The Tax Roll is a stray manuscript available at the Long Island Historical Society. James M. McPherson, introduction, *Anti-Negro Riots in the North, 1863* (New York, 1969), pp. 7, 30-31. See also the manuscript works of Robert Swan: "Welcome to Weeksville: An Historic Reconstruction of the Past" (1971); "Weeksville: The Macroscopic Study of a Microscopic Community" (1971); "Carrville: The Other Black Settlement in Brooklyn" (1977).

12. United States Census Bureau, *Seventh Census, 1850* (manuscript); Samuel R. Scottron, "The Industrial and Professional Pursuits of the Colored People of Old New York," *The Colored American Magazine*, 13 (October 1907): 265; *New York Age*, Oct. 19, 1905; Robert Swan, "The Brooklyn Directories: Stochastic History," *The Journal of Long Island History* 11 (Spring 1975): 42.

13. Census Bureau, *Ninth Census, 1870* (manuscript). These 1870 employment figures are selective rather than complete. They are derived from the five wards with the largest black population—the Fourth, Ninth, Eleventh, Sixteenth, and Twenty-first Wards. Within this study area there were 848 male and 341 female workers.

14. Rev. Edwin Warriner, *Old Sands Street Methodist Episcopal Church of Brooklyn* (New York, 1885), pp. 13, 15, 21, 22; Bridge Street AWME Church, *Centennial Anniversary Celebration* (Brooklyn, 1918), pp. 11, 17; W. E. H. Chase, "History of Bridge Street A.M.E. Church Brooklyn, N.Y.," *The Colored American Magazine* 7 (November 1904): 674-75; Ralph Foster Weld, *Brooklyn Village* (New York, 1938), pp. 71, 285.

15. Siloam Presbyterian Church, *Semi-Centennial* (Brooklyn, 1899), pp. 6-7; Wesley Curtwright, "Rise of Negro Churches in New York, 1828-1860" (WPA research papers, Schomburg Collection); photocopy of the incorporation papers of the Bethel AME Church (Long Island Historical Society); Bridge St. AWME Church, *Centennial*, p. 27.

16. Jacob Judd, "The History of Brooklyn, 1834-1855; Political and Administrative Aspects" (Ph.D. dissertation, New York University, 1959), p. 32; Weld, *Brooklyn Village*, pp. 224, 231, 285, 327; Carleton Mabee, "Brooklyn's Black Public Schools; Why Did Blacks Have Unusual Control Over Them?," *The Journal of Long Island History* 11 (Spring 1975); *Complete History of Widow's Son Lodge No. 11 F. & A.M. Prince Hall* (Brooklyn, 1970), pp. 15-17; Swan, "Weeksville." Relations between the Woolman and Tompkins societies were not always cordial as the following excerpt from the *Long Island Star* (Oct. 4, 1827) indicates:

The cornerstone of the African School House was laid on the 25th day of September under the immediate direction of the African Woolman Benevolent Society; at which time a company of men who call themselves the African Tompkins Society marched through the streets of Brooklyn with music. A Committee was dispatched from the Woolman's Society, requesting the Tompkins not to form a procession, nor to have music on the occasion; for the Woolmen saw wherein it would prove injurious to them in their enterprise. But the Tompkins very obstinately rebelled against them and did come out with music, and caused much disturbance in the streets. We hope, therefore, that the respectable population of this village will not impute those irregularities to the Woolmen Society, for we aim at the general good of the people of color of this village, and have been associated for that purpose more than seventeen years.

17. Mabee, "Brooklyn's Black Public Schools;" Carleton Mabee, "Early Black Public Schools," *Long Island Forum* (November 1973): 214-16; (December 1973): 234-36.

18. Benjamin Quarles, *Black Abolitionists* (New York, 1969), p. 229.

19. Weld, *Brooklyn Village*, pp. 118, 298-99; *Long Island Star*, June 8, 1831, June 15, 1831.

20. *The Brooklyn City and Kings County Record: A Budget of General Information* . . . (Brooklyn, 1855), pp. 200-202.

21. Prior to the New York State Constitution of 1821, property and resident requirements for New York voters applied equally to both races. The new constitution required Negroes not only to meet the general age and residence requirements but also to possess a freehold estate worth $250. This latter restriction contrasted with the virtually universal white manhood suffrage. It had the effect of practically disenfranchising black citizens. Leon Litwack, *North of Slavery: The Negro in the Free States, 1790-1860* (Chicago, 1961), pp. 180-84.

22. *Long Island Star*, Nov. 17, 1846; "Speech of Hon. Theophilus C. Callicot of Kings County Against Granting Equal Suffrage to Men of Color, Feb. 10, 1860" (Albany, 1860), pp. 3-12. In 1846, white voters in Kings County voted 4,896 to 1,494 against removing the property qualification for black suffrage. The vote in 1860 was 23,399 to 5,534 aganist extending the franchise. Following this resounding defeat, the *Brooklyn Daily Eagle* commented in a similarly hostile manner: "If the union is to be preserved, if the nation is to exist, there must be no more truckling to this disgusting and contemptible negro worship. Not only is it a war upon the ineradicable laws of nature, but it is a practical falsehood wherever it exists. In this state the black man is a political pariah and a social outcast" (Esther A. Ohlsson, "Brooklyn During the Civil War as Reported by *The Brooklyn Daily Eagle*, September, 1860-April, 1865" [M.A. thesis, New York University, 1957], p. 14).

CHAPTER 2

# Recognition and Deprivation: 1870-1900

## POST-CIVIL WAR EXPANSION

During the post-Civil War era of industrialization and immigration, Brooklyn City attained the apex of its independent existence. This was the period of the construction of the Brooklyn Bridge, one of the most remarkable technological feats of an era replete with technological marvels; of the arrival of mass transit that both contracted the city by reducing commuting time and enlarged it by extending its geographic zone of intensive settlement; of an urban imperialism that saw Brooklyn expand to absorb the outlying towns of Kings County and become coterminous with the county; of the flowering of such lasting indigenous cultural institutions as the Brooklyn Museum, the Brooklyn Academy of Music, and Prospect Park. It was a time when Brooklyn ranked behind only New York City and Philadelphia, and after 1890 Chicago, in population and economic development. All this did not, of course, suddenly evaporate in 1898 when Brooklyn became part of New York City, but the loss of political independence did mark the end of an era.[1]

Between 1870 and 1900 Brooklyn's population nearly tripled from 396,099 to 1,166,582. Like New York, Newark, Chicago, and other northern cities, Brooklyn remained a substantially "foreign" city throughout this period, although some shift in the countries of origin of the immigrants—from Germany and Ireland to Italy and Russia—was evident by 1900. At each decennial census between 1870 and 1900, approximately one-third of the city's population was foreign-born and at least that proportion were their progeny. In 1890 native-born whites of native-born parents constituted only 28 percent of Brooklyn residents. The reciprocal relationship between immigration and industrialization accelerated Brooklyn's growth as a leading urban center. In their quest for economic well-being, the immigrants provided the fuel to feed Brooklyn and New York's expanding industrial economy; this growth in turn attracted additional foreign workers to the city.[2]

During this same period Brooklyn's black population grew consistently, if not spectacularly, from 4,931 in 1870 to 18,367 or 1.6 percent of the city's total in 1900. Before the Great Migration of the twentieth century, however, blacks did not generally constitute a significant numerical component within Brooklyn's diverse ethnic minorities. The 10,287 Negroes residing in Brooklyn in 1890 were overshadowed by the 94,798 German-born residents and the nearly 90,000 of Irish birth. By 1900 blacks had substantially expanded their numbers to 18,367, but even more rapid had been the increase in "new" immigrants from Southern and Eastern Europe. Italian-born Brooklynites nearly quadrupled from 9,600 to 37,200, while the Russian-born grew sevenfold from 3,400 to 24,400. Thus, the primary demographic reality confronting Brooklyn during the second half of the nineteenth century was the assimilation of European immigrants, not local blacks.

Generally speaking, no spatial black ghetto such as would develop in all major northern cities existed in Brooklyn at this time. Ward statistics, an admittedly less-than-perfect instrument for measuring racial segregation, reveal a rather broad distribution of blacks throughout the city. In 1890, for example, blacks did not exceed 10 percent of the total population of any ward, although a more detailed study by sanitary districts did reveal one area where the "colored population" did reach 10.2 percent. By 1900, one major node of black settlement had clearly emerged in the Fort Greene Park area, but most blacks still lived dispersed about the city. Many resided in that lineal community that extended radially from the Fort Greene center along the commercial arteries of Fulton Street and Atlantic Avenue through the middle-class Bedford and Stuyvesant neighborhoods. In contrast, most of the immigrant groups were considerably more concentrated.[3] This pattern paralleled that prevalent in most northern cities. Blacks in Chicago did live in enclaves in the early twentieth century, but these pockets were well distributed. In 1910 blacks were less segregated from native whites than were Chicago Italians. In Du Bois's Philadelphia, blacks were "scattered in every ward of the city" with the "great mass" living "far from the whilom centre of colored settlement." [4]

## A DISTINGUISHED GROUP OF LOCAL BLACKS

As indicated in Chapter 1, prominent blacks had resided in Brooklyn in the prewar period. James McCune Smith (1816-65), a persistent protester, was one of the first Negro physicians in the United States. Although he practiced in New York City, he lived in Brooklyn. William J. Wilson, teacher, writer, and militant; Thomas Hamilton, founder of the *Anglo-African Magazine;* George Hogarth, teacher, editor, and church official; and Junius Morrell, principal, teacher, and protester, all had lived in Brooklyn. Indeed, Brooklyn had developed a favorable reputation among blacks in the New York City area.[5] In 1861, a writer for the *Weekly Anglo-African* claimed expansively that "Brooklyn offers as great, if not much greater advantages for improving the temporal, the social, and the intellectual condition of colored men as any place in this broad land." This pattern of prestigious black residence in Brooklyn persisted in the latter years of the century. The *New York Times* in 1895 lamented that as soon as Negroes "amass a comfortable fortune they move from the city across the East River" where living conditions were somewhat better and prejudice less marked. During this period Brooklyn did serve as home for an especially distinguished coterie of blacks whose lives extended back into the antebellum era or forward into the twentieth century.[6]

Peter W. Ray (1825-1906) attended Bowdoin College and Vermont Medical College and became the first black physician to become a member of the Kings County Medical Society. For fifty years he operated a pharmacy in the Williamsburg section. He was one of the founders of the Brooklyn College of Pharmacy, later a part of Long Island University, and served as its treasurer for twenty-three years.[7] Philip A. White (d. 1891) operated a pharmacy in lower Manhattan while residing in Brooklyn. His popularity and esteem were attested to when the local Irish residents protected his store during the 1863 draft riots. Brooklyn officially recognized White's ability and stature by appointing him to the board of education in 1882.[8] The first black female physician to practice medicine in New York State was Susan Smith McKinney (1847-1918), daughter of Sylvanus Smith, the trustee of the Brooklyn African Public School in the 1840s. She was graduated from the New York Medical College for Women in 1870 and practiced in Brooklyn from then until the mid-1890s. She was a member of the Kings County and New York State Homeopathic Medical Societies and one of the founders of the Brooklyn Women's Homeopathic Hospital and Dispensary in 1881.[9]

Samuel R. Scottron exhibited remarkable entrepreneurial talent and inventiveness in becoming a successful businessman and manufacturer. His first patent was obtained for an adjustable mirror—mirrors arranged opposite each other to permit a barber to view both sides of the customer's head at once. Expanding from this base, Scottron manufactured looking glasses, pier and mantel mirrors, and wood moldings. Putting his mirror patents out on royalty, he next embarked upon the manufacture of extension cornices, only to have them become obsolete by the "capriciousness of fashion," which replaced cornices with curtain poles. In 1892, a "chance discovery" launched him in still another direction, the manufacture of imitation onyx, which was utilized by lamp and candlestick manufacturers. By 1904 Scottron's reputed annual business income equaled $25,000. In addition to his business ventures, Scottron participated actively in civic and social affairs. Prior to Brooklyn's merger with New York City, he served as the last Negro member of the Brooklyn Board of Education. He was active in the Colored Citizens Protective League and served as secretary of the Committee for Improving the Industrial Condition of Negroes in New York. Many columns in the *Colored American Magazine* and the *New York Age* carried his byline.[10]

For a period during the 1880s Lewis Latimer (1848-1928) resided in Brooklyn. He was associated with the pioneering inventions of Thomas A. Edison and Alexander Graham Bell, producing the original drawings for Bell's first telephone and directing Edison's street-lighting contract in London.[11]

T. McCants Stewart (1854-1923) achieved local prominence as a lawyer and intellectual. He was active in politics as the leading local black Democrat and was appointed a member of the Brooklyn Board of Education in 1891. His militant championing of equal rights may have resulted in his subsequent removal in 1894. He also participated in the various activities of Brooklyn's black literary groups. Stewart later emigrated to Liberia where he became a justice of its Supreme Court.[12]

Although Fred R. Moore (1857-1943) ultimately became associated with Harlem, he resided in Brooklyn for three decades. After working as confidential messenger in the Treasury Department in Washington, Moore accepted a position with the Western National Bank in New York City in 1887 and settled in Brooklyn. Even prior to his editorship of the *Colored American Magazine* and the *New York Age*, Moore had achieved local repute in Republican politics. In 1900, his party nominated him for the assembly in a primarily white district. Moore actively participated in the operations of the Association for the Protection of Colored Women, the Colored Citizens Protective League, and the Committee for Improving the Industrial Conditions of Negroes in New York.

As his own connections to Harlem life became tighter and as Harlem emerged as America's "Negro Mecca," it became expedient for him to move. His change of residence in 1919 was eventually rewarded in 1927 when he was elected to the New York City Board of Aldermen, an achievement he could not have expected in Brooklyn.[13]

William L. Bulkley (1861-1934) taught in the Brooklyn public school system during the 1890s. After consolidation he became the first Negro principal of a racially mixed New York City school. Like Scottron and Moore, Bulkley participated in the formation of black self-help organizations during the early twentieth century. He was the prime mover in the establishment of the Committee for Improving the Industrial Conditions of Negroes; a founding member of the National Association for the Advancement of Colored People (NAACP); the first vice-chairman of the National League on Urban Conditions among Negroes, the initial name of the National Urban League.[14]

Jerome B. Peterson (1859-1943) was a native Brooklynite and married Philip White's daughter. In the 1880s he became associated with T. Thomas Fortune in editing the *New York Globe* and *New York Age*. After 1900 he obtained a variety of federal patronage posts until he retired in 1931.[15] Rufus L. Perry (1868-1930), son of the Reverend Rufus L. Perry, was graduated from New York University and its law school. He practiced law locally, authored a number of books in both English and French, and followed an erratic course in his religious and political beliefs. His ultimate apostasy lay in his becoming both a Jew and an avowed Socialist, under which banner he sought elective office in 1927.[16]

Three black Brooklyn clergymen deserve special mention. The Reverend Rufus L. Perry, (1834-95) founded and edited between 1872 and 1895 a religiously oriented monthly publication, the *National Monitor*. He founded Messiah Baptist Church and authored a book entitled *The Cushite: or the Descendants of Ham*. The Reverend William Dixon, pastor of Concord Baptist Church from 1864 to his death in 1909, was elected moderator of the interracial Long Island Baptist

Association in 1905. The Reverend William A. Alexander of
Siloam Presbyterian Church was accorded a similar leadership
honor by the Brooklyn Presbytery.[17]

## BLACK INVOLVEMENT IN BROOKLYN INSTITUTIONS

The presence in Brooklyn of such prominent black individuals and of a visible black elite may have facilitated
governmental, political, social, and cultural recognition of local
Negroes. In a number of instances, in fact, Brooklyn adopted a
distinctly more favorable attitude toward its resident blacks
than did its larger neighbor across the river. It seems clear
that prior to the 1898 consolidation, Brooklyn blacks received
more recognition than they did after the merger with New
York City.

### Schools

This was especially evident in the sphere of education. As
early as 1869 Negroes in the Weeksville community had
petitioned, but to no avail, for the appointment of a black to
the Brooklyn Board of Education so that blacks could have
some say about the governance of the five "colored" schools.
Following the election of the reform candidate, Seth Low, as
mayor in 1881, local blacks again sought recognition. Low said
he would consider their petition if they submitted the name of
a qualified Negro. After due consideration he appointed in
1882 the dignified Philip White, a longtime Brooklynite and
successful pharmacist, to one of the forty-five board positions.
White was one of only a handful of blacks to be appointed to
local boards of education in New York State in the nineteenth
century and probably the only black to be selected in a major
American city. Whether anyone but an independent-minded,
reform mayor of Yankee ancestry like Seth Low would have
taken this initiative seems doubtful. However, once the
precedent had been established, succeeding Negro appointments by perhaps less adventuresome mayors were facili-

tated. Following White's death in 1891, Mayor Alfred Chapin, a Democrat, solicited nominations and selected T. McCants Stewart, a lawyer and the city's leading black Democrat. Chapin's Republican successor was persuaded to replace Stewart in 1894 with a black Republican, Samuel Scottron. While politics undoubtedly influenced this decision, Stewart's militant championing of school integration may also have contributed to his nonreappointment. Scottron retained the position until the Brooklyn Board of Education ceased to exist with the formation of Greater New York. He continued until 1902 as a member of the less powerful School Board of the Borough of Brooklyn.[18]

Separate "colored" schools, as we have seen, had existed in Brooklyn long before the Civil War. Their existence, however, had not precluded the possibility of occasional Negro attendance at a white school. According to Scottron, the school superintendents were "opposed to putting colored children to great inconvenience in walking long distances to colored schools." In 1873 Negro integrationists sought the "immediate abolition of all distinctions, founded on race or color, in our public schools." Reflecting the persistent tension between integration and separatism, an opposing black group was less convinced of the social and educational benefits to be derived from such a policy. They accused the integrationists of being "ashamed [or] afraid of being known as colored persons." Complete integration, they feared, might only agitate black parents and children who felt more comfortable in a segregated environment. More practically, abolition of the separate school system might well eliminate the positions of the black teachers who presided over the black schools.[19] The official policy of segregation remained unchanged until 1883, when Philip White successfully sponsored a resolution that allowed Negro children to attend the public school in their district rather than one of the three undistricted "colored" schools. Simultaneously, with White again supporting the majority, the board rejected another proposal that would have abolished entirely the separate schools. White's permissive desegregation plan satisfied most interested parties. Whites were not necessarily threatened since the "colored" schools still absorbed most black pupils. Blacks were offered a choice of schools for their children, and Negro teachers' positions were protected. "In a sense, this formula provided public support for black 'parochial' schools, while removing any infringements on the rights of black citizens." Similar desegregating legislation had been adopted by Newark in 1872, Chicago in 1874, and Philadelphia in 1881.[20]

The three separate schools continued to survive throughout the 1880s, although their names were changed in 1887 from Colored Schools, 1, 2, and 3 to the more anonymous Numbers 67, 68, and 69. These schools remained conspicuous for their absence of definite boundaries, permitting them to admit Negro pupils residing anywhere in the city.[21] Within the Negro community opinion remained divided on the retention of these segregated schools. T. Thomas Fortune, long a foe of separatism, reluctantly admitted that black parents generally were "satisfied with their present [separate] educational status." A significant step toward the full integration of Brooklyn schools, however, did occur in 1893. The Brooklyn Board of Health had twice condemned the old wooden and "woefully deficient" structure of PS 68 in the Weeksville area. Instead of constructing a new separate school, the board of education voted to consolidate PS 68 with PS 83 in a large new building already housing a white school. T. McCants Stewart, the Reverend Rufus Perry, and the Brooklyn Literary Union strongly supported such desegregation. Some white parents objected to this mixed school, preferring the construction of a building "devoted solely to the use of colored children." The board rejected this plea, and PS 83 opened harmoniously in 1893 with 1,000 white and 200 black pupils. The staff consisted of a white principal, a black head of department or assistant principal, Maritcha Lyons, and black and white teachers. The four Negro teachers even had a "larger percentage of white pupils than colored in their classes." The policy of dismantling the separate school structure was reinforced in 1894 when Brooklyn annexed Flatbush and the board of education closed the Flatbush "colored" school. In 1900, twenty-two blacks taught in Brooklyn classes, all of which contained white pupils. Although New York City's black population was double that of Brooklyn, black teachers and pupils were somewhat more common in the Brooklyn public school system than in the larger New York City one. In 1890 there were eighteen black teachers in Brooklyn but only sixteen in New York. Similarly, black pupils in Brooklyn (1,636) outnumbered those in New York (1,612).[22]

## Politics and Patronage

Official recognition of blacks was not limited to the field of education. Long before New York City acted, Brooklyn had appointed Negroes to its police and fire department. The appointment of Wiley Overton as the first black policeman in 1891 brought protests from his white colleagues against sleeping in the same room with him. The police commissioner, however, staunchly upheld the selection: "I slept upon the decks of a war ship when fighting with colored men to save the Union, and you can't convince me that you should be allowed to draw the color line against this officer." [23]

In 1887 and again in 1900 Brooklyn Republicans nominated black candidates for the New York state assembly. Such designations were intended to quiet internal dissent about the nonrecognition of loyal Negroes by the Republican party and to contravene any black flirtation with the Democrats.[24] Victory seemed rather secondary. Thus in 1887, James W. Mars, president of the Kings County Colored Citizens Republican League, received the regular party designation for the Third Assembly District, a traditionally Democratic area. Not surprisingly, the Democratic candidate soundly thrashed Mars 4,417 to 2,868. In 1900, under almost identical circumstances, the Republicans nominated Fred R. Moore in the Eighth Assembly District, an area "so strongly Democratic that a Republican candidate there has little chance of election." Moore's anticipated defeat was accomplished. Nevertheless, despite the obviously self-serving character of these candidacies, two blacks did possess sufficient credibility in the

Republican party and the community at large to be selected to
run for public office. Nor did any general obloquy attach itself
to the party that dared to name a black man. After all, a black
had served in Brooklyn in a major appointive office since 1882.
After 1900, however, despite and sometimes because of
Brooklyn's growing black population, the public recognition of
Negroes in elective politics ceased. Only with the emergence
of a black belt of significant proportions more than forty years
later would a major political party again dabble in interracial
politics.[25]

## BLACK-RUN INSTITUTIONS

In addition to the recognition accorded them by whites,
blacks demonstrated initiative, determination, and self-con-
sciousness in establishing and running Negro-directed institutions. In this respect they often proved more adventuresome
and adept than their more numerous fellow blacks in New
York City. Three major black charitable institutions, located
in the Weeksville area, operated under Negro direction and
supervision. The African Civilization Society had operated in
New York City from at least the later 1850s, but in 1865 it
moved its headquarters to its own building on Dean Street
near Troy Avenue in Brooklyn. The society operated schools
for freed blacks in the South. The New York Freedman's
Relief Association of New York City, which pursued similar
ends, was white-run.[26]

Similar to the African Civilization Society, the institution
that was to evolve into the Brooklyn Howard Colored Orphan
Asylum commenced operations in New York City. It originated as a response to the influx to the city of freewomen and
their children following emancipation. Since these migrants
were frequently unable to procure adequate accommodations
for themselves, and the city asylum would not accept the
youngsters, it became necessary to establish some institution
willing to care for these displaced persons. To this end the
Home for Freed Children and Others was founded. In 1866, at
the behest of General O. O. Howard and H. H. Howard, the

organization moved to Brooklyn where it was incorporated as the Brooklyn Howard Colored Orphan Asylum. The home aimed "to shelter, protect and educate the destitute orphan children of colored parentage, and to instruct said children in useful trades and occupation...." The initial building was situated on Pacific Street near Ralph Avenue in the Weeksville area. In 1884 a new brick structure equipped with "all the modern improvements," including steam heat, was constructed in the same neighborhood. The Howard Orphanage occupied this building until 1911, when the entire operation moved to Kings Park, Long Island. During much of its existence, and especially at the beginning, blacks supervised and operated the institution, though with white financial support. The comparable New York City orphanage was white-dominated in its staff and directors.[27]

At the other end of the age spectrum, the plight of aged blacks could be equally as harsh as that of the children. The Zion Home for Aged Colored People, founded in the 1860s, sought to ameliorate this situation. It too was black-run, unlike New York City's Colored Home.

Black initiative in establishing publications, realty companies, and literary societies further illustrated the broad scope of local black life. The *Anglo-African Magazine* was founded in 1859 by Thomas Hamilton of Brooklyn. The *Sunbeam* was a local weekly journal published between 1865 and 1867. The African Civilization Society issued *Freedman's Torchlight* beginning in 1866. Between 1872 and 1895 the Reverend Rufus L. Perry edited the *National Monitor*. Another Brooklynite, Jerome Peterson, was closely associated with T. Thomas Fortune in editing and publishing the *New York Age*, which regularly devoted some of its space to Brooklyn news. Late in the 1880s and continuing into the 1890s Augustus M. Hodges issued a weekly journal entitled the *Brooklyn Sentinel*, "which for three years was the leading race paper in New York State." Early in the twentieth century Fred R. Moore bought and edited both the *Colored American Magazine* and the *New York Age*.[28]

Although only a small percentage of Brooklyn blacks were

financially capable of purchasing a house, a number of local Negro land-investment companies prospered. The earliest endeavor was the Excelsior Land Association, founded in 1871. By 1887 two other organizations—the Mercantile Association and the Kings County Pioneer Land and Improvement Association—also operated in the real estate market. The most prominent of these collective businesses was the Afro-American Investment and Building Company of Brooklyn, "one of the most reliable financial institutions owned by members of the race." With real estate operations extending beyond Brooklyn to Greater New York and even New Jersey, its investments enabled blacks "to buy homes on the monthly installments plan, and [assisted] others to pay off small mortgages" without charging exorbitant interest rates. Among its officials were such prominent Brooklynites as Fred R. Moore, president in 1905, Samuel R. Scottron, William L. Bulkley, and Sully McClellan, businessman.[29]

Brooklyn also gained a reputation as an "aristocratic" and cultured center of Negro settlement. In 1892 the *Brooklyn Eagle* observed that no class of its city's people were "fonder of literary pursuits than the Afro-Americans." The Brooklyn Literary Union of the Siloam Presbyterian Church pursued an active program of concerts, lectures, and discussions of a "very high character" in addition to running a lending library. It was the black cultural "Mecca to which all Brooklyn looked with a peculiar pride." Among its active contributors were Maritcha R. Lyons and Charles A. Dorsey, both principals of Brooklyn "colored" schools, T. McCants Stewart, and William F. Johnson, the director of the Howard Orphan Asylum. Imitators of the Brooklyn Literary Union included the Turner Lyceum, the Star Lyceum, the Concord Literary Circle, and the Progressive Literary Union. The *Eagle* also noted the existence of a "Negro 400" in Brooklyn.[30]

Viewed from this perspective, we see a kind of golden era for blacks in Brooklyn. The city emerges as a residential refuge for both well-off and poor blacks because of its "quiet avenues and streets, its cheaper rents and general house comforts, and the prevalence of a general moral atmosphere."

"Here in Brooklyn a family may be reared with healthful surroundings and without contamination by those gaudy viceful influences, which seem to keep with Negro colonization in New York City. . . . Here, also, is an entire absence of the great tenement system." Brooklyn appears to be a place of some racial openness where advancement and recognition were possible for black individuals, where Negro residents could create and operate an institutional network sufficiently varied and effective to shape their social, religious, cultural, political, and economic lives. Such an array of individuals and organizations implies a society of some sophistication, prominence, and prosperity.[31]

## THE OTHER BLACK BROOKLYN

The recognition, status, and well-being just described did not extend, regrettably but not unexpectedly, to the bulk of Brooklyn blacks. Their relationship to the economic mainstream was often tenuous. They were generally denied equal status by whites, and the social-benefit institutions that blacks had developed were usually impoverished and oftentimes only a step removed from bankruptcy.

### Employment

Most northern, urban blacks, in the latter nineteenth century labored outside the economic mainstream of America and consequently languished in poverty and deprivation. Du Bois's observations on the fate of black workers in Philadelphia were probably generally applicable:

Without doubt there is not in Philadelphia enough work of the kind that the mass of Negroes can and may do, to employ at fair wages the laborers who at present deserve work. The result of this must, of course, be disastrous, and give rise to many loafers, criminals and casual laborers.

The first class [Negro] ditcher can seldom become foreman of a gang; the hod-carrier can seldom become a mason; the porter cannot have much hope of being a clerk, or the elevator-boy of becoming a salesman.[32]

Most black workers were relegated to what some current economists would call the secondary labor market, where jobs were physically demanding, menial, low-paying, and without the probability of occupational upgrading. The types of employment available to blacks were severely circumscribed. Brooklyn and nearby New York City, like Chicago or Newark, were still heavily industrialized cities, yet blacks were virtually excluded from their factories, were, to use Du Bois' phrase, disenfranchised from full participation in the economic process, which did, however, offer work to 150,000 Brooklyn whites in 1900. In contrast, half the employed black males in Brooklyn were engaged in domestic or personal-service occupations, predominantly as servants, waiters, and unspecified laborers. Only one in six white males engaged in such pursuits. In the trade and transportation category black and white males did approach statistical parity with slightly more than one-third of each racial group so employed. Within this broad category, however, the types of work for whites and blacks differed perceptibly. Whites generally occupied white-collar positions as clerks, copyists, and merchants, while most blacks tugged, hauled, and pushed as draymen, teamsters, hostlers, porters, and helpers. Nor were blacks able to utilize the avenue of self-proprietorship as a means to economic improvement. Among the more than 24,000 Brooklyn males enumerated as merchants and dealers, only 64 were Negro.[33]

For black women the prospects were even bleaker and more restricted. They were limited almost exclusively to domestic and personal-service employment as laundresses, servants, or waitresses. Less than 10 percent of black females labored outside this general category, with the bulk of these exceptions in the traditional Negro trades of dressmaking and sewing. White women were more equally distributed among the various occupational categories. Furthermore, Negro women were far more likely than whites to be in the work force, owing to a variety of factors, including the depressed nature of black male employment, the greater acceptability of Negro women to white employers, and the excessive number of unattached Negro women needing to support themselves. Thus, despite the presence of prominent blacks resident in Brooklyn, most black men and women in 1900 were concentrated in low-status and low-paying manual employment.

## Health

"The Negro death rate is largely a matter of condition of living," wrote Du Bois in 1899. Given poverty, overcrowded housing, and the lack of local health care for blacks, it is scarcely surprising that blacks suffered excessively from ill health. The death rate for Brooklyn blacks consistently exceeded that for whites, and the interracial differential actually increased during the latter part of the nineteenth century. During a six-year period (1884-90) the general black death rate equaled 30.54, while that of whites was 25.90. Yet in the final year of that span, the gap was more substantial than the six-year average (34.99 to 25.54), and by 1900 the Negro death rate exceeded the white rate by nearly 50 percent. One life insurance company even refused to pay off at par value a ninety-dollar policy it held on a black. Since the "death rate was so great" among blacks, the company unilaterally decided, it would pay only fifty dollars. Especially susceptible to disease and death were black babies and youths. The infant mortality rate for Negroes in 1890 exceeded that for whites by 83 percent and by 1900 it was more than double the white level. In addition to infant mortality, consumption, pneumonia, and diseases of the nervous system were especially deadly for blacks, and all three also exhibited increasing interracial differentials. As a result of this terrible winnowing out of blacks, especially among the youthful, Negro population expanded only modestly. It seems probable that virtually the entire increase in the number of blacks in Brooklyn between 1870 and 1900 resulted from migration to the city from

Manhattan or other parts of the country. Had the Negro population been left to increase naturally, it might instead have shrunk. Life for blacks often tended to be nasty, brutish, and short.[34]

## Prejudice and Discrimination

While no pervasive system of residential segregation prevailed in Brooklyn, the physical proximity of blacks was not always welcome. In 1894, for example, when a "prosperous" Negro bought a home in a "highly respectable ... neighborhood," local property owners reportedly "boiled with indignation" at this "calamity." On another occasion a white resident considered it an "outrage" to have Negroes move into "that part of the street which has been kept clear of colored families until the present." Such opposition focused primarily on the anticipated depreciation in property values resulting from the presence of a black family. Indeed, a favorite form of neighborly vengeance was to threaten to sell or rent one's property to blacks. Such spite tactics remained popular for several decades.[35]

It is salutary to recall that the Fifteenth Amendment, adopted in 1870, enfranchised most northern as well as southern Negroes. Even on the eve of its implementation, Brooklyn still remained sharply divided on the question of black voting rights. At the 1867 New York State Constitutional Convention, Brooklyn's Democratic boss, Henry Cruse Murphy, opposed extension of the franchise to blacks since it would only "confound the races and tend to destroy the fair fabric of democratic institutions which had been erected by the capacity of the white race." Even worse, "political equality ... will lead to ... social equality with the white race." Two years later Congressman William E. Robinson of Brooklyn twisted Negro enfranchisement in order to argue for similar rights for immigrants. If Negroes, "the lowest and most ignorant of the descendants of Ham," were allowed to vote, then naturalization should not be a prerequisite for recent white European arrivals. In that same year New Yorkers again voted on the question of Negro suffrage and again rejected the concept, with the majority of Brooklynites still registering anti-Negro sentiments. Two decades later, however, such attitudes had modified sufficiently to permit the Republicans to nominate a black for public office.[36]

Although blacks did achieve recognition in public education as teachers, principals, and members of the board of education, and although the mandatory separate school system was abandoned in 1883, serious shortcomings existed in black Brooklyn education. An 1888 attendance survey of the old Weeksville area revealed extensive nonattendance by black children. Ordinarily the board would have required their attendance, but both the white and "colored" schools in the area were overcrowded. The "colored" school in that area contained only four classrooms to accommodate its 242 registered pupils and was repeatedly labeled "not fit for school purposes" and a "disgrace to the city of Brooklyn." Appropriations for the three separate schools for fuel, books, stationery supplies, and general maintenance invariably ranked among the lowest in the entire school system.[37]

### Problems of Black Charitable Institutions

The black-founded and black-directed social work institutions represented an impressive achievement, indeed, but these organizations were also plagued by endemic difficulties. Especially grim was the unmitigated financial struggle that confronted them. In its 1872 annual report the Brooklyn Howard Colored Orphan Asylum complained of its "insufficient" treasury. Owing to the "insufficiency of the patronage of our Brooklyn public," the orphanage was compelled to solicit aid in other cities and states. When not worried about acquiring an adequate level of funding, the directors often expressed concern about the physical state of the building. The Howard Orphanage moved into a newly constructed home in 1884; yet by the early twentieth century the institution had become "overcrowded" and "dilapidated." This dilapidation led the State Board of Charities to withhold additional commitments and payments to the orphanage, and ultimately determined the decision to sell the Brooklyn property in 1911 and remove the institution to Suffolk County, Long Island.[38]

By 1890 the Zion Home for Aged Colored People had apparently fallen into bankruptcy and disrepair. At that time a white circle of King's Daughters visited the home; they found it in such sad condition that they determined to "lend a hand." The physical structure itself had already been condemned by city authorities. To publicize the plight of the Zion Home and to interest their friends in remedying the situation, the King's Daughters sponsored a mass meeting at the white Washington Avenue Baptist Church in the Bedford section. Since the existing institution had "no adequate means of support and the inmates are not properly fed, clothed, warmed or cared for in case of sickness," the group immediately resolved "to raise a fund for a new and suitable Home." On March 14, 1891 the new organization took possession of the home and assumed its management. Because of the "low condition" of the building fund, the new directors were forced to compromise their initial plan to construct a sanitary, airy, and bright new home. Instead they purchased a used structure in the same neighborhood to solve the immediately pressing problem of condemnation. In 1899 the cornerstone of a new building was finally laid, but the structure contained only thirty beds, scarcely adequate for an expanding black population.[39]

Both the Howard Orphanage and Zion Home had been black-directed in their origins; however, this characteristic was diluted or altogether lost by the 1890s. The Zion Home's management was taken over by a white group; the board of directors of Howard became increasingly interracial. Blacks, however, retained responsibility for the daily operation of these institutions. Given the aggregate poverty of the black community, these institutions could not have survived without substantial white financial support. To be sure, such notable local Negroes as Samuel Scottron, Lewis Latimer, T. McCants Stewart, Jerome Peterson, Mr. and Mrs. Frank Gilbert, and Miss Anna Hawley, as well as some black religious congregations, donated money and goods, but they could not long have sustained these institutions. As early as 1872 the bulk of the Howard Orphanage's funds were solicited by the institution's "faithful and unwearied agent," W. F. Johnson, from white churches in Brooklyn and throughout the country. The large donations to the home for the aged came from such prominent white philanthropists as Alexander Orr, George Foster Peabody, William Hoople, and Mrs. Julia Brick. Frank Jones underwrote the costs of the black Ministers' Kindergarten. White financing and white direction in conjunction with black needs and black operation became a common feature of not only these nineteenth-century Brooklyn institutions, but also of those early twentieth-century national civil rights organizations, including the NAACP and the Urban League.[40]

Among the white supporters of these black institutions, a kind of interlocking relationship was evident. The William G. Hoople family, for example, was extremely generous in its gifts of money, goods, and time to the Home for Aged Colored People. In the first report, Mrs. Hoople was cited for contributing $100, running a lawn party, a parlor fair, and a cake sale for the benefit of the home, and serving as chairman of the House Committee and as a member of the Executive Committee. This close association continued until her death in 1915. In 1897 Mrs. Hoople presented to the Brooklyn City Mission and Tract Society a house at 1699 Atlantic Avenue, which eventually became a Negro mission. Mr. Hoople focused his attention on the Howard Orphanage and served as its president.

Mrs. George F. Stone was primarily responsible for the foundation of the Ministers' Kindergarten. She also served on committees for both the home for the aged and the Howard Orphanage. Her husband donated his services to direct the construction of the new home for the aged. Other benefactors associated with almost the entire spectrum of private social work agencies operating in Brooklyn at the turn of the century included Alfred T. White (the most consistently generous individual), George Foster Peabody, Frank S. Jones, and Alexander Orr.[41]

These underfinanced and limited charitable institutions scarcely met the needs of the local black community, which was steadily expanding throughout this period. Yet, narrow and separate as these facilities may have been, they were necessary in an institutional world that generally ignored the existence of blacks. For example, such homes for the aged as the Brooklyn Home for Aged Men and the New York Congregational Home for the Aged probably excluded blacks altogether. The Baptist Home of Brooklyn did accept blacks as early as 1877 and allotted periodic regular monthly ministrations to the black Concord Baptist Church. Such interracial fraternity gradually diminished, with the last Negro resident dying in 1894 and none subsequently admitted. One wonders whether the existence of the rejuvenated Home for Aged Colored People encouraged this exclusionary policy, since blacks could now utilize their own separate facility. For Negro youngsters who came into contact with the Brooklyn Society for the Prevention of Cruelty to Children because of a variety of offenses ranging from professional begging by children to barbarous practices perpetrated by parents and guardians, the agency acted as a conduit, referring cases requiring institutional treatment to the Howard Orphanage. An occasional Negro child attended one of the many schools directed by the Brooklyn Free Kindergarten Association, but blacks were generally expected to attend the segregated Ministers' Kindergarten after its establishment in 1896. The Brooklyn Home for Consumption admitted anyone "irrespective of creed, color, sex or nationality." Because of the particularly ravaging impact of this disease upon blacks, it is hardly surprising that they were included among its patients from the earliest years. Never, however, were they represented in numbers commensurate with their need.[42]

Despite some exceptions these general charitable institutions either ignored and excluded Negroes or adopted a separatist policy. One suspects that to some extent the existence or nonexistence of an identifiably black facility may have influenced institutional attitudes. Where separate race institutions existed, Negroes were expected to avail themselves of these services. The presence of a black kindergarten, orphanage, and old age home, for example, facilitated Negro exclusion from other similar agencies. Conversely, in the absence of a home for black consumptives, the general institution extended its care across racial lines.

## THE BEDFORD AREA

The histories of the Bedford-Stuyvesant area of Brooklyn and of Manhattan's Harlem have reflected a curiously parallel pattern over time. Both originated as remote, sleepy, agricultural communities, developed into solid, middle-class white residential neighborhoods in the later nineteenth century, then evolved into predominantly black slum-ghettos.

The settlement of Bedford dates from the latter years of Peter Stuyvesant's administration of New Netherland. Like the rest of Kings County, its economy was then based primarily upon agriculture, but its location at a major highway intersection linking the Brooklyn ferry with the settlements of Jamaica, Flatbush, and Newtown also facilitated some early commercial development. In 1668 Thomas Lambertse received authorization to keep an "ordinary, for the accommodation of strangers, travellers, ... with diet and lodging and horse meals." The settlement itself probably covered a quarter-mile radius about the intersection. During the eighteenth century the bucolic character of Bedford was little disturbed. After the Battle of Long Island the British occupied the area and quartered invalids in houses of the vicinity. Letters from such soldiers commented on the prosperous condition of the local farms.[43]

A substantial number of blacks lived in Bedford throughout this early period. In 1790 slightly over one-third of the area's total population of 204 was slaves. Blacks in Harlem constituted approximately the same proportion at this time. Thirty years later Bedford's proportions remained little changed, with 103 blacks enumerated out of a total of 310 persons. Sixty-five of these Negroes were still slaves. Although many free blacks continued to live on as parts of white households, two large free black families, headed by Sarah Keer (or Kur), and Phillip Hicks, also resided in the area. The Negro settlements of Weeksville and Carrsville were located in the general Bedford vicinity, and mid-nineteenth century maps located a Negro burial ground in the area, just as one had existed in Harlem since colonial times.[44]

When Brooklyn was incorporated as a city in 1834, Bedford became part of the Ninth Ward, an enormous tract of underpopulated, rural land on the outskirts of the city. Only 666 persons lived there in 1835. In 1840 the first seven wards of the city constituted a fire-watch district, but exclusion of the Eighth and Ninth Wards indicated their lower susceptibility to extensive fire damage, owing to the more scattered nature of the dwellings. These "agricultural wards" maintained separate interests from the rest of Brooklyn, objecting, for example, to paying for municipal improvements such as street paving or lighting, which barely affected their area. This rural character underwent a progressive metamorphosis as Brooklyn grew in numbers and space. By 1855 the Ninth Ward's population had increased to over 9,000 and the area was being touted as the "garden of Brooklyn," ideal for "genteel suburban residences." Casualties of this overall growth and white encroachment upon the area were the previously separate black communities of Weeksville and Carrsville, which were gradually diluted.[45]

Despite obvious demographic expansion, the area was still considered "sparsely settled" in the 1860s. These open spaces attracted the attention of a variety of charitable institutions that required substantial tracts of land for their buildings and surrounding grounds. In 1858 the Church Charity Foundation purchased twenty-three lots at the corner of Albany and Herkimer as a site "healthy, and easily reached by the Fulton or Atlantic cars." Here it erected an orphan asylum and a home for the aged. The Brooklyn Orphan Asylum migrated in 1872 from its inadequate building in the downtown area to larger, more commodious quarters in the Bedford area. In the

1880s the Brooklyn Home for Aged Men, the Brooklyn Home for Consumptives, and St. Mary's Hospital erected new facilities in this section. Similarly, such black institutions as the Howard Colored Orphan Asylum and the Zion Home for Aged Colored People located their operations in the same vicinity.[46]

During the last quarter of the nineteenth century, the Bedford and Stuyvesant sections emerged as solidly middle-class and sometimes even upper-class residential areas, that were inhabited by "people of moderate fortune, intelligent, temperate, thrifty." The role of improved transportation facilities cannot be overestimated in this demographic growth. The completion of the Brooklyn Bridge in 1883 provided convenient transportation to New York City and spurred a population increase for all Brooklyn. More particularly for the Bedford and Stuyvesant neighborhoods, the construction in the late 1880s of an elevated railway along Fulton Street made the area ripe for rapid and general development by bringing it within reasonable commuting time of downtown Brooklyn and New York City. Such residential construction both anticipated and followed the completion of the "El." The Twenty-third Ward, the heart of the Bedford neighborhood, tripled in population between 1875 and 1890, and by 1900 the general area was fully developed. The quality of this burgeoning section was indisputable. In 1890, the private dwellings of the Twenty-third Ward were classed among the "best in the city." Neighboring wards merited only slightly more modest appraisals for their generally "good class" of residences and the absence of tenements and small dwellings. The *New York Times* commented in 1894 on the "fine architectural attractions" along Bedford Avenue. In both the chronology of its development and the interrelation of this growth with rapid-transit innovations, the Bedford and Stuyvesant areas strikingly resembled Harlem in the later nineteenth century. Both emerged as solid residential communities during a "long spurt of energy" that spanned the 1870s through the early 1900s.[47]

As we have noted previously, blacks had lived in this part of

Brooklyn since colonial times. Despite the white invasion of their areas as Brooklyn's expanding populace sought living space, blacks continued to reside there even as the section was transformed. Indeed, the black population of the broadly defined Bedford and Stuyvesant area increased proportionately as rapidly as that of the whites. By 1900, approximately 40 percent of Brooklyn's blacks lived in the area. However, they were not concentrated in a particular quarter, but resided along Atlantic Avenue and Fulton Street, both less than desirable locations because of the noisome presence of the Long Island Railroad on the former and the El on the latter. Negroes had not yet extensively overflowed this narrow strip along these heavily commercial thoroughfares into the primarily residential streets beyond. Although blacks were living in the area in larger numbers than ever before, they were dwarfed into near insignificance by the area's overwhelming whiteness. In 1900 one certainly could not have predicted the ultimate influx and concentration of blacks in Bedford-Stuyvesant.[48]

## NOTES

1. Some representative works about Brooklyn during this period would include Harold C. Syrett, *The City of Brooklyn, 1865-1898, A Political History* (New York, 1944); David McCullough *The Great Bridge* (New York, 1972); Clay Lancaster, *Prospect Park Handbook* (New York, 1972); Donald Simon, "The Public Park Movement in Brooklyn, 1824-1873" (Ph.D. dissertation, New York University, 1972); Robert Smith, "Brooklyn at Play: The Illusion and the Reality, 1890-1898" (Ph.D. dissertation, University of Indiana, 1973).

2. United States Census Bureau, *Ninth Census, 1870, Population* (Washington, 1871), p. 211; United States Census Bureau, *Tenth Census, 1880, Population* (Washington, 1883), pp. 402, 422; United States Census Bureau, *Eleventh Census, 1890, Population* (Washington, 1892), 1: 562-63; United States Census Bureau, *Twelfth Census, 1900, Population* (Washington, 1901), 1: 631. Brooklyn's population during this era was:

| Year | Total Population | Negro Population | Percentage Negro |
|------|-----------------|------------------|------------------|
| 1870 | 396,099 | 4,931 | 1.2 |
| 1880 | 566,663 | 8,095 | 1.4 |
| 1890 | 795,397 | 10,287 | 1.3 |
| 1900 | 1,166,582 | 18,367 | 1.3 |

3. United States Census Bureau, *Eleventh Census, 1890, Vital Statistics of New York and Brooklyn* (Washington, 1894), pp. 238-41.

4. Census Bureau, *Twelfth Census, 1900, Population*, 1: 631; Allan H. Spear, *Black Chicago: The Making of a Negro Ghetto, 1890-1920* (Chicago, 1967), pp. 14-15; W. E. B. Du Bois, *The Philadelphia Negro: A Social Study* (New York, 1967), p. 7.

5. William Wells Brown, *The Black Man, His Antecedents, His Genius, and His Achievements* (New York, 1863), pp. 205-7; Carleton Mabee, "Brooklyn's Black Public Schools: Why Did Blacks Have Unusual Control Over Them?," *The Journal of Long Island History* 11 (Spring 1975); William Katz, ed., *The Anglo-African Magazine*, Vol. I, 1859 (New York, 1968).

6. *New York Weekly Anglo-African*, Sept. 7, 1861; *New York Times*, July 14, 1895.

7. Herbert M. Morris, *The History of the Negro in Medicine* (New York, 1967), p. 31; Harry A. Williamson, "Folks in Old New York and Brooklyn" (New York, 1953), pp. 1-2 (Schomburg Collection); Walter N. Beekman, "Address Sponsored by the Brooklyn Catholic Interracial Council," February 13, 1946.

8. Brooklyn Board of Education, *Proceedings, 1882*, p. 484; Williamson, "Folks in Old New York," pp. 2-3; Sidney H. French, "Biographical Sketch of Mr. Jerome Peterson" (WPA research papers, Schomburg Collection).

9. Leslie L. Alexander, "Susan Smith McKinney, M.D. 1847-1918," *Journal of the National Medical Association* 67 (March 1975): 173-75. After her husband, the Reverend William S. McKinney, died in 1895, she married Theophilus G. Steward. In 1898 she joined Wilberforce University in Ohio as resident physician and faculty member. She remained there until her death in 1918.

10. Samuel R. Scottron, "Manufacturing Household Articles," *The Colored American Magazine* 7 (October 1904): 621-24; "A New Organization in New York That Deserves the Sympathy and Support of the Masses," *The Colored American Magazine* 9 (September 1905): 467-68; "Work for the Committee for Improving the Industrial Condition of Negroes in New York," *The Colored American Magazine* 12 (June 1907): 464; Ralph Foster Weld, *Brooklyn Is America* (New York, 1950), p. 164.

11. Louis Haber, *Black Pioneers of Science and Invention* (New York, 1970), pp. 49-60; "Lewis Howard Latimer: A Black Inventor" (Thomas Alva Edison Foundation, 1973); Beekman, "Address."

12. Seth Scheiner, *Negro Mecca: A History of the Negro in New York City, 1865-1920* (New York, 1965), pp. 184-85, 190; Brooklyn Board of Education, *Proceedings, 1891*, p. 282.

13. Clement Richardson, ed., *The National Cyclopedia of the Colored Race* (Montgomery, Ala., 1919), p. 226; Frank L. Mather, ed., *Who's Who of the Colored Race* (Chicago, 1915), pp. 195-96; Odette Harper, "Biographical Sketch of Fred R. Moore" (WPA research papers, Schomburg Collection).

14. Ralph Ellison, "William L. Bulkley" (WPA research papers, Schomburg Collection); Gilbert Osofsky, *Harlem: The Making of a Ghetto* (New York, 1966), pp. 63-66.

15. Waring Cuney and Carl Offord, "Interview with Mr. Jerome B. Peterson, January 30, 1939" (WPA research papers, Schomburg Collection); French, "Biographical Sketch."

16. Joseph J. Boris, ed., *Who's Who in Colored America* (7 vols.; New York, 1927-50), 1:156; *Who's Who of the Colored Race*, p. 215. In their obituaries both the *Amsterdam News* (June 11, 1930) and the *New York Age* (June 14, 1930) mentioned Perry's being an assistant district attorney in Brooklyn around 1894, but I found no verification of this statement. Among Perry's books were *L'homme d'après la science et la Talmud* (n.p., n.d.); *La situation actuelle en Haiti* (New York, 1913); *Sketch of Philosophical Systems* (n.p., 191?).

17. *Who Was Who in America, Historical Volume, 1607-1896* (Chicago, 1963), p. 406; *New York Age*, June 15, 1905, Feb. 3, 1910. The full title of Perry's book was *The Cushite: or the Descendants of Ham as Found in the Sacred Scriptures, and in the Writings of Ancient Historians and Poets from Noah to the Christian Era* (Springfield, Mass., 1893). During its early years, the title of the black newspaper that was to be known as the *New York Age* varied. From 1880 to November 8, 1884 it was known as the *New York Globe*. From then until October 8, 1887 its title was the *New York Freeman*. Subsequently it became the *New York Age* and continued publication until 1960.

18. Brooklyn Board of Education, *Proceedings, 1882*, p. 484; Mabee, "Brooklyn's Black Public Schools."

19. David Ment, "School Segregation in Brooklyn, N.Y. 1850-1897" (typescript, 1971), pp. 1-4, 11-12, 14-15; Mary White Ovington, *Half a Man: The Status of the Negro in New York* (New York, 1911), p. 17; *Age*, July 13, 1905.

20. Ment, "School Segregation," p. 18; Spear, *Black Chicago*, p. 6; Du Bois, *Philadelphia Negro*, p. 88; Harold Connolly, "A History of Blacks in Newark" (typescript, 1975).

21. Brooklyn Board of Education, *Proceedings, 1887*, p. 545; *1890*,

pp. 46a, 154-55; Department of Public Instruction, *Thirty-Eighth Annual Report of the Superintendent of Public Instruction of the City of Brooklyn for the Year Ending December 31, 1892*, pp. 126-41.

22. Brooklyn Board of Education, *Proceedings, 1891*, p. 648; *1892*, pp. 288, 595; *1893*, pp. 135, 183-87, 223; *1894*, pp. 468, 522; Ment, "Segregated Schools," pp. 19-21; United States Census Bureau, *Eleventh Census, 1890, Report on Education in the United States* (Washington, 1893), table 22; *New York Times*, Sept. 8, 1892, Feb. 19, 1893, June 8, 1893; *Age*, Jan. 4, 1900. Brooklyn had more black teachers than any other northern city except Philadelphia, which had twenty-eight. Chicago and Detroit had none, Boston one, and Newark and Cleveland four each.

23. T. McCants Stewart, "The Afro-American in Politics: An Address," Oct. 27, 1891, p. 9; *New York Times*, March 15, 1891, March 28, 1891, April 4, 1891; *Age*, April 25, 1891. New York City appointed its first black policeman in 1911 (Mabee, "Brooklyn's Black Public Schools," p. 25).

24. Symbolizing this black disaffection for the Republican party was T. McCants Stewart, who spearheaded the establishment of the first black Democratic club in Brooklyn in 1889. In an 1891 speech, Stewart lauded the Democratic leaders of Brooklyn as "men of broad and liberal views." He contrasted the local Republican failure to provide political jobs for blacks to the Democratic performance that saw "over forty Afro-Americans in the public service, drawing an aggregate salary of $40,000." These included twenty teachers and principals, four doormen at police precincts, two clerks in the Department of City Works, plus assorted messengers, watchmen, laborers and janitors (Stewart, "Afro-American in Politics," pp. 5-13). In 1895 Stewart switched back to the Republican party, viewing the Democrats as too hampered by their southern wing.

25. *Brooklyn Daily Eagle, Almanac, 1888*, p. 165; *1900*, p. 588; *Age*, Oct. 22, 1887, Nov. 5, 1887; *New York Times*, Oct. 21, 1900. The Democratic character of the Eighth AD is revealed by the election returns for that district from 1896 to 1904.

| Year | Republican | Democrat |
|------|-----------|----------|
| 1896 | 2,216 | 2,621 |
| 1897 | 2,537 | 3,479 |
| 1898 | 1,817 | 4,203 |
| 1899 | 2,681 | 2,939 |
| 1900 | 2,002 | 4,516 |
| 1901 | 2,612 | 3,494 |
| 1902 | 1,666 | 4,190 |
| 1903 | 2,105 | 3,839 |
| 1904 | 2,315 | 4,025 |

26. Carleton Mabee, "Charity in Travail: Two Orphan Asylums for Blacks," *New York History* (January 1974): 55-77; Mabee, "Brooklyn's Black Public Schools," pp. 28-29.

27. Brooklyn Howard Colored Orphan Asylum, *Annual Reports*, 1885, 1912-13; "The Howard Orphan Asylum," *The Colored American Magazine* 10 (April 1906): 238-43; Mabee, "Charity in Travail."

28. Irving Garland Penn, *The Afro-American Press, and Its Editors* (Springfield, Mass., 1891), p. 292; Elmore Brock, "Augustus M. Hodges," *The Colored American Magazine* 2 (December 1900): 146-47; Armistead Scott Pride, "A Register and History of Negro Newspapers in the United States: 1827-1950" (Ph. D. dissertation, Northwestern University, 1950), p. 305.

29. "The Afro-American Investment Company," *The Colored American Magazine* 9 (July 1905): 390; Fred R. Moore, "Negro Business Enterprises in New York," *The Colored American Magazine* 7 (July 1904): 518-20; *New York Freeman*, Jan. 22, 1887.

30. Scheiner, *Negro Mecca*, p. 101; Williamson, "Folks in Old New York," p. 11; *Age*, Feb. 27, 1908; *Eagle*, Sept. 16, 1892, Dec. 18, 1892.

31. Scheiner, *Negro Mecca*, pp. 20, 34; *New York Times*, July 14, 1895.

32. Du Bois, *Philadelphia Negro*, p. 134.

33. United States Census Bureau, *Twelfth Census, 1900, Occupations* (Washington, 1904), pp. 648-55.

34. Du Bois, *Philadelphia Negro*, p. 156; Census Bureau, *Eleventh Census, 1890, Vital Statistics*, pp. 13-15, 38-41, 444-47, 498-99; United States Census Bureau, *Negro Population in the United States, 1790-1915* (Washington, 1918), p. 334; W. E. B. Du Bois, *Some Notes on the Negroes in New York City* (Atlanta, 1903), p. 3; *New York Globe*, May 26, 1883.

35. *New York Times*, Oct. 1, 1894, Oct. 2, 1894, Oct. 3, 1894, June 12, 1895; *Eagle*, Oct. 1, 1894, Oct. 2, 1894, Oct. 3, 1894, Oct. 23, 1894, Nov. 22, 1898, Sept. 21, 1900.

36. Scheiner, *Negro Mecca*, p. 171; "Speech of the Hon. William E. Robinson of Brooklyn, N.Y., in the House of Representatives, March 2, 1869," p. 31; Mabee, "Brooklyn's Black Public Schools," p. 26. In 1869 only 42 percent of Brooklyn voters favored giving blacks equal voting rights.

37. Brooklyn Board of Education, *Proceedings, 1888*, pp. 638-39; *1891*, p. 594. For examples of inadequate appropriations, see Brooklyn Board of Education, *Proceedings, 1887*, p. 178; *1888*, p. 172a; *1889*, p. 154; *1890*, p. 400.

38. Brooklyn Howard Colored Orphan Asylum, *Annual Reports*, 1872, 1906-10, 1912-13. The orphanage closed its doors in 1918 and never reopened (Mabee, "Charity in Travail," pp. 74-75).

39. Brooklyn Home for Aged Colored People, *Annual Reports*, 1892-97; *Eagle*, May 8, 1892, June 25, 1899.

40. Brooklyn Howard Colored Orphan Asylum, *Annual Report*, 1872; Brooklyn Home for Aged Colored People, *Annual Reports;* Brooklyn Free Kindergarten Association, *Annual Reports.*

41. White served as president of the Brooklyn Bureau of Charities from 1885 until 1920. He actively supported control of tuberculosis, aided the foundation of the Brooklyn Botanical Garden, donated land for public parks, and built the initial low-rent housing project in Brooklyn in 1878. He became a helpful friend of Booker T. Washington and a building at Tuskegee was named after White.

George Foster Peabody supported the Brooklyn Kindergarten Society and the Brooklyn Bureau of Charities. He was also a devotee of Hampton Institute and aided the founding of a Negro YMCA in Brooklyn. He also contributed $16,000 to a black YMCA in Montgomery, Alabama.

Frank S. Jones contributed money and time to the Brooklyn Society for the Prevention of Cruelty to Children.

Alexander Orr, a prominent member of the New York Produce Exchange, was president of the New York Chamber of Commerce in the 1890s.

42. The Brooklyn Home for Aged Men, *Annual Reports*, 1879, 1903; New York Congregational Home for the Aged, *Annual Reports*, 1910-25; Baptist Home of Brooklyn, *Annual Reports*, 1876-1910; Brooklyn Society for the Prevention of Cruelty to Children, *Annual Reports*, 1882-1910; Brooklyn Home for Consumptives, *Annual Reports*, 1882-1910.

43. New York State Local History Leaflets prepared by the Division of Archives and History, "Bedford Corners, Brooklyn" (Albany, 1917), unpaged; Henry R. Stiles, *A History of the City of Brooklyn, the Town of Bushwick, and the Village and City of Williamsburgh* (3 vols.; Brooklyn, 1867), I:158; John C. Brown, "Old Brooklyn and Its Vanishing Roads," *Valentine's Manual of Old New York*, 3: 178, 205; Watson B. O'Connor, *Bedford in Breuckelen Town from 1667 to 1868* (Bangor, Me., 1926), pp. 3-8; Lois Gilman, "The Development of a Neighborhood, 1850-1880: Bedford, A Case History" (MA thesis, Columbia University, 1971).

44. United States Census Bureau, *Fourth Census, 1820* (manuscript); O'Connor, *Bedford in Breuckelen Town*, pp. 7-10; Osofsky, *Harlem*, p. 83.

45. Jacob Judd, "The History of Brooklyn, 1834-1855: Political and Administrative Aspects" (Ph.D. dissertation, New York University, 1959), pp. 4-5, 63, 196-97; Gilman, "The Development of a Neighborhood," pp. 20-21.

46. William E. Fales, *Brooklyn's Guardians: A Record of the Faithful and Heroic Men Who Preserved the Peace in the City of Homes* (Brooklyn, 1867), pp. 320-21; Henry J. Cammann and Hugh N. Camp, *The Charities of New York, Brooklyn and Staten Island* (New York, 1868), pp. 521, 546, 560; Brooklyn Home for Consumptives, *Annual Report*, 1888; Brooklyn Home for Aged Men, *Annual Report*, 1887; Lois J. Gilman, "The Development of a Neighborhood;" *Eagle*, Dec. 19, 1930, April 22, 1931, May 4, 1931, April 6, 1932.

47. New York State Secretary of State, *Census of the State of New York for 1875* (Albany, 1877), p. 19; Census Bureau, *Eleventh Census, 1890, Population*, 1: 562-63; *Eleventh Census, 1890, Vital Statistics*, pp. 174-76, 212-15, 219-21, 224-28; *Twelfth Census, 1900, Population*, 1: 631; Gilman, "The Development of a Neighborhood," p. 44; Osofsky, *Harlem*, ch. 5; *New York Times*, April 22, 1894. In the 1890s the boundaries of the Twenty-third Ward were expanded, making any comparisons between 1890 and 1900 impossible.

48. Census Bureau, *Twelfth Census, 1900, Population*, 1: 631.

PART II

# Foundation Building: 1900-1940

# CHAPTER 3

# Black Influx, White Response

## BLACK INFLUX

In 1900 the 18,367 black residents of Brooklyn formed less than 2 percent of the borough's total population. The growth of this Negro community during the next twenty years was a relatively modest 74 percent, lagging substantially behind the skyrocketing black populations of most other major northern urban centers. Cities like Detroit and Cleveland, virtually devoid of blacks in 1900, became the destination of thousands of southern blacks following the railroads northward from the southcentral region. In Chicago, Philadelphia, Newark, and Los Angeles, the black population doubled, tripled, and more between 1900 and 1920. Similar growth occurred in New York City, but most of it was concentrated in Manhattan, as Harlem established itself during this period as the black capital of the United States and the focus of black settlement in New York City. Brooklyn's share of the city's total Negro population declined from 30 percent in 1910 to 21 percent in 1920, at which time Manhattan contained nearly three-fourths of the city's blacks.[1]

The migration of blacks to the North was an already perceived phenomenon in 1910, but World War I provided a vigorous stimulus to this process.[2] The European conflict created a new market for American manufactures while restricting the flow of immigrants who had traditionally supplied the human power to operate America's factories. European armies sucked up excess population and wartime priorities disrupted normal maritime intercourse. The previous policy of unrestricted European immigration resumed briefly after the war, but national phobias and prejudices and economic factors coalesced to impose severe restrictions upon the influx of European immigrants.

Faced with a decreasing labor supply and needing an expanding labor force, northern employers looked to that vast, generally untapped, internal human resource, the southern American Negro. By default, blacks for the first time found themselves welcome to participate extensively in the northern industrial economy. Attracted by real employment possibilities and encouraged by northern labor recruiters, blacks migrated northward in unprecedented numbers to perform the heavy, unskilled tasks previously assigned to Italians, Poles, and Hungarians.

In addition to these pull-factors, a number of push-factors, both general and specific, facilitated this movement. Rural Americans, both black and white, had long been abandoning their farms to seek a new life in urban centers. Oppressive southern laws and customs kept blacks in near-servitude and poverty. A number of southern agricultural disasters around this time further depressed already grim conditions. The boll weevil ravaged thousands of acres of cotton; low cotton prices led to a curtailment of cotton acreage and thus to the demise of many sharecroppers; devastating floods in 1915 and 1916 only compounded the difficulties of an already weakened southern economy.

All these factors begat what Gunnar Myrdal termed "accumulated migration potentialities." Yet without a corresponding pull-factor, what Dorothy Thomas called "apparent economic opportunity," the Great Migration would not have occurred, or certainly not in the volume it did. Thus black migrants sought the industrial cities of the North for the same reasons earlier European immigrants had—jobs. If this goal was to prove illusory at times, it was not because blacks did not seek employment.[3]

The sharp upsurge in black migration generated by World War I gained momentum during the 1920s. This was the crucial decade during which the geographical base of many of the major northern ghettos was laid. In Detroit, Newark, Manhattan, Cleveland, and even several suburban communities, the black population more than doubled between 1920 and 1930. The resultant racial distribution and concentration formed the core area out of which emerged the ghettos of many northern urban centers. Brooklyn joined this array of burgeoning black centers, as its Negro population more than doubled from 31,912 to 68,921.[4] This black increase drew its primary impetus from the South and, to a lesser degree, the West Indies. In 1930 over 60 percent of Brooklyn blacks had been born in the southeastern United States, especially Virginia and the Carolinas, or outside the country, while the proportion of Negroes born in New York State and residing in Brooklyn had declined from 39 percent in 1910 to 30 percent in 1930. Despite such an absolute increase and a demographic growth rate more than four times that of local whites, Negroes remained overshadowed by Brooklyn's vast white population, which had increased by 500,000 during this same decade.[5]

The salient feature of Brooklyn's black demography during the 1920s, however, was not the actual increase in population but the emerging geographic distribution of that populace. In 1920, Brooklyn's Negroes were most heavily settled along a lengthy narrow axis extending along Fulton Street and Atlantic Avenue from the downtown and Fort Greene areas through the Bedford and Stuyvesant sections. Blacks rarely penetrated beyond these major thoroughfares and their immediately adjoining streets. Beyond lay the primarily white districts of Bedford, Stuyvesant, and Crown Heights.[6] By 1930, however, although Brooklyn had no contiguous, compacted ghetto such as existed in Harlem or South Side

Chicago, the demographic distribution of blacks pointed toward the possible evolution of Central Brooklyn into the primary place of residence for that borough's black population. While the Fulton-Atlantic axis retained its residential primacy, significant numbers of blacks had moved into the area north of Fulton Street for the first time. The racial composition of some blocks shifted dramatically. Areas that had no black residents in 1920 became home for substantial black minorities by 1930. Furthermore, there developed a degree of racial concentration hitherto unknown in Brooklyn. Thus, given hindsight, one can see in skeletal form by 1930 the outline of the future Brooklyn ghetto.[7]

The general northward migration of blacks slowed during the Depression, but Brooklyn's black population expanded at a more rapid rate than most northern urban centers. While the rate of growth (56 + percent) for Brooklyn Negroes was only half that for the 1920s, their absolute increase exceeded that for the previous decade. Furthermore, the white population expanded only 5 percent. Thus, by 1940, Brooklyn's 107,263 blacks formed 4 percent of the borough's total population, the highest proportion since a century before. This continued black growth reinforced the already emerging pattern of black residency. In areas in Bedford-Stuyvesant that had contained modest numbers of blacks in 1930, their population increased. More significant for the process of ghettoization was the appearance of areas almost exclusively black in character. Moreover, Negroes moved into parts of Bedford-Stuyvesant adjoining those sections that were becoming saturated with blacks. Thus the skeletal outline of 1930 was gradually being fleshed out and expanded.[8]

## WHITE REACTION

Since their intensive development in the late nineteenth century, the Bedford and Stuyvesant neighborhoods had been viewed as solid, middle-class, residential communities. In 1920 the area still retained a reputation for "miles and miles of

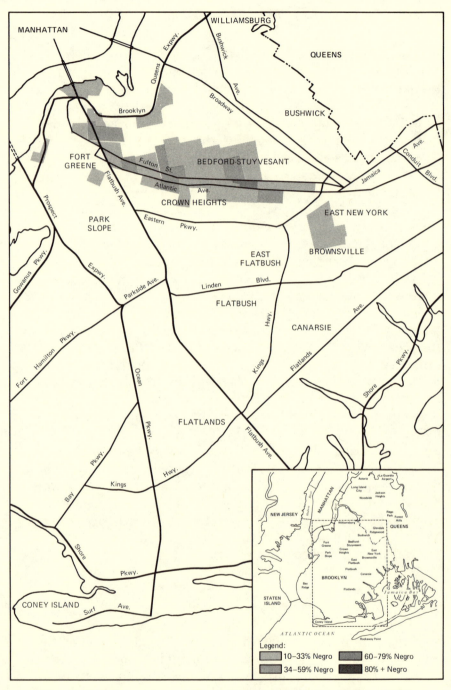

Map 2. Concentration of Black Population in Brooklyn, 1930.

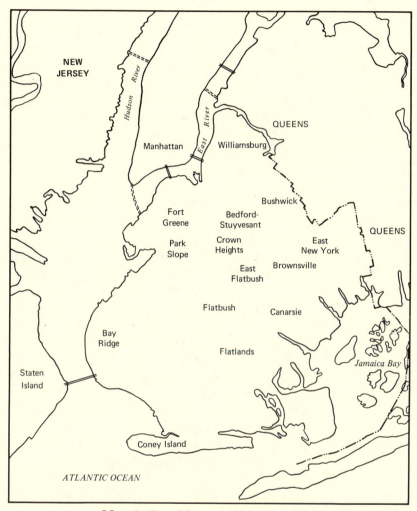

Map 3. Brooklyn neighborhoods.

stately mansions, ..." which housed a "cultured and church going population." The presence of beautiful churches with famous pastors, of splendid schools, clubs, and libraries made them among the "most attractive home sections of the entire borough," inhabited by "as fine a body of middle class citizens as are to be found anywhere." Nevertheless an incipient, if not yet overly visible, decay lay near at hand. Since most of the local housing stock had been constructed prior to 1900, Bedford-Stuyvesant belonged essentially to the Brooklyn that had emerged before the extensive expansion of rapid-transit lines throughout the borough. Subsequently other newer, more attractive or convenient areas such as Bay Ridge, Coney Island, and Flatbush had been developed. New rapid-transit construction bypassed Bedford-Stuyvesant both to stimulate and to tap settlement in these outlying areas. Furthermore, the section's architectural mode—featuring large rooms, high ceilings, and numerous stairs—belonged to a previous era that had made considerable use of no-longer-plentiful immigrant servant help. Some of these homes had been converted into two-family residences, but the majority remained occupied by single families. While substantially constructed, these houses had become functionally undesirable, if not yet obsolete. Thus residential fashion and mass-transit construction cooperated to reduce the appeal of Bedford-Stuyvesant as a middle-class settlement, while the presence of blacks in the proximate area facilitated their succession to any vacant housing stock.[9]

## The Gates Avenue Association

The white residents of Bedford-Stuyvesant perceived the black influx as a threat to their neighborhood and reacted with fear, anger, hostility, and discrimination. Traditionally, white opposition had usually focused upon isolated incidents of residential incursion by blacks into white areas. It tended to be specific and directed against a definite sale or rental. The newer, more extensive and continuous black influx into Bedford-Stuyvesant threatened the existing character of the entire area and hence required a more organized and continuing opposition to stem the black tide. For this purpose white block associations came into existence. A rare insight into their activities is provided by the Gates Avenue Association, founded in 1922. During the 1920s this organization expended more time and talk on the "Negro question" than on any other topic. Essentially it aimed to prevent the movement of blacks into its neighborhood. One member urged a propaganda campaign aimed at the board of aldermen for the enactment of restrictive zoning, and at one executive meeting excerpts were read from the zoning law of Atlanta, Georgia, "showing how the city is zoned for colored and white residents." [10]

In the absence of any such legal sanctions, however, only voluntary cooperation offered hope. The "widening spread of the black belt" required neighborhood solidarity and care in the disposal of property. Residents were urged to utilize only "reliable" realtors and to refrain from selling to "people one does not know." Such a universal tacit conspiracy would prevent blacks from purchasing local property and assure the continued high quality of residents and realty values. The possibility of supplementing voluntary cooperation with restrictive covenants forbidding the sale of property to Negroes was also discussed. Furthermore, the attention of the Gates Avenue Association to non-racial local civic matters was frequently motivated by racial concerns. Support for the construction of the Fulton Street subway and the corresponding razing of the Fulton El was based on an anticipated rise in property values that would lead to the reclamation of depreciated property and the "driving out of less desirables." Opposition to a proposed playground derived in part from the increasing blackness of the blocks immediately adjoining the area. When this much-needed facility was proposed in 1922, Bedford property owners opposed it because it would be financed by a local property tax assessment instead of a boroughwide levy. By 1928, with the financing no longer a local problem, the ostensible reason advanced in opposition to the project was the "heavy traffic" in the vicinity. Others concernedly commented on the steep, unsafe terrain, the opposition of local residents, the needless extravagance. An added but perhaps underlying excuse was fear of "the race riot which a playground will invite." Blacks bitterly assailed this reasoning, arguing that the real reason was the influx of Negroes into the area near the proposed playground and the consequent reluctance of whites to provide an amenity that would primarily benefit blacks.[11]

The activities and attitudes of the Gates Avenue Association were not unique. Its *Minute Book* abounds with references to other block organizations whose representatives expressed a similar concern about the Negro invasion. These groups reflected white apprehensions that as black neighbors increased and multiplied whites would flee from the section. Only total exclusion of Negroes offered a satisfactory solution and stable realty values.

## The Blackshear Affair

The single most dramatic and publicized act of racial discrimination during this period, however, was religious in nature. On September 15, 1929 the Reverend William Blackshear, rector of St. Matthew's Protestant Episcopal Church in Bedford-Stuyvesant, announced that Negroes were no longer welcome in his church. In the parish bulletin he stated: "The Episcopal Church provides churches for Negroes. Several of these churches are within easy reach of this locality. They are in need of the loyal support of all true Negro churchmen, and therefore the rector of this parish discourages the attendance or membership in this church of the members of that race."

When challenged and attacked, Blackshear elaborated and elucidated his position. As a southerner he rejected the concept of social equality among the races in favor of the notion of "parallel civilization." Separate facilities permitted Negroes to develop their own leadership, an impossibility in a white church. This "concern" for black growth was augmented by simple racism; "my church" is "a white church for white people, and I intend to keep it so." Such racism was cloaked in self-protection; increasing numbers of black parishioners would only turn St. Matthew's into a black church. Thus self-interest, racism, and encouragement of Negro civilization coalesced to buttress Blackshear's determination to "keep my church a white church." [12]

Condemnations thundered down upon Blackshear for his outrageous action. One local white minister denounced Blackshear for turning "his back on Jesus." "The church that excludes Negroes, excludes Christ. Exclusive Christianity is not Christianity. A white man's church is not a church of Christ," proclaimed the Reverend L. Bradford Young. The Reverend S. Parkes Cadman, longtime friend of the Negro, stated simply that the "house of God is for prayer and prayer is independent of race or creed." Blackshear's fellow Negro Episcopalian divines in Brooklyn damned his "Jim Crow Christianity." The Reverend George Frazier Miller branded him a "gross misfit" while the Reverend N. Peterson Boyd characterized his pronouncements as "un-Christlike, un-Christian and positively indecent to the point of cruelty." At a rally of the National Afro-Protective League, Rev. Thomas Harten consigned Blackshear to the depths of hell. George E. Haynes of the Federal Council of Churches stated that any churchmen who advocated or adopted racially discriminatory policies "betray the glorious Christ who called all men unto Himself. ... There should be no color line at Christ's altar." [13]

The words of outrage reverberated beyond Brooklyn. According to Congressman Hamilton Fish, "It is inconceivable that any Episcopal congregation north of the Mason and Dixon Line should permit such bigotry and intolerance to be transported into ... Brooklyn, noted for its famous divines, such as Henry Ward Beecher, and the Rev. Dr. Parkes Cadman, ... who have constantly preached the cause of humanity and brotherhood." Fish added that "Abraham Lincoln would turn in his grave" if public opinion in the North upheld this action. A group of forty-two prominent Protestant clergymen, including Harry Emerson Fosdick, John C. Bennett, Henry Sloan Coffin, and Reinhold Neibuhr, condemned Blackshear and the implications of his action.

We join in condemning the wide and more pervasive attitude of racial exclusiveness of which this is only one instance. What he [Blackshear] and his congregation have done openly many of us have tended to do subtly though perhaps unconsciously.

While attention is being fastened upon a single instance, we confess a more general guilt and perplexity. If the Church seriously intends to make her congregations spiritual fellowships she must look squarely at this by no means easy question by rendering it homelike to folk of various races.[14]

No other single event so galvanized the Brooklyn Negro community into a unified, massed voice of protest. Similarly, notable white spokesmen could join with blacks in condemning this blatant example of discrimination. Such interracial protest was obvious and simple, given the clarity of the case. After the initial reactions of shock and horror, however, additional perspectives and views surfaced. The *Age* expressed little surprise with the "sentiments expressed by the Rev. William S. Blackshear ... except that he was a trifle brutal and coarse in his manner of proclaiming them." "Probably it was this crudity and roughness that offended the public sense of decency and prompted the editorial rebukes ... and indignant letters. ..." In his weekly column, Kelly Miller admitted a certain grudging admiration for Blackshear, who had "the moral courage, or ... the immoral courage, of his conviction. What he did in the open, 999 out of 1,000 white ministers believe and practice by overt or covert contrivance." At least Blackshear was not hypocritical as well as prejudiced.[15]

The attitude of the *Eagle* seemed to justify black suspicion of the credibility of outraged white sentiment. Although duly deploring Blackshear's actions and warning that race prejudice was not the sole property of the South, the paper was not without understanding for Blackshear's plight. "No one familiar with the race question will deny that there is a serious problem facing a rector in Mr Blackshear's position," sympathized the *Eagle*. As deplorable as his statements may have been, the *Eagle* seemed equally, if not more, upset with his public expression of them. "Ordinary consideration" should have restrained his utterances and "spared the feelings of the colored people." The implication was clear: had the rector acted more discreetly and secretively he would not have merited opprobrium.[16] Furthermore, a majority of the letters from the local citizenry that were published in the *Eagle* revealed more hostility to blacks than condemnation of Blackshear. They exhibited traditional white attitudes of superiority and antipathy. One writer generously accorded Negroes divine creation and "a place in the world, if they would only keep in their place." Another admitted that if in Blackshear's position he would have made the "same utterances" as that "fine, clean, true, outspoken" man. In an incredible juggling of logic, he even blamed the victims themselves for causing the problem. "As it is, the area in which the church lies is becoming populated with Negroes and as time goes on the Negroes will outnumber the whites and compel many to leave their dear church. Such an act on the part of the Negro is not just." A third writer warned against allowing "our perhaps warped Northern prejudices in behalf of the Negro race to run away with our common sense." After all, how willing would those self-righteous ministers be to perform an interracial marriage or call in a Negro physician? The message and implication were clear; let racial separatism prevail in religious matters, and by extension, let it apply to all aspects of life.[17]

The only prominent individual openly to commend Blackshear's courage was Msgr. John Belford, the white pastor of the Roman Catholic Church of the Nativity. Belford had come to Nativity in 1905 and had built it into a substantial parish. Located in Bedford-Stuyvesant, this parish had been confronted by a rising black population and declining parish resources and had supported the erection in 1922 of a separate Catholic church, St. Peter Claver's, to serve Brooklyn's Negroes. Belford's views thus reflected his own experience with and reaction to Negroes. Both he and Blackshear feared for the future integrity of their churches given shifting demography. In his monthly parish paper Belford asserted that there had been an excess of nonsense in "the denunciation of the minister who boldly announces this church has been built by and is maintained by white people. That minister is well within his rights and he deserves applause for his honesty." Belford compared a church to a home or a private corporation from which certain people could be excluded. If too many Negroes started attending his own church he would ask them to leave, and, if necessary, bar the door with ushers. Quite simply, "Our people do not want the Negroes in their church, in their homes or their neighborhood." St. Peter Claver's Church afforded ample service and required black attendance. Such sentiments expressed Belford's personal biases, but also indicated that the churchmen who condemned Blackshear so freely might not have been so hostile if their churches were being "overrun" by blacks.[18]

These varied responses revealed that Blackshear's decision was not simply the act of a single perverse individual. While Blackshear's southern background undoubtedly influenced his decision, especially the explicit form it took, his act struck a sympathetic chord among local whites, many of whom did approve of this blatant form of segregation. Brooklynites might not lynch Negroes, but many scarcely considered them equals. It was also symptomatic of northern racial relations that both black and white communities could become so agitated over an essentially minor incident. The endemic Negro problems of employment, housing, poverty, and so on failed to arouse even passing notice. This particular dramatic event attracted public attention beyond its intrinsic worth. "Behold what a great fire a little matter kindleth," observed Kelly Miller. It did, however, expose underlying northern attitudes that usually lay hidden beneath pious pronouncements and noncontroversial acts.[19]

## Institutional Succession

During the 1930s, institutional religion acted as a barometer of shifting demography and of temporizing, rationalization, and resistance by whites. The interactive relationship between black influx and white flight was reflected in the changing pattern of ownership of Bedford-Stuyvesant's churches. For many years before 1930 local white churches had contained small Negro memberships. The influx of Negroes in the 1920s and the flight of whites caused a large increase in black attendance at these white churches since relatively few black churches yet existed in the section. The Brooklyn Federation of Churches sympathized with the dilemma faced by such congregations. "While these [white] churches welcomed the few, they find a problem in serving the increased number [of blacks]. Such situations are grave, for they threaten the life of these churches." Clearly implied was the federation's preferred solution to the problem—segregated black churches to relieve white churches of this burden. Similarly, the Reverend J. Henry Carpenter, executive secretary of the Brooklyn Church and Mission Federation, urged the establishment of "good strong Negro churches" in the Bedford area. These semiofficial endorsements of separatism contrasted sharply with the outraged pious pronouncements that had marked the recent Blackshear case.[20]

As their parishioners died or fled, white churches faced financial strains that were further compounded by the Depression. Merger of two white churches offered temporary relief, but the continued "residential changes" (a typical white euphemism for the Negro influx) had only one logical conclusion, the purchase and physical takeover of these churches by black congregations. The case of the white Grace Presbyterian Church offered a prime example of this dynamic. In 1937 this Brooklyn institution voted to merge with a Queens congregation and sell its property to a Negro congregation. Residents of the immediate vicinity protested such a sale because it would lower realty values and damage the general quality of the neighborhood. The Midtown Civic League, a white citizens' organization, bitterly denounced the proposed sale. Clothing himself in the mantle of righteousness, the group's president Sumner Sirtl addressed the Brooklyn-Nassau Presbytery:

Surely, you gentlemen have a moral obligation to the
residents of the Stuyvesant section of Brooklyn who may
see their life savings, which are invested in their homes,
dwindle to less than half of their real value.

It is a prime tenet of equity that one should so use his
own property as not to injure that of another. How much
more forceful is this tenet when looked at from a
standpoint of Christian ethics.

The Presbytery rejected such reasoning, although they issued
no striking declaration of purpose. It had already accepted a
binder and feared a civil law case if it refused to complete the
sale. In addition, the group viewed its primary duty as the
meeting of Grace Church's debts through sale of the property.
The Bridge Street AME Church decisively concluded the
controversy by purchasing the structure in 1938.[21]

Shortly afterward, the Marcy Avenue Baptist Church followed a similar pattern. It was located in a neighborhood
"that has so rapidly become a Negro section that there seems
no alternative to abandoning the property and giving every
possible assistance to establishment of a strong Negro
church." The black Concord Baptist Church purchased this
property. Similarly, in the early 1940s the First AME Zion
Church purchased the Tompkins Avenue Congregational
Church, and Siloam Presbyterian Church moved into the heart
of Bedford-Stuyvesant, acquiring the property of the Central
Presbyterian Church. The prominent Negro congregations
thus followed the flow of black residents to Bedford-Stuyvesant, leaving behind the older, increasingly deserted downtown section. An occasional voice questioned this almost
automatic racial shift in ownership and its resultant separatism. The Reverend John Lathrop, white, former president of
the Brooklyn Urban League, urged that the churches of
Bedford-Stuyvesant, "instead of getting out or selling out to a
Negro organization, ought to make themselves over into
interracial churches." Such a recommendation depended on a

continued white presence in an area that was increasingly becoming an example of *de facto* segregation.[22]

## Other Signs of Discrimination

Racial separatism was not limited to religious institutions in Bedford-Stuyvesant. In PS 35 the Glee Club was formed into separate black and white units with the approval of the principal. It was argued that black boys' voices did not blend with those of white youths. Adding further insult was the restriction of the Negro unit to "mammy" and southern songs. Local hospitals often segregated their patients. Movie theaters discriminated against blacks, usually refusing to sell them orchestra seats.[23]

For a brief period the Ku Klux Klan supplied an added dimension to local race relations. During the early 1920s the Klan prospered in many urban areas of the North. These branches tended to emphasize their pro-Protestant, Prohibitionist, anti-Semitic, and anti-Catholic views, although the Negro was not entirely ignored. While the Klan was more active and successful in Nassau and Suffolk counties on Long Island, it did inaugurate a Brooklyn Klavern in mid-1921. Sporadic support from the local clergy lent an air of respectability to the Klan. Canon William S. Chase of Christ Episcopal Church praised the organization as a band of men "organized to resist the corruption of politics and the lawlessness of our times." The Reverend N. Dwight Hillis, pastor of the historically liberal Plymouth Congregational Church and author of *The Battle of Principles: A Study of the Heroism and Eloquence of the Anti-Slavery Conflict,* urged that "the Klan . . . be defended by every white American who is not under the domination of the Church of Rome." A robed Klansman delivered a Sunday sermon at the Washington Avenue Baptist Church and its pastor, the Reverend Robert McCaul, cited the Klan as necessary to preserve right and order. The Reverend Roy E. Manne of Grace Methodist Episcopal Church defended the Klan as pro-Protestant, prowhite, pro-Gentile.[24]

Although many Klan statements did not stress the racial aspect of the Klan's ideology, Brooklyn Klansmen did occasionally remind blacks of their proper place in American society. The white forefathers who had brought blacks to America gave to them "their civilization and Christian religion and caused them to become the most civilized and useful Negroes the world has known." Despite their civilization, however, Negroes must still recognize that they "are living in the land of the white race and by courtesy of the white race...." Indicative of the Negro's invisibility was the *Eagle's* condemnation of the "Invisible Empire" for its prejudice "against foreigners, against Jews, against Roman Catholics." While the paper allotted space to anti-Klan spokesmen for Jewish and Catholic groups, it generally forgot blacks.[25]


## GRAVEN IMAGES OF HOPE

As the cutting edge of the black frontier advanced more swiftly and surely through Bedford-Stuyvesant during the 1930s, the entrenched white residents reacted with increased alarm. They hoped to halt the racial "blighting" of their neighborhood and preserve its white middle-class tradition. This opposition tended to be more vocal than violent, resorting to a standard set of suggestive phrases and euphemisms such as "desirable," "high quality," "right kind," "certain elements," and so forth, which attempted to gloss over underlying anti-Negro sentiment. When applied to Bedford-Stuyvesant, however, the racial implications were obvious. In addition, plans were advanced to remove the black presence by legal, upright means. White Brooklynites rarely based their opposition to blacks simply on racial prejudice, but sought other plausible reasons—Negroes were lawless or dirty or immoral or caused a decline in property values. Northern propriety and decorum required such euphemistic and legalistic circumlocutions.

An example of this indirect but real racism may be seen in the persistent emphasis by white residents and organizations of Bedford-Stuyvesant on maintaining realty values. Some white spokesmen charged that the racial transformation of Bedford-Stuyvesant was causing a decline in property values. To counteract this development whites formed the Midtown Civic League. According to its president, Sumner Sirtl, the organization's primary purpose was to "better conditions in our section and stabilize real estate values." In testimony before the New York State Temporary Commission on the Condition of the Urban Colored Population, he attributed the decline in local realty values and the reluctance of mortgage companies to loan money to homeowners to the influx of Negroes into the section:

> White people can't raise money on their homes. Banks are afraid the area is going to develop into a slum. Millions of dollars of real estate are at stake. Why? Because of a changing character of the neighborhood. If this keeps on it will have a direct bearing on the income of the city. But there are thousands of white families who won't be driven out. Don't think that Central Brooklyn will become a second Harlem!

That the banks through their loan policies were serving as accomplices in the "decline" of local realty values was not mentioned. Banks were respected and respectable institutions while Negroes were simply Negroes.[26]

In order to maintain property values and preserve Bedford-Stuyvesant as a "desirable" neighborhood, whites proposed a variety of schemes that aimed to remove blacks permanently from the area. Sirtl urged that relief recipients, many of whom were Negroes, be returned to their original townships. He later joined with local realtors in advocating the establishment of an "ideal community for the colored people" on empty land owned by the city near Jamaica Bay, removed from extensive direct contact with whites. Another eager helper suggested a "settlement" for Negroes in the Myrtle Avenue vicinity, since "colored people would rather live in a section populated by their own." Even more helpfully, Msgr. John

Belford suggested "colonizing" Negroes "in an agricultural area somewhere in New York where they could learn how to live and act like other people." Failing these direct relocation schemes, the Midtown Civic League in conjunction with Edward Richards, the president of the East New York Savings Bank, proposed, in prototypical urban renewal fashion, the construction of a "privately financed low cost housing project" in the middle of Bedford-Stuyvesant's black community. It was anticipated that such a project would fragment the concentration of blacks in the area and discourage their future influx.[27]

If such resettlement schemes proved unfeasible, Bedford-Stuyvesant whites hoped that certain local structural transformations would create conditions unconducive to continued black residency. The construction of the Fulton Street subway provided the most persistent image of hope. Since the 1880s, the section had been linked to downtown Brooklyn by means of the Fulton Street Elevated Railroad. The El had contributed to the growth of Bedford-Stuyvesant by providing mass transit between there and the downtown business section of the borough. Unfortunately, the "Fulton Street Spider" also constituted an ugly scar the length of that avenue. Agitation for its removal dated to 1910, although this proved feasible only with the proposed construction of a parallel subway line that would offer more rapid transportation between Central Brooklyn and the downtown areas of Brooklyn and Manhattan. Coupled therefore with the construction of this new transit facility was the congruent demand for the demolition of the existing El.

The beginning of construction of the Fulton Street subway in 1927 raised expectations of a "new, rehabilitated, revitalized, thriving business and residential community," no longer haunted by "drab dilapidated brownstones and vacant stores." One local resident foresaw a "bigger and better Bedford" composed of "residents and businessmen of high character." The Depression, however, interrupted the construction of the subway, and renewed efforts had to await the granting of federal loans in 1934. This again prompted wishful thinking that Central Brooklyn was "on the verge of a structural transformation and a strong real estate revival." In place of the old brownstones, outmoded apartment houses, and dilapidated business buildings, "there will be built modern residences, small unit multi-family houses and attractive looking shopping centers." Such extensive changes would allow "this great section" to "again come into its own" and "rebound back to old-time real estate values." [28]

The expectation was that Central Brooklyn realty values and expansion would emulate the experiences of the Bronx and the Bay Ridge section of Brooklyn following transit improvements in these areas. Such hopes, however, ignored certain realities. Prior to subway construction, Bay Ridge had been an underpopulated area with substantial vacant tracts available for development. Furthermore, its incorporation into the city transit network had antedated an era of prosperity and booming residential construction during the 1920s. The Bronx was similarly underpopulated before its transit links to Manhattan were constructed. In spectacular fashion the population of the Bronx nearly tripled between 1910 and 1930. The subsequent construction of the Independent subway line in the late 1920s had less demographic impact on the Bronx because of the borough's previous growth. Subways had been instrumental in opening outlying areas to intensive development and population. Bedford-Stuyvesant, however, already stood fully constucted with little open land for speculation and building. Furthermore, neither the Bronx nor Bay Ridge possessed a substantial, indigenous Negro population to cause prospective buyers to hesitate in committing themselves. Finally, the economic conditions of the Depression militated against these sanguine predictions of rising realty values. Thus Central Brooklyn's anticipated growth and transformation could not be predicated on the essentially dissimilar situations of Bay Ridge and the Bronx.

After what must have seemed an eternity to local residents, the Fulton Street subway was finally opened on April 8, 1936. A spate of articles again appeared, all hopeful of a "modernization ... and enhancement of real estate values," both commercial and residential. *Brooklyn Realty Magazine*, the organ of the Brooklyn Real Estate Board, editorialized glowingly:

> April the 8th will mark a red letter day in the history of Brooklyn, for on that date another important extension to the city's municipal subway will be placed in operation.
>
> For many years we have been hearing and reading about the new transit line under Fulton Street, and now we are about to see this dream become a reality. What the opening will mean to the section to be served by the new line . . . can easily be imagined. Rapid transit brings with it the erection of new buildings and the rehabilitation of existing structures. Fulton Street should prove no exception to this rule, and during the next few years many improvements will be made in the territories within walking distance of the Fulton Street subway.

Unfortunately for these local boosters, the expected second stage, the razing of the Fulton El, became mired in legal and political entanglements. Continually, local civic organizations and prominent residents sought its immediate removal in order to salvage the community from further deterioration and drive out "the undesirables." Not until the mid-1940s, however, was the demolition work completed in Bedford-Stuyvesant.[29]

Another method that local realtors and civic leaders advocated for the salvation of Bedford-Stuyvesant was the structural transformation of existing buildings. In 1930 this section was extensively covered by rows of brownstone houses. These dwellings, it was argued, had become "obsolete" as homes for the average family but could be modernized by "intelligent remodeling" that would prevent the development of slums. In addition to such individual renovation, this territory was also viewed as "ripe for modern apartment developments and business structures" which would replace the old brownstones and tenements.[30] Primary propaganda, however, focused upon converting one- and two-family brownstones into multifamily dwellings. One such typical structure, located at 27 Halsey Street in Central Brooklyn, contained eight large rooms on four floors. The monthly rent of twenty-five dollars did not cover taxes, interest on the mortgage, insurance, water charges, and upkeep. After modernization, rearrangement, and reconstruction, the building contained six apartments ranging in size from two to four rooms and complete with modern plumbing, heating, and kitchen facilities. Such improvements increased rental income a potential tenfold. This was billed as an exemplary "solution of the housing problem in Brooklyn," a means of stemming the migration of "desirable population" to the suburbs. Attractive renovation increased property values and permitted the owner to charge higher rents, which would effectively discourage or even bar many blacks from purchasing or renting homes in Bedford-Stuyvesant.[31]

The fundamental purpose of these various schemes was to create an atmosphere conducive to rising property values and consequently rising rents. The section would thereby become the white middle-class neighborhood of Sirtl's and Belford's dreams, and the neighborhood would be restored "to what it once was" twenty years previous, "the backbone of our borough." Rising realty values would lead to the improvement of properties, the attraction of "desirable" tenants, and the charging of higher rents for modern facilities that poor blacks (and whites for that matter) could not afford. By means of this economic squeeze play, Bedford-Stuyvesant would be preserved.

Ironically, both schemes contained the seeds of their own destruction. The anticipated savior of Bedford-Stuyvesant, the Fulton Street subway, contributed manifestly to the racial transformation of the neighborhood. For ten years Fulton Street was scarred not only by the eyesore of the El but also by the presence of subway construction of varying dimensions and permanent uncertainty. While the underground transportation might ultimately make the area more attractive, its lengthy and interrupted construction was a temporary blight. Furthermore, the linking of Central Brooklyn to Manhattan by convenient transit, which was expected to attract white-collar workers to the area, also made Bedford-Stuyvesant convenient to Harlem. A rider could now travel from 125th Street and Eighth Avenue in Harlem to Central Brooklyn in half the time previously required. One could live in the less crowded atmosphere of Bedford-Stuyvesant and yet be reasonably proximate to the pleasures and entertainment of Harlem and the employment opportunities of Manhattan. The possibility of black homeownership was much greater in Brooklyn than Manhattan, and rental costs were considerably more modest. One black realtor predicted that "with the coming of the new subway, we expect a great influx of people [Negroes] in this borough." Already he possessed a long list of Manhattan residents desiring to live in Brooklyn when transportation was improved.[32]

While structural modernization might have salvaged some of the pre-1900 vintage brownstones, it also created the possibility of imminent decay. The construction of four two-room apartments in a single building offered the opportunity for instant overcrowding. To place any more than a single couple in such surroundings would mean more than one person per room. The temptation to allow the number of occupants to expand despite health, sanitary, and structural hazards and to realize the maximum return in the shortest time could be both persuasive and destructive. As blacks increasingly moved into Bedford-Stuyvesant, this opportunity was seized and the prospect of slum prevention was overwhelmed by overcrowding, blight, and poverty.

Between 1900 and 1940 in Brooklyn, the process of urban black ghettoization, which is central to twentieth-century United States urban history, proceeded apace. If it had not yet attained the dimension of subsequent years, neither had any effective resistance or counterbalance been forthcoming. The factors of black migration, urbanization, and concentration had achieved an internal momentum, which was abetted by such aracial factors as restrictive immigration legislation, which afforded blacks limited economic opportunities and housing units to occupy, and suburbanization, especially significant during the 1920s, which was to evolve into the functional national land-use policy after World War II. While new technological and economic forces most definitely affected subsequent developments, what occurred demographically and spatially in Brooklyn, and much of urban America after 1940, was the logical growth and intensification of an already existent dynamic.

## NOTES

1. United States Census Bureau, *Negro Population in the United States, 1790-1915* (Washington, 1918), p. 101; United States Census Bureau, *Negroes in the United States, 1920-1932* (Washington, 1935), pp. 32, 55, 62. The basic demographic data for Brooklyn during this period were:

| Year | Total Population | Negro Population | Percentage Negro |
|------|------------------|------------------|------------------|
| 1900 | 1,166,582 | 18,367 | 1.6 |
| 1910 | 1,634,351 | 22,708 | 1.4 |
| 1920 | 2,018,356 | 31,912 | 1.5 |
| 1930 | 2,560,401 | 68,921 | 2.7 |
| 1940 | 2,698,285 | 107,263 | 4.0 |

2. Suggested titles on black migration might include: Louise Venable Kennedy, *The Negro Peasant Turns Cityward: Effects of Recent Migrations to Northern Centers* (New York, 1930); Clyde Vernon Kiser, *Sea Island to City: A Study of St. Helena Islanders in Harlem and Other Urban Centers* (New York, 1932); Arna W. Bontemps and Jack Conroy, *They Seek a City* (New York, 1945); Thomas J. Woofter, *Negro Problems in Cities* (New York, 1928).

3. Gunnar Myrdal, *An American Dilemma* (New York, 1944), pp. 191-96.

4. Census Bureau, *Negroes in the United States*, pp. 32, 54. In 1930 Brooklyn ranked sixth in northern urban Negro population behind New York City, Chicago, Philadelphia, Detroit, and Cleveland. However, the vastness of Brooklyn's population (it ranked third in total population behind only New York City and Chicago) dwarfed these 69,000 blacks. Brooklyn's black population proportion (2.7

percent) represented the lowest level in the thirty cities with the largest Negro populations.

5. Ibid., pp. 32-36. In 1930, 11,266 of New York City's 54,754 foreign-born Negroes resided in Brooklyn. This constituted the largest black immigrant community in the country outside Harlem. In 1930, 28,883 Brooklyn blacks had been born in the Southeast with Virginia contributing 9,604, North Carolina 8,023, and South Carolina 5,824.

6. The Bedford-Stuyvesant section lacks any legal standing or boundaries. Originally it encompassed the distinct sections of Bedford and Stuyvesant that centered about the avenues of the same names. The earliest reference that I have found to the hyphenated union of the two areas is in a *Brooklyn Daily Eagle* article of February 21, 1931. This designation attained a permanency and pervasiveness in the late 1930s, replacing the separate terminology and the title "Central Brooklyn" in popular usage. In 1938, the New York State Temporary Commission on the Condition of the Urban Colored Population used the hyphenated terminology. After the 1943 grand jury hearings on crime conditions in Bedford-Stuyvesant, the linkage of the two names was assured. Subsequently, the imprecision of the section's boundaries allowed them to expand in popular conception to encompass most of black Brooklyn.

7. Walter Laidlaw, ed., *Population of the City of New York, 1890-1930* (New York, 1932), pp. 130-31.

8. United States Census Bureau, *Sixteenth Census, 1940, Census Tract Data on Population and Housing; New York City* (New York, 1942), pp. 52-70.

Bedford-Stuyvesant's population in 1940 was to some extent a polyglot reflection of the new immigration. Parts of the area were heavily Jewish with large numbers of foreign-born persons from Russia, Poland, and Austria living there, but no area seemed to be without its Italian element and in some corners of Bedford-Stuyvesant Italians formed the dominant ethnic group. Some residual pockets of Germans and Irish also still persisted. These immigrants together with their offspring represented a clear majority of local whites although older native white families were not uncommon in some parts of the section. In addition to this white population, a considerable black population constituted approximately one-quarter of Bedford-Stuyvesant's population.

9. *Eagle*, Jan. 11, 1920, April 11, 1920, July 29, 1923. Of course, not every structure in the area attained such solid middle-class standards. According to a 1918 study, workingmen's homes in the Bedford district contained many of the same deficiencies as those located elsewhere in Brooklyn. Less than half the apartments possessed interior toilets, only 23 percent had bathrooms, over 60

percent contained interior rooms. These figures approximated borough averages. John C. Gebhart, *Housing Standards in Brooklyn: An Intensive Study of Housing Records of 3227 Workingmen's Families* (Brooklyn, 1918), pp. 9, 13.

10. Gates Avenue Association, *Minute Book.* This important document is in the collection of the Long Island Historical Society.

11. Ibid.; *Eagle*, June 2, 1922, June 4, 1922, Feb. 21, 1929, Feb. 28, 1929, March 7, 1929; *Amsterdam News*, July 11, 1928, March 13, 1929, April 10, 1929.

12. *Eagle*, Sept. 16, 1929, Sept. 17, 1929, Sept. 19, 1929, Sept. 26, 1929, Oct. 14, 1929; *New York Times*, Sept. 17, 1929, Sept. 27, 1929, Sept. 30, 1929.

13. *Amsterdam News*, Sept. 25, 1929; *Eagle*, Sept. 17, 1929, Sept. 18, 1929, Sept. 23, 1929, Sept. 28, 1929, Oct. 1, 1929.

14. *Eagle*, Sept. 18, 1929, Sept. 24, 1929; *New York Times*, Sept. 18, 1929, Sept. 25, 1929.

15. *New York Age*, Sept. 28, 1929; *Amsterdam News*, Oct. 2, 1929. Kelly Miller was former dean of Howard University and a regular contributor to the black press.

16. *Eagle*, Sept. 18, 1929.

17. *Eagle*, Sept. 20, 1929, Sept. 28, 1929, Sept. 30, 1929, Oct. 12, 1929.

18. *Amsterdam News*, Oct. 23, 1929; *Eagle*, Sept. 20, 1929, Oct. 7, 1929, Oct. 18, 1929. Msgr. Belford was a prominent, outspoken cleric, who deserves to be studied in some detail.

19. *Amsterdam News*, Oct. 16, 1929; *Eagle*, Sept. 19, 1929. Blackshear remained in Brooklyn until 1933 when he resigned his pastorate to become archdeacon in a Texas diocese (*Eagle*, Sept. 8, 1933).

20. Brooklyn Federation of Churches, *Yearbook*, 1932, p. 33; *Eagle*, March 23, 1938. Because of the "increasing Negro population" in the borough, the Brooklyn Federation of Churches formed a race relations committee in 1932.

21. *Amsterdam News*, July 3, 1937, Dec. 3, 1938; *Eagle*, June 24, 1937, June 28, 1937, July 7, 1937, July 13, 1937, Dec. 10, 1938.

22. *Age*, Jan. 7, 1939, Sept. 12, 1942, Sept. 24, 1948; *Amsterdam News*, Feb. 4, 1939; *Eagle*, Jan. 3, 1939, March 26, 1939, May 20, 1942, Sept. 26, 1942, Feb. 29, 1944, Oct. 2, 1944.

23. *Age*, March 21, 1925; *Amsterdam News*, Sept. 1, 1926, Dec. 22, 1926, Jan. 23, 1929, Jan. 30, 1929, Feb. 6, 1929.

24. Kenneth T. Jackson, *The Ku Klux Klan in the City, 1915-1930* (New York, 1967), pp. 90-91, 175-77; *Eagle*, Feb. 5, 1923, July 7, 1924, June 9, 1925.

25. *Eagle*, Aug. 20, 1923, Nov. 20, 1923, May 14, 1924.

26. *Age*, Jan. 22, 1938, Sept. 3, 1938; *Amsterdam News*, Jan. 22, 1938. The belief that banks "redlined," that is, refused to make loans

in certain sections of Bedford-Stuyvesant at this time, has been often expressed and is indeed probably accurate though I have seen no study that has specifically addressed this issue. The evidence thus far seems somewhat fragmentary, impressionistic, and personal, which is why I have refrained from making more of this factor.

27. *Age*, Nov. 20, 1937, Jan. 22, 1938, Sept. 3, 1938, March 9, 1940, June 22, 1940; *Amsterdam News*, July 16, 1938, Nov. 27, 1943.

28. *Eagle*, June 16, 1931, May 20, 1934, Aug. 26, 1934, June 16, 1935.

29. *Eagle*, March 15, 1936, April 5, 1936.

30. *Eagle*, Sept. 6, 1931, March 27, 1932, Dec. 17, 1933, March 15, 1936.

31. *Brooklyn Realty Magazine* 12 (July 1937): 5-9; *Eagle*, Sept. 29, 1937. Undoubtedly not all white realtors in Bedford-Stuyvesant opposed the black influx. Some profited from blockbusting and panic sales. Local Negro realtors advertised houses for sale or rent in the New York Negro press. However, the role of black and white realty activities in attracting blacks to Bedford-Stuyvesant is less clear than in the case of Harlem in the early 1900s when Philip Payton's Afro-American Realty Company was operating (see Gilbert Osofsky, *Harlem: The Making of a Ghetto* [New York, 1966], pp. 92-104, for a detailed account of the Harlem scene).

32. *Amsterdam News*, April 4, 1936. In 1940 black median rent in Brooklyn was $24.49; in Manhattan it was $33.85 (United States Census Bureau, *Sixteenth Census, 1940, Population and Housing: Statistics for Health Areas* [Washington, 1942], pp. 104, 154.

# CHAPTER 4

# Creating an Institutional Framework

## ORGANIZATIONAL FLOWERINGS

The early twentieth century was a time of institutional ferment and fermentation throughout the North, both among the black community and among sympathetic whites. Northward black migration was a continuing phenomenon that demanded some organizational response in those cities to which blacks flocked. Even prior to the Great Migration during and after World War I, the need for positive action and institution building was already clear. The formation of those organizations that were eventually to coalesce to form the Urban League began in 1905 with the formation of the Association for the Protection of Colored Women. In the same year the Niagara movement, the forerunner of the NAACP, held its initial conference. New or refurbished Negro YMCAs were constructed, especially through the benevolence of Julius Rosenwald, president of Sears Roebuck, in numerous northern cities. Much of the organizational framework that would form the foundation of black institutional life in northern urban

centers was constructed during the first two decades of the
century.

Not only national headquarters but local branch offices were
established, including several in Brooklyn. As indicated previously, black institutional life in Brooklyn had achieved a
certain maturity during the nineteenth century. In the 1890s
blacks could participate in an extensive array of political,
social, cultural, religious, and social work organizations. To be
sure, these institutions undoubtedly attracted the active
participation of only a minority of the local citizenry, mainly
the better-off, but such has always been the nature of
organizational life. With the exception of the existing
churches, the centrality of most of these older institutions to
black life in Brooklyn diminished during the first part of the
twentieth century. Between 1900 and 1920 that network of
new organizations developed that was to form the institutional framework of black Brooklyn for the next fifty years.
By 1920 the Urban League, NAACP, Negro YMCA and
YWCA, and the Elks had all established Brooklyn branches.

## The YMCA and YWCA

The possibility of establishing a Negro branch of the YMCA
had been discussed during the 1890s under the prodding of the
Reverend Alexander J. Henry, pastor of the Nazarene Congregational Church. During this time a small number of blacks
did meet regularly at the central branch of the Y. In 1901,
Henry renewed his efforts in a conference with W. Frederick
Trotman, Norman D. Johnson, J. C. DeVillis, and W. E.
Johnson. These four gentlemen canvassed the black population and enrolled 250 men who pledged to support such an
enterprise. Organizational meetings were held at the central
branch, but the fundamental question of a permanent meet-
ing-place remained a vexing problem. White philanthropy
provided the solution. George Foster Peabody, a longtime
supporter of Negro causes and a Brooklyn resident, purchased
and furnished a three-story and basement brownstone building on Carlton Avenue near Fulton Street in the Fort Greene

Park section for this new branch of the YMCA. On June 15, 1902 the Carlton Y opened its doors amidst impressive ceremonies that were the "talk of the town among Brooklyn Negroes for days and weeks afterwards." [1]

The formation of such a racially separate branch created a philosophical dilemma. Some blacks had met at the Central YMCA prior to 1902, but it seems doubtful that their numbers approached the eventual membership of the distinct Carlton facility. Given prevailing white attitudes, anything more than token integration of institutional facilities would have been most surprising. When one black writer complained later of the "Jim Crow" YMCA, the *Age* replied that the primary consideration must be the existence of some sort of Y, segregated or not, catering to Negroes. The growing black population created the need for such a facility; white prejudice assured its separateness.[2]

The Y building contained sitting rooms, a reading room, library, game room, and a limited number of furnished rooms. Additional equipment was modest, consisting of one pool table, two checker tables, and a few boxes of dominoes. Activities tended strongly toward exhortatory moral uplift with regular Sunday meetings and other lectures and educational programs. The primary purpose of the branch was "purely religious," its object "to save and develop young men." However, the Y also functioned as a social-service and community center. Beginning in 1911, it operated an employment service, the first such program in a Negro YMCA; it sponsored a glee club and orchestra and a baseball team. The building served as headquarters for a variety of Negro organizations from the Boy Scouts to the Ministerial Alliance. The first black Scout troop in the United States began in 1910 under the direction of James R. Spurgeon in cooperation with the Carlton Y. It pioneered the development of summer-camp life for black children beginning in 1910 and subsequently purchased a 156-acre farm in upstate New York to expand this program.[3]

Shortly after the establishment of the Carlton Y, a parallel branch of the YWCA was founded at 112 Lexington Avenue near Bedford Avenue. This was only the second YWCA branch in Brooklyn. While its program was heavily leavened with spiritual exercises, it also offered "practical help to its members." The Department of Household Training offered a series of courses intended to serve as a thorough preparation for domestic employment, encompassing such skills as cooking and the care of the kitchen, laundering, general cleaning, sewing, childcare, and home nursing. In addition, there was instruction in such traditional Negro trades as dressmaking and millinery. Such training prepared students for a limited job spectrum in personal and domestic service. The Lexington Y also operated an employment service to assist its members in finding work. Although it may be argued that this program reinforced the occupational stereotyping of black women, it was also a pragmatic acknowledgment of existing employment opportunities. Overwhelmingly, black females were relegated to domestic work at this time. In addition to employment work, the Y met the varied needs of Negro girls and women by providing dormitory rooms, Bible study and inspirational talks, athletics and drama, and classes in citizenship, flower making, and Negro music.[4]

The pressures of northward migration during World War I strained the limited facilities and resources of these Ys. Both the Carlton and Lexington branches conducted successful building campaigns at this time to expand their facilities. The new YMCA, still located on Carlton Avenue, opened in 1918 and shortly thereafter the YWCA relocated to new quarters on Ashland Place, near the Carlton Y. The YMCA benefited substantially from the philanthropy of John D. Rockefeller and Julius Rosenwald, each of whom donated $25,000 toward the construction of the new building. At the time of its completion, the building, land, and furnishings, valued at $215,000, represented the most expensive Negro Y in the country. The new structure provided vastly expanded facilities, including a swimming pool, bowling alleys, and seventy dormitory rooms.[5] The modern equipment drew new members to the Y, but membership did not keep pace with the multiplying Negro populace and its needs. Furthermore, the emergence of Bedford-Stuyvesant as the focus of black residence in the 1920s reduced the effectiveness of the Carlton Y, which had been built in the old downtown center of black settlement just before the growth of the uptown community. It therefore existed increasingly in semi-isolation from the community it was designed to serve. Moving from Lexington Avenue to 221 Ashland Place, the YWCA also obtained more commodious quarters. The four-story brick structure contained a library, a large meeting-hall, cafeteria, and thirty-one rooms. Its initially convenient location, however, was similarly undermined by the migration of blacks to Bedford-Stuyvesant. Thus neither male nor female Ys accomplished what they might have had their new locations been more fortuitous.[6]

## Social-Service Organizations

Late nineteenth-century organizational efforts to deal with Negro social problems concentrated on particular aspects of black life. The Howard Orphanage and the Prince Street Kindergarten assisted young blacks; the Home for Aged Colored People dealt with the elderly. The first social-service organization to attempt to deal with the needs of the black population on a more comprehensive scale was the Lincoln Settlement, which opened on May 15, 1908 at 105 Fleet Place in the center of the downtown black community. Dr. Verina Morton-Jones, its sponsoring advocate, felt that "something must be done" for the people of the area whom she had found "in dire need of physical and moral uplift." In the immediate vicinity were located some of the worst slum dwellings in the borough "where the bravest efforts at cleanliness meet with discouraging results." [7]

While unable to attack effectively the entire range of social problems that required attention, the Settlement did undertake an extensive program that brought it into contact with a larger number of blacks than any previous organization. It operated, at a nominal fee, a safe and secure day nursery for working mothers. The already existing Negro kindergarten operated by the Brooklyn Free Kindergarten Society relocated to the Lincoln Settlement. Afternoon and evening classes and clubs aimed to meet the needs of girls and boys. The Settlement offered classes in embroidery, cooking, folk dancing, and carpentry and sponsored debating and choral clubs. This work was supported by voluntary contributions, primarily of white origin, although these proved scarcely munificent, and lack of funds occasionally forced the temporary closing of the day nursery. In 1915 the Lincoln Settlement operated on a marginal budget of $3,400; to meet even this sum it urgently required more contributions. According to the customs of the times the officers and board of directors were overwhelmingly white, headed by Mary White Ovington. However, the daily administration of the work rested in black hands.[8]

In 1913 a local branch of the National League on Urban Conditions Among Negroes opened at 185 Duffield Street under the direction of Paul. F. Mowbray. In its initial phase the league concentrated on improving black housing conditions by cooperating with the Tenement House Commission and the board of health in correcting abuses and violations. It also listed rooms and apartments "which may be rented by colored persons." Through Big Brother and Big Sister work it sought to assist boys and girls and keep them out of court. The seeking of employment received little attention. This particular organization disappeared within two years.[9]

Following a lapse of three years and under a new name, the Urban League, the organization reappeared in Brooklyn in November 1917 on a permanent basis. Initially, the League lacked an office of its own, operating from space lent to it by the Juvenile Probation Society, located in the children's court building. Such a location handicapped the organization's work, by associating it "too closely in the public mind as distinctly a child welfare organization." In addition, limited space made extensive visiting to the office difficult, thus hindering industrial and housing advisement. The hope to open an office in a "colored section" of Brooklyn and bring its work more visibly before the public reached fruition in 1920 with the partial merger of the Urban League with the Lincoln Settlement. This permitted the League to move its operation to the settlement house and concentrate Negro social service organizations in one location. The weak financial condition of the Settlement forced it to seek such a merger or face collapse. For a period the two groups maintained separate offices, boards of directors, and financial statements, although employing a unified professional staff. These formal distinctions ended in 1927 with complete integration into a single institution.[10]

The work of the Urban League covered a broad spectrum of activities. As the primary black social work agency in Brooklyn, it was expected to handle all the black problems of the borough. In its early years it investigated Negro housing conditions, conducted health meetings at churches, provided temporary relief for deserving families. A major part of its work concerned children; the children's court and Juvenile Probation Society referred black cases to its jurisdiction; the League arranged summer camp vacations. While some job placements were made, the lack of space and staff prevented the organization of a full-time industrial department. Throughout the 1920s and 1930s the League remained a social-service agency with primary emphasis on court work, family visits, health, relief, and travelers' aid, although a separate industrial department with its own director was created in 1926. The continued activities of the Lincoln Settlement in nursery and kindergarten care, and as a center for clubs and meetings, added further diversity to 105 Fleet Place. The building also acted as headquarters for Negro visiting nurses serving the neighborhood. In 1927, the League expanded its settlement services when it acquired an old church for use as a clubhouse and gymnasium to "carry on a comprehensive program of boys' work." The Hudson Avenue Boys Club opened on March 1, 1928. Further diffusing the League's energies was the establishment of the Snyder Avenue Boys Club in 1929, which served as a recreational and community center for the growing black population of the Flatbush section. This social-service orientation continued unabated into the 1930s. In 1936, for example, such diverse public and private institutions and agencies as nine hospitals, seven public schools, two high schools, the district attorney's office, the local courts, the Society for the Prevention of Cruelty to Children, the Visiting Nurse Association, and the British consul general all referred cases to the League.[11]

National Urban League officials were not sympathetic with such settlement-house activities, which they considered diversionary. The Urban League traditionally viewed employment as the "crux of the situation" with the primary objective "the development of industrial opportunities for Negroes in cities." L. Hollingsworth Wood, president of the National Urban League, expressed the fear that settlement programs would "inevitably swamp and cramp" the other activities of the League. This industrial primacy was never established in the Brooklyn branch, where the settlement work was allowed to continue in order to prevent the "catastrophe" that would result from giving up the only local settlement for blacks. The employment work of the Brooklyn branch was therefore often submerged under its social-welfare activities, even after the establishment of the industrial department enabled the League to collect and publish employment information and statistics, offer vocational guidance, and provide a free employment service. Such placements as the League was able to make, however, rarely extended beyond traditional "Negro" jobs. It maintained a list of "dependable" women willing to perform day work, and secured employment for Negroes as janitors, chauffeurs, laborers, mothers' helpers, messengers, waitresses, elevator men, and so on. Moreover, such work as was available for blacks was quite sensitive to general economic conditions. Even prior to the stock market cataclysm of 1929, Robert Elzy, executive secretary of the Brooklyn League, was predicting a dim occupational future with few additional employment possibilities for Negroes in firms not already using them.[12]

Nowhere was it ever admitted, publicly at least, that the Brooklyn Urban League was fundamentally a product of negativism, that it was performing tasks that other organizations, catering to a general (i.e., white) clientele, should have been performing. The "dependence" of courts, agencies, schools, and relief organizations on the League was but tacit witness to the failure of these other groups to respond to black needs. That the League stood so majestically alone was more a reflection of the moral and material poverty of white and black communities respectively, than evidence of brilliant racial cooperation.[13] Furthermore, one may legitimately question the quality of some of the services provided by the League for the benefit of its constituents. How adequate were the facilities and staff after one pried behind the rhetoric of annual reports? For example, while the Hudson Avenue Boys Club may have created an environment preferable to the dirty and dangerous streets of one of the worst slum districts in the borough, the structural limitations and defects of this pre-Civil War, antiquated, and abandoned Baptist church could scarcely be ignored in assessing the general effectiveness of the club. The League itself complained about operating from an "outmoded and inadequate building" that was "ill-adapted to service as headquarters for a modern social service program." A series of studies sponsored by the Welfare Council of New York City further emphasized the limitations imposed by institutional penury. An inventory of the arts-and-crafts activities of thirty-one settlement houses in the city indicated that those conducted by the Brooklyn Urban League were of low quality. An intensive examination of eleven settlement nurseries was extremely critical of the health standards, physical plant, cleanliness, limited equipment, and overly restrictive discipline in the one conducted by the League.[14]

In addition to these structural and practical limitations, the increasing geographical separation of the Fleet Place office from the bulk of the black population further hindered the League. Nevertheless, the efforts of the Brooklyn Urban League to ameliorate the grim life of local blacks, however restricted and stunted, stood out starkly when compared with the lack of other efforts. It provided a modicum of social betterment and individual happiness by sending children to summer camp, distributing food baskets, placing blacks in jobs, and running recreational and educational facilities for youths of all ages. Without the League, black life in Brooklyn would have been more difficult than it was.

Given the reliance of the League and the other local black organizations upon white funding for both capital and operating expenses, the funneling of some of these dollars to the support of southern Negro educational institutions reduced the amount of money available for Brooklyn-based institutions. Even before the establishment of a local branch of the Armstrong Association in 1906, Brooklyn whites had long been providing scholarship assistance to students at Hampton Institute. The association attracted white support for Hampton from the White, Peabody, Pratt, and Babbott families, all prominent in Brooklyn charity work. Booker T. Washington appeared periodically in Brooklyn soliciting funds. In 1908, both Secretary of War William Howard Taft and Washington visited Brooklyn and spoke on the association's behalf. Between 1910 and 1920 the Armstrong organization usually donated at least $3,000 annually to Hampton. In 1914 it served as the conduit for a gift of $40,000 to establish a scholarship fund. A wealthy Brooklyn Negro even willed $10,000 to both Hampton and Tuskegee Institutes while reserving only $500 for the Carlton Y. Had a greater portion of this money been provided to the Lincoln Settlement or the Negro Ys, they would have been able to offer expanded service to their local constituencies.[15]


## PROTESTS AND PASTORS

In addition to these uplift and social work organizations, a chapter of the fledgling NAACP was founded in Brooklyn, the initial step being taken in 1914, when Oswald Garrison Villard and W. E. B. Du Bois addressed a mass meeting at Concord Baptist Church. The association grew slowly, its membership remaining under 100 in 1920. During the 1920s and 1930s, under the direction of such blacks as Dr. Walter N. Beekman, Mrs. Maria C. Lawton, O. D. Williams, and Stanley Douglas, it protested discriminatory acts perpetrated against Negroes in Brooklyn and throughout the country. It sponsored an anti-lynching meeting at the Brooklyn Academy of Music at which Walter White and James Weldon Johnson of the national office spoke. It protested and won an apology for the use of the term "darkies" by a local newspaper; it opposed acts of discrimination by local movie theaters, insurance offices, and stores; it repeatedly demanded a cessation of police brutality against Negroes.[16]

The most visible and flamboyant source of protest activity during the 1920s, however, was the Reverend Thomas S. Harten, pastor of Holy Trinity Baptist Church. Following a fiery four-week revival at Brooklyn's Fleet Street AME Zion Church in 1922, he was called to Holy Trinity. Originally something of an unknown quantity except for his preaching ability, Harten wasted little time in impressing his personality upon Brooklyn. Within a year he was conducting a mass meeting at his church denouncing a proposed Jim Crow educational institution in New York State. In subsequent years such protest meetings became commonplace at Holy Trinity. On the local level, Harten repeatedly clashed with the police over their alleged mistreatment of blacks. Under the auspices of the National Equal Rights League, of which he was national organizer, he demanded that the Brooklyn police cease their policy of going into homes and dragging men to prison. Harten's attempt to protect a Negro woman being roughly treated by a white policeman led to his own brief arrest in 1928. Harten's prominence by this time was demonstrated by the offer of Congressman Emanuel Celler to assist his defense.[17]

After President Coolidge appointed C. Bascom Slemp, a "lily-white" Republican, as his secretary, Harten called a protest rally and headed a delegation to Washington which met with Coolidge. He also presided at mass meetings, addressing such black concerns as the continued incarceration of black soldiers convicted after the so-called Houston riot in 1917; lynching; the anti-Negro comments of Federal Judge William Atwell in a Brooklyn court; the Scottsboro case; and the Jim Crow policies of the United States War Department. Harten became known as a "staunch race man," "outrageous," "militant," and "fearless in his stand for the rights of the race." Among Brooklyn's black leaders he stood as the primary example of protest and militancy. His statements at times verged on the revolutionary for that era. He demanded that "every right and privilege that is guaranteed to white citizens by the Constitution of the United States be given my patriotic race." To secure these equal rights, blacks must "fight with every moral and legal weapon at our hands and when that fails we should be willing to make even the supreme sacrifice of death." He urged blacks to "make larger demands on the officials of the city" to obtain employment as subway guards, ticket sellers, and cashiers and as gas-meter readers for the local utility company.[18]

By 1930 Harten had become a force to be courted or at least acknowledged in local politics. A 1930 meeting attracted to Holy Trinity such white politicians as John McCooey, Democratic boss of Brooklyn, Edward Cadley, Democratic leader of the Seventeenth AD, Assemblyman Irwin Steingut, and Judge Edward Wynne. Harten had long supported the Democrats on the local level because of their greater recognition of blacks in Brooklyn. "We've got to leave the Republican party once in a while to get their nerve up," he reasoned. Nationally, he remained loyal to the Republicans through 1928 but switched his allegiance for the 1932 campaign.[19]

Despite his prominence in protest and political circles, Harten never achieved lasting success. He did not win elective office despite some vague promises offered by McCooey. His militant words were stronger than his actions, and he was unable to create an ongoing organization as a vehicle for protesting white discrimination and uniting Negroes for race objectives. His militancy and involvement in the black protest movement faded during the 1930s, although he remained active and controversial in Baptist church politics. Nevertheless, Harten remained uniquely important among Brooklyn ministers not only for his verbal protests but also for his willingness to march and actively back up his words.

In sharp contrast to Harten was Rev. Henry Hugh Proctor, pastor of the Nazarene Congregational Church from 1920 to his death in 1933. The white press and community accorded him attention, praise, and honor, thereby revealing their ideal of a black leader. In 1926, Proctor was elected moderator of the New York Association of Congregational Churches. He served as a member of the board of directors of the Brooklyn Urban League. He exchanged pulpits with white ministers, and once, when the renowned Rev. S. Parkes Cadman could not present his traditional Sunday afternoon sermon at the Bedford YMCA, which did not admit blacks, Proctor addressed this white audience. He was the lone Brooklyn Negro listed in *Who's Who in America*. All these credentials verified Proctor's position in the white world.[20]

Before coming to New York, Proctor had headed Atlanta's First Congregational Church for twenty-six years. He had secured a prominent position there, maintained excellent relations with the white community, and built up a model institutional church, which contained a gymnasium, library, high school, vocational training school, employment agency, kindergarten, and working girls' home. This successful experiment attracted widespread attention, including visits by President Roosevelt and President Taft and praise and support from Booker T. Washington. After his call to Brooklyn, Proctor did not abandon the accommodationist and gradualist philosophy that had succeeded so well for him in the South. His favorite themes were progress, responsibility, and spirituality.He urged upon his black listeners the traditional American virtues of thrift, work, duty, responsibility, dignity. Proctor asked whites to provide equal opportunity for Negroes. "Give us nothing because we are black. Deny us nothing because we are not white." He stressed the spiritual solution of all man's problems—"from birth to death including education, work, sin, worship and race." Through work and spirituality progress would result.[21]

Such "incredible optimism" rarely faltered. Proctor blithely praised his adopted city:

> In the application of the Christian spirit Brooklyn may be a working model for the relation between the races throughout the country and the world. There has never been any residential segregation of the races in Brooklyn, public facilities are open alike to all, and there is a fine spirit of inter-racial fraternity in this city.

His "faith in the better element of the white men of America" had a hollow ring when local realities of discrimination and segregation were considered. It is scarcely surprising that such moderate views received widespread white approbation. Proctor became in effect the *Brooklyn Eagle*'s "Negro in residence." Until his death, his were the only sermons by black preachers reported in that paper. Their bland spirituality could hardly be deemed objectionable by whites. In contrast, Harten received scant attention.[22]

Despite continued white approval, Proctor's prestige within the black community declined during the late 1920s. Negroes denounced him bitterly for a newspaper interview wherein he was quoted as saying that "colored folk go into the white houses as domestic servants. And they carry their disease and crime with them." At a mass meeting an estimated 3,000 blacks booed and hissed Proctor's name. Harten complained that "every time he [Proctor] speaks to anyone of the white race he apologizes for the black race." Despite a subsequent explanatory column stating that Proctor merely was expressing a fear for the future, his position within the black community continued to deteriorate. Nevertheless, he retained his prestige among whites. He was, said the *Age*, "more a favorite among the whites than among his fellow people." The white community was willing to accept a black man on its own terms: Proctor's emphasis on Negro progress and his shunning of militant protest secured him a place among whites.[23]

Another black clergyman worthy of notice was the Reverend George Frazier Miller, pastor of St. Augustine's PE Church. An avowed socialist and pacifist, he had refused to raise the American flag over his church during World War I and in 1918 ran on the Socialist party ticket for Congress. He served as an editor of the radical magazine, *Messenger*, during the 1920s. He viewed religion as dealing with both theological salvation and the salvation of "the whole man while he is yet on this side of the grave." To this end he looked upon "the whole teaching of Christ as socialistic. Christ was fundamentally a revolutionist, revolutionizing society from one in which the powerful suppressed the poor for their own enrichment to one where all could live abundantly." [24]

A number of black protest organizations surfaced during the Depression. Such groups sought to expand black employment opportunities either through direct negotiation with local proprietors or by more visible methods of picketing, boycotts, and publicity. Most notable among these groups were the Crispus Attucks Community Council headed by George Wibecan; the misnamed National War Veterans Association directed by Elvia Sullinger and composed mostly of women; and the Citizens Civic Affairs Committee led by Alexander Clayborn and Eugenia Wright. These organizations did obtain employment for some blacks, but their impact was limited, since the general level of unemployment restricted real possibilities for work. Moreover, since any strength that these groups manifested derived essentially from the expanding ghetto, their impact beyond the ghetto was negligible. Eventually the war-related prosperity of the early 1940s deprived them of their function and they quickly faded from the local scene.[25]

A number of fraternal and social groups prospered along with these protest and social-service institutions. The first branch of the "colored" Elks in New York State was established in Brooklyn in 1903; this "mother lodge of Elkdom in the East" hosted the 1906 national convention. The southern migration had led to the formation of such social and benevolent groups as the Sons of North Carolina and the Sons of Virginia. Further prominent social activity focused on the Comus Club, the Convivial Coterie Club, and the Charleston Club, all founded in the early years of the century. Additionally, Negro Republicans and Democrats formed their own political groups, and new black churches sprang up. Mention should also be made of two black professional organizations. The Provident Clinical Medical Society of Brooklyn was founded in 1906 by eleven black physicians, dentists, and pharmacists including Peter Ray, Verina Morton, and Walter Beekman. The corresponding legal group, the Brooklyn and Long Island Lawyers Association, was established in 1930 with Lewis Flagg as president. Other charter members were Lennie George, Clarence Johnson, James R. Spurgeon, Ernest Miller, and Hutson Lovell. What existed in 1920 in Brooklyn was a comprehensive array of organizations and institutions that touched all areas of black life, if not all blacks.[26]

Since institutions usually reflect the social, demographic, and cultural milieu of their time, it is not surprising that the history of black organizational life in Brooklyn between 1900 and 1940 was frequently distinguished by poverty, racial separation, discrimination, and, sometimes, paternalism. Indeed, black institutional existence on any other terms would have been quite unexpected. What was striking about the organizational growth in the early decades of the century was that the resultant groups formed not only the institutional infrastructure for the black community of that period in Brooklyn, but for nearly fifty years to come. To be sure, ghetto growth spawned some institutional growth, especially in the number of churches, but not until the emergence of the antipoverty agencies of the 1960s was a new stratum of organizations created to service the community.

## NOTES

1. Barnett Dodson, "Carlton Avenue Branch of the Brooklyn, N.Y., Y.M.C.A.," *The Colored American Magazine* 7 (February 1904): 117-20; Wilfred R. Bain, "Carlton Avenue Branch YMCA" (WPA research papers, Schomburg Collection).

2. *New York Age*, Oct. 21, 1909, Jan. 6, 1910.

3. Dodson, "Carlton Avenue Branch"; Bain, "Carlton Avenue Branch"; R. P. Hamlin, "Work of the YMCA among the Young Colored Men of Brooklyn, N.Y.," *The Colored American Magazine* 14 (June 1908): 338; Baxter R. Leach, "Colored Boy Scouts of Brooklyn" (WPA research papers, Schomburg Collection); *Amsterdam News*, July 29, 1925. James Spurgeon had been first secretary of the United States Legation in Monrovia, Liberia. He later was one of the founders of the Brooklyn and Long Island Lawyers Association.

4. "Young Women's Christian Association of Brooklyn—Lexington Avenue Branch," *The Colored American Magazine* 10 (February 1906): 99-101; *Age*, Nov. 29, 1906; *Amsterdam News*, Jan. 17, 1923.

5. Bain, "Carlton Avenue Branch"; *Age*, Nov. 11, 1915, May 10, 1917, Sept. 13, 1917, June 1, 1918; C. H. Tobias, "The Work of the Young Men's and Young Women's Christian Associations with Negro Youth," *The Annals of the American Academy of Political and Social Science* 140 (November 1928): 284. The 10 percent of the total cost of the new Y that Brooklyn blacks subscribed was low compared to other cities. This was due to both the high cost of the structure and the relatively small number of blacks in the borough. A more accurate measure of local Negro contributions would be the ratio of total black population to the money subscribed by blacks. This yields a per capita average of eighty cents in Brooklyn, which approximated a middle position between Chicago and Cleveland (one dollar), and Manhattan and Baltimore (thirty cents).

6. Wilfred R. Bain, "Ashland Place Branch YWCA" (WPA research papers, Schomburg Collection).

7. "The Lincoln Settlement" [pamphlet] (Brooklyn, 1915), pp. 2-4. Dr. Morton-Jones was active in other Negro organizations before the establishment of the Lincoln Settlement, including the Committee for Improving the Condition of Negroes in New York and the Association for the Protection of Colored Women.

8. Ibid., pp. 4-7; *Age*, Nov. 26, 1908, March 9, 1911.

9. Clinton Avenue Congregational Church, "Community Study" (Brooklyn, 1915), pp. 49, 56; *Age*, Oct. 30, 1913.

10. Brooklyn Urban League, *Annual Report*, 1919, p. 8; Wesley Curtwright, "History of the Brooklyn Urban League" (WPA research papers, Schomburg Collection); *Age*, Nov. 13, 1920, Jan. 22, 1921; *Amsterdam News*, March 9, 1927.

11. Brooklyn Urban League, *Annual Report*, 1919, pp. 2-7; 1923, pp. 2-13; 1924, pp. 7-16; 1925, pp. 11-15; 1929, pp. 5-14; 1936, pp. 9-10; *Age*, Jan. 28, 1928, Aug. 3, 1929; *Amsterdam News*, Jan. 25, 1928, March 1, 1928, Aug. 7, 1929.

12. Guichard Parris and Lester Brooks, *Blacks in the City: A History of the National Urban League* (Boston, 1971), p. 134; Abram Hill, "History of the New York Urban League" (WPA research papers, Schomburg Collection); Brooklyn Urban League, *Annual Report*, 1923, pp. 6-7; 1925, p. 16; *Age*, Jan. 28, 1928. Feb. 6, 1929.

13. Commenting on the New York scene generally, Frances Blascoer observed in 1915 that social work agencies either differentiated their work among Negroes or entirely excluded them from their activities. Frances Blascoer, *Colored School Children in New York* (New York, 1915), p. 34.

14. Arnold de Mille, "Hudson Avenue Boys Club" (WPA research papers, Schomburg Collection); Albert J. Kennedy, *The Visual Arts in New York Settlements* (New York, 1931), pp. 26-27; Mary M. Read and E. Mae Raymond, *Preschool Education in New York City Settlements* (New York, 1931), pp. 15-21, 24, 33-41.

15. The Brooklyn Armstrong Association, *Annual Report*, 1911, 1914, 1916; *Age*, Dec. 3, 1914; *Brooklyn Daily Eagle*, March 15, 1892, Feb. 13, 1899, Nov. 14, 1920, Nov. 19, 1920; *New York Times*, Feb. 23, 1903.

16. *Age*, March 12, 1914, Dec. 18, 1920, Nov. 15, 1924; *Amsterdam News*, Nov. 17, 1926, March 30, 1927, April 13, 1927, Sept. 18, 1929, Feb. 12, 1930; *Eagle*, May 23, 1922.

17. William Welty, "Black Shepherds, A Study of the Leading Negro Clergymen in New York City, 1900-1940" (Ph.D. dissertation, New York University, 1969), pp. 188-89; *Age*, July 25, 1925; *Amsterdam News*, March 31, 1926, April 3, 1926, Jan. 18, 1928, Jan. 25, 1928; *Eagle*, April 16, 1923, March 15, 1926, March 29, 1926, March 30, 1926. The National Equal Rights League included such personages as the Reverend George Frazier Miller, socialist and pastor of St. Augustine's PE Church in Brooklyn, as president and Monroe Trotter of Boston as corresponding secretary.

18. Welty, "Black Shepherds," p. 192; *Age*, April 22, 1933, April 29, 1933; *Amsterdam News*, July 21, 1926, June 1, 1927, Aug. 10, 1927, Nov. 2, 1927, Jan. 18, 1928, Aug. 29, 1928, Jan. 30, 1929, Sept. 25, 1929; *Eagle*, June 9, 1931, April 17, 1933; *New York Times*, Aug. 23, 1928.

19. *Age*, Oct. 11, 1930, Oct. 8, 1932, Oct. 15, 1932; *Amsterdam News*, July 13, 1932, Aug. 31, 1932, Oct. 12, 1932; *Eagle*, Oct. 29, 1932.

20. *Age*, May 29, 1920; *Amsterdam News*, May 19, 1926; *Eagle*, Jan. 29, 1922, May 22, 1922, June 8, 1925, May 17, 1926, Feb. 18, 1929, Dec. 1, 1930, Nov. 7, 1931.

21. Henry Hugh Proctor, *Between Black and White: Auto-*

*biographical Sketches* (Boston, 1925), pp. 91-170; Welty, "Black Shepherds," pp. 180-84; *Age,* Jan. 26, 1924; *Amsterdam News,* May 19, 1926, Sept. 22, 1926, Oct. 20, 1926.

22. Welty, "Black Shepherds," p. 186; *Amsterdam News,* Oct. 13, 1926; *Eagle,* May 16, 1921, May 11, 1925, July 27, 1925, Sept. 24, 1925, Dec. 12, 1927, Jan. 30, 1928, April 23, 1928, Jan. 21, 1929, Feb. 18, 1929, July 6, 1931, Feb. 27, 1931, April 9, 1932.

23. Welty, "Black Shepherds," p. 181; *Age,* March 8, 1930, March 29, 1930; *Amsterdam News,* March 12, 1930, April 2, 1930; *Eagle,* March 19, 1930, March 25, 1930.

24. *Age,* Dec. 13, 1919; *Amsterdam News,* Feb. 29, 1936.

25. Louis B. Bryan, "The Crispus Attucks Community Council of Brooklyn, N.Y." (WPA research papers, Schomburg Collection); S. Michelson, "The National War Veterans Association" (WPA research papers, Schomburg Collection); *Age,* June 17, 1933, June 24, 1933, Aug. 26, 1933, Sept. 29, 1934, Oct. 13, 1934, July 31, 1937, Aug. 7, 1937, Feb. 10, 1940; *Amsterdam News,* April 26, 1933, Aug. 16, 1933, July 24, 1937, Aug. 14, 1937, Sept. 11, 1937, Aug. 20, 1938, Nov. 18, 1939, Jan. 27, 1940, March 23, 1940; *Eagle,* July 7, 1933; interview with Lewis Flagg, a local black politician, July 24, 1970.

26. W. Preston Moore, "Elkdom in the State of New York," *The Colored American Magazine* 11 (August 1906): 129-39; "The History of the Society of the Sons of Virginia," *The Colored American Magazine* 2 (November 1900): 42-43; Baxter R. Leach, "The Comus Club of Brooklyn (WPA research papers, Schomburg Collection); Baxter R. Leach, "The Charleston Club of Brooklyn" (WPA research papers, Schomburg Collection); *Age,* Aug. 18, 1928; *Amsterdam News,* Oct. 7, 1925, April 23, 1966.

# CHAPTER 5

# The Politics of Invisibility

Following the Republican nomination of Fred R. Moore for the assembly in 1900, neither major party endorsed a black candidate for office until the 1940s. Negroes remained on the fringe of the political party structure, occasionally accorded patronage positions, but more often ignored or exploited. While black political clubs existed, especially in Republican ranks, the established party leaders in Brooklyn, as in Manhattan, preferred generally to deal through individual blacks whose power and influence resulted from friendship with and approval by the white power structure. This pattern prevailed into the 1930s, when the first permanent effective black political organization was established. The recognized leader among the Democrats for most of this period was Wesley Young, a whitewasher by trade before he secured a minor patronage position in the city jail. George Wibecan, a postal worker of impressive bearing, vigorous oratory, and lengthy Republican lineage, was Young's Republican counterpart.

Black appointments had to be cleared through them, and they were accorded at least a touch of respect by regular party leaders. The organizations behind these men functioned, if at all, only around election time.[1]

## CUTTING REPUBLICAN TIES

Given such a modest political foundation, given the still insignificant proportion of blacks in Brooklyn's population, given ingrained white indifference or even hostility to blacks, it is not surprising that both the Republicans and Democrats usually ignored the existence of blacks. Occasionally such neglect produced open rebellion, especially within Republican ranks, since most blacks were nominally Republicans and expected more equitable treatment from the party of Lincoln. Thus, for example, a Negro Republican political club was organized in 1919 in the First AD with Franklin W. Morton, son of Verina Morton-Jones, as president. It aimed to counteract the "present apathy of the Party on matters of concern of the colored voters."[2]

In 1920, Morton challenged the local party leadership by running against the official Republican nominee for the assembly. The First AD was usually a Democratic district, but not so overwhelmingly that a Republican could not carry the district in a strong Republican year. Initial primary returns indicated a narrow seventeen-vote victory for Morton, but political organizations do not respond kindly to challengers, black or white—the official recount stripped Morton of his success by a single vote. While Morton's race may have been a factor in his official defeat, his insurgency probably angered the regular organization equally, and, in an era of paper ballots, election fraud was neither uncommon nor difficult. Morton had savored victory momentarily but then saw it snatched away. Such was his punishment for opposition. To add to his frustration, the landslide proportions of the 1920 general election swept Republicans, including Morton's primary opponent, into office. It seems reasonable that Morton, having overcome the disadvantage of race in the primary, might well have won the general election. By the slightest and most questionable of margins Morton failed to become the second black legislator in Albany. It would be twenty-eight years before Brooklyn would be represented by a black elected official at any governmental level. Morton never forgave this Republican perfidy and eventually switched allegiance to the Democrats.[3]

The continued failure of George Wibecan to receive appropriate patronage positions during the 1920s angered Brooklyn black Republicans and disillusioned Wibecan himself, although he did not defect from the party. "We are learning," he commented sadly, "that the Republican Party of today is not the party of Lincoln." Most blacks, however, did remain loyal to the Republicans through 1930. The Reverend Thomas Harten supported Hoover in 1928, as did most other prominent black Brooklynites. In what was to prove to be the last gasp of black loyalty, black votes were responsible for the Republicans' narrowly regaining what had once been a traditionally Republican district, the Seventeenth AD, in 1930. The district became increasingly Negro during the 1930s, but no Republican was elected. By 1932 Harten was heading a Roosevelt-for-President club and by the mid-1930s the first effective black political organization had developed, not among the Republicans but among the Democrats of Bedford-Stuyvesant. By 1940 blacks generally, and the Seventeenth AD specifically, had clearly shifted loyalties to the Democratic party.[4]


## PATRONAGE AND THIRD-PARTY EFFORTS

Both parties bestowed occasional recognition upon loyal blacks in the form of patronage. The first position of prominence went to Summer Lark, a local printer and newspaperman. With Young's blessing he was appointed a deputy assistant district attorney in 1923. He resigned the position the next year, but, as in the selection of a black member for the Brooklyn Board of Education in the 1880s, the precedent of reserving the position for a black had been established. Lark was succeeded by Samuel Pease, who was replaced by Clarence Wilson in 1939. On the Republican side Francis F. Giles became assistant United States attorney for the eastern district of New York in 1929. After Roosevelt's election, Clarence Wilson, a Democrat, succeeded Giles. Brooklyn blacks gained two additional patronage positions in the 1930s. In 1938 Phillip Jones was appointed an assistant attorney general of New York State. George Wibecan was finally rewarded for his lengthy Republican service by being appointed confidential inspector for Borough President Raymond Ingersoll. When John Cashmore, a Democrat, succeeded the Fusionist Ingersoll in 1940, he replaced Wibecan with a white, to the anger of local black politicians. In 1944, however, Cashmore did name Bertram Baker to this post. Prior to this appointment Baker, the leader of local black Democrats, had merited a miserly $1,800 position in the Internal Revenue Service, scarcely commensurate with his value and loyalty.[5]

The most persistent patronage request of the 1930s was for the appointment of a Brooklyn Negro to a judgeship. The black Brooklyn and Long Island Lawyers Association repeatedly pressed Mayor La Guardia to recognize the legitimacy of their claims. Not until 1940 did La Guardia respond positively when, to the chagrin of Brooklyn's black lawyers and politicians, he appointed Myles Paige, a prominent Harlem politician, as justice of the court of special sessions. In order to meet the legal requirements of the office, Paige had to move from Manhattan to Kings County. While unanimous in their praise for Paige, the local lawyers insisted (to no avail) that his appointment did not fulfill their request for judicial recognition of Brooklyn blacks. Paige remained the sole Negro on the Brooklyn bench until the 1950s.[6]

Not suffering from the constraints of possible victory or public image, the Socialist party was not inhibited from nominating blacks for office. In 1918 they selected the Reverend George Frazier Miller, rector of St. Augustine's Episcopal

Church, to run in the Twenty-First Congressional District. In 1927 the Socialists named Rufus L. Perry, Jr. for county judge. Not unexpectedly, both Miller and Perry were soundly defeated. Such recognition, gratuitous or sincere, availed neither the Socialists nor Negroes. This minority party had little to lose nominating a black; since black voters did not flock to the Socialist banner, the major parties simply ignored such provocations.[7]

## INCIPIENT INSURGENCY

During the 1930s black political effort became regular if not successful. The growing number of blacks in Brooklyn and their increasing concentration in Bedford-Stuyvesant (Seventeenth AD) provided the raw material-potential votes-necessary for political activity. Beginning in 1932 when Lewis Flagg ran as an independent candidate for the assembly, one or more Brooklyn blacks sought office in nearly every subsequent election. Black voters did occasionally influence internal Democratic contests for local office, but generally their activity wrought little external change. No black secured elective office; patronage rewards remained scarce; the major parties continued to ignore or exploit blacks for their own advantage. Despite their mounting numbers and geographical concentration, Negroes remained outsiders in the related games of politics and patronage.[8]

In 1932 Robert Hargraves, head of the Negro Non-Partisan Organization, persuaded Lewis Flagg, a lawyer and a recent migrant from Baltimore, to run for the assembly in the Seventeenth. It required a certain temerity and daring for a Negro to challenge the major parties. Flagg ran on a blatantly black platform, urging his fellow Negroes to vote for one of their own kind. The results were, in Flagg's words, "calamitous"—Flagg's 254 votes approximated 1 percent of the total cast—but Flagg and his supporters were not dismayed by these returns. They were sufficiently realistic to know that their inexperienced organization could not challenge the entrenched parties and win, but they were determined that some protest against black exclusion from politics be manifested. Significantly, Flagg's candidacy did generate a tradition of blacks' seeking elective office, a tradition he himself helped affirm by running again in 1933. This time he received 301 votes.[9] In 1935 Lennie George, a native West Indian and a local lawyer, ran as an independent in the Seventeenth AD. Both the American Labor party (ALP) and the Fusion party endorsed Oliver D. Williams, a lawyer and former president of the Brooklyn branch of the NAACP, for the same seat in 1937. The ALP repeated its racial tactics the following year, nominating Rev. Theophilus Alcantara. Not unexpectedly, all these candidates proved unsuccessful, although they polled creditable vote totals. Williams, for example, received over 4,000 votes, or 21 percent of the district's total vote.[10]

These unsuccessful independent and third-party candidacies illustrated a basic ideological and practical dilemma facing black politicians—whether to work within the framework of the two-party system or to abandon it and support a race candidate no matter what his party affiliation. Could black voters be welded into an effective, unified voting bloc to support with near unanimity black candidates for office? Would it be wiser instead to attempt to utilize the existing political structure, or was this system too unreceptive to black candidates? During the 1930s Negro candidates for the assembly were forced to follow the route of independency in seeking elective office since neither major party, despite increasing black pressure, would yield its rigid stance against becoming more interracial. Given the reality of the two-party system, however, these independent campaigns seemed most unlikely vehicles for success. Black politicians and voters were thus forced to choose between a black independent with doubtful possibilities of victory and the regular organization's white nominee.

The assembly race of 1937 perhaps best illustrated this dilemma. O. D. Williams received substantial community support from prominent black clergy and Republican party stalwarts. Arthur Q. Martin, second only to George Wibecan in prestige in local black Republican circles, pledged his full support: "I was a colored man long before I was a Republican, and as such my entire allegiance must go to the members of my race, regardless of party affiliations." The majority of Williams's black endorsements, however, came from Fusionists or Republicans who had little to lose by supporting a black candidate in an increasingly Democratic district. The decision was far more complex for the fledgling black Democrats who had recently demonstrated their strength in local primary races. The United Action Democratic Association, the only effective black political organization in Brooklyn, had just achieved some standing in Seventeenth AD Democratic ranks. Given the dual movements of blacks into Bedford-Stuyvesant and into the Democratic party, the effective power of United Action and its leader, Bertram Baker, could be expected to expand in the immediate future. Baker refused to back Williams, supporting instead the regular Democratic candidate, Fred Moritt, a white. Moritt's election, he advised, "will show the solidarity of the Negro vote ... and if he is not elected, the Negroes' only weapon—organization—will have been dealt a severe blow." Baker clearly preferred to practice politics within the established system rather than rely upon doubtful appeals for racial solidarity. He hailed Moritt's subsequent victory as a demonstration of "the power of the organized Negro vote."[11]

In assessing the probability of black success in elections, it has been hypothesized that the likelihood of black victory varies inversely to the size of the electoral unit.[12] The larger the unit, the more likely whites will be able to unite and thwart black ambitions. Conversely, small, compact geographic districts, as exemplified by the ward system in Chicago, can facilitate Negro entrance into local office by concentrating black voters in, and excluding most white voters from, a narrowly defined area. Prior to 1937 New York City's aldermanic districts coincided with its assembly districts and were relatively modest in size. Harlem had long been represented by both a black alderman and a black assemblyman. Brooklyn Negroes had not yet achieved either the numerical superiority or sufficient concentration to capture a district as their Harlem counterparts had done.

Commencing with the 1937 election, however, New York City embarked on a short-lived experiment in proportional representation (PR).[13] The essential feature of this new system, which theoretically militated against black political advancement, involved the boroughwide character of these elections. Obviously the white voters of Kings County could easily overwhelm any black candidate.

In the initial proportional-representation election two blacks joined the optimistic stampede of 99 Brooklyn candidates. Chester Thomas, a youthful lawyer, ran on an independent ticket, while Ben Butler, a longtime borough resident, local businessman, and active civic worker, ran with the support of La Guardia's Fusion party. Butler's race took on unexpected, even spectacular, proportions and was the most successful campaign waged by a Negro in this era. Initial returns gave Thomas 2,378 and Butler a respectable 14,883 votes. Thomas was eliminated quickly, but Butler's tally mounted steadily and surprisingly with each recount. Most of these additions represented the transfer of votes by whites who selected Butler as their second or third preference. Ultimately Butler more than doubled his initial tally, a feat unmatched by any subsequent black candidate, before being eliminated with a total vote of 32,427. Butler's unexpectedly impressive performance was viewed as a "moral victory" and brought praise for the PR system as a vehicle for future Negro political success.[14]

In achieving this remarkable performance, however, Butler had benefited from a unique coalescence of nonracial forces. Since the 1937 election was the first held under the new system of proportional representation, the regular parties had not yet perfected their strategy for controlling this electoral process. Furthermore, the apparent ease of entering and even winning had induced nearly 100 contestants to enter the race, thus diffusing white votes among numerous candidates. Most important, however, was a totally nonpolitical, accidental factor that induced many whites to vote for Butler. At that time there existed in the New York area a chain of food stores, the James Butler Stores, with a predominantly Irish clientele and Irish employees. The name Butler itself had a distinctly Irish ring. This apparently induced numerous Irish, who were traditionally among the more antiblack elements in the population, to vote unknowingly, and most ironically, for a Negro.[15] Butler ran again in 1939 but failed to replicate even remotely his initial impressive performance. The factors that had contributed to Butler's previous success no longer stood in alignment. Fewer candidates sought the councilmanic seats; Butler's race was more generally known; the Democratic and Republican parties had adjusted their strategies to assure their control of the PR system.

It was hoped that all blacks might unite in support of a single councilmanic candidate in 1941. Instead for the first time since 1900, a major party nominated a black for office. A citizens' committee of distinguished blacks had selected the nonpartisan Rev. George Thomas, pastor of Brown Memorial Church, to be the black candidate for the city council. However, 1941 was a mayoral year, and the Democrats, who had been out of office since Fiorello La Guardia's victory in 1933, were determined to use whatever means necessary to regain City Hall and its patronage. Their tactics extended even to the nomination of Bertram Baker, president of the United Action Democratic Association, for city council. Faced with this challenge, the Republicans dusted off and trotted out the venerable George Wibecan. The "political history" made by these selections was based on obvious self-serving premises. Baker received virtually no support from the Democratic organization, one local leader even flatly refusing to distribute his campaign literature. Despite such nonsupport and ultimate electoral defeat, the very selection of blacks by the major parties signified a certain coming of political age, or at least the recognition of the political reality of more than 100,000 Negro residents in Brooklyn. Their numbers could no longer be completely ignored.[16]

Mere perfunctory support from Republicans was the fate for Norman Johnson's unsuccessful efforts in the 1943 election.

Disgusted with the shabby treatment accorded him in 1941, even Bert Baker temporarily defected from the Democrats and supported Johnson's councilmanic candidacy. Baker headed Johnson's petition committee and his careful scrutiny of the lists led to the elimination of false signatures obtained by Republican workers or saboteurs.[17] The last election conducted under PR was in 1945; in form it resembled that of 1941. A new mayor was to be chosen to succeed La Guardia. The Republicans endorsed Mrs. Maude B. Richardson, a longtime civic and social activist, who had been selected by a committee of prominent blacks. Sensing victory for the first time in twelve years, the Democrats were again prepared to nominate a prominent Brooklyn black for the city council. Baker was unenthusiastic about seeking office, but the white political bosses rejected his request not to run and Baker yielded to their importunity. The American Labor party joined in his support, and, given Baker's presidency of the only effective Negro political organization in Brooklyn, Baker's chances of victory exceeded those of any previous black candidate. Baker ran reasonably well but did not come close to being elected.[18]

## INTERNAL POLITICS

While Negroes failed to secure elective office or even to have an impact on general elections, they did exert some influence upon internal Democratic party affairs. Blacks did not initiate these intraparty fights, but their votes helped to decide them. These contests centered upon the Seventeenth AD with its growing Negro population. In 1936 blacks, including Bertram Baker, J. Daniel Diggs, Phillip J. Jones, and Elvia Sullinger, supported the insurgent candidacy of Stephen Carney and Minnie Abel against Edward Cadley, the Democratic leader of the Seventeenth. It was an often vicious contest that found Carney and Abel wooing black votes by appointing some to office within their political organization, and Cadley supporters retaliating with ominous warnings that a Carney-Abel victory would result in an expanded black belt. To the surprise of most political analysts, Carney unseated Cadley. The *Age* exulted in this demonstration of political power. "Never before in the history of Kings County had the colored vote played so important a part in a district fight." An estimated 95 percent of the black voters had supported Carney.[19]

Almost immediately Carney's black supporters felt themselves aggrieved as Carney allied himself with Cadley's assemblyman, George Stewart, who was unpopular among Negroes for his opposition to legislation proposed by Harlem assemblymen. Carney further insulted his black supporters by selecting an all-white slate of officers for his county committee. Local blacks had been aroused by the recent fight to a level of keen vigilance and anticipation, and, as one Baker aide warned, "if Carney wants war, he shall have it." Carney's neglect of local blacks was particularly upsetting because he owed his victory to them—if Cadley had previously denied blacks recognition, at least he had not been in their debt. This resentment focused upon Carney's support of Assemblyman Stewart for reelection in 1937. In its anti-Stewart mood, the United Action Democratic Association and other leading black Democrats supported the challenge of Fred Moritt, who was being sponsored by their former nemesis Cadley. Again Negro votes contributed heavily to an upset victory as Moritt squeezed in by 4,592 to 4,172. Baker warned that "this victory is a public notice to all office holders that we expect them to keep faith, and further, that our political patience is short-lived." [20]

Internal politics in the Seventeenth AD continued turbulent in 1938. Stewart, with Carney's support, challenged Moritt to regain his former position. Moritt retaliated by supporting Martin Kelly for the leadership of the district against Carney. This alliance brought the wrath of Negroes down upon Moritt, since Kelly acted as attorney for the infamous, racist Midtown Civic League and was a member of its executive board. Baker accused Moritt of having "broken faith" by running with Kelly; he "has proven himself unworthy of the confidence placed in him." Moritt barely escaped the results of this black dissatisfaction. In 1940 when two insurgents challenged Carney, the issue of race again surfaced. Harry Wolkof's demand for a black assemblyman from the district was branded as an "appeal to racialism" by supporters of Carney. Carney won, and local Democratic turmoil diminished with Carney and Moritt temporarily secure in their positions. Although the Seventeenth was nearly half black in 1940, Negroes had made few inroads into party governance. Leadership in both the local Republican and Democratic organizations continued to be a white monopoly. When white politicians clashed and their strengths were near parity, black voters could influence electoral results. Yet the contempt in which black political support was held was indicated by the rapidly shifting alliances among white politicians who frequently forgot their recent black supporters.[21]

Despite occasional examples of recognition and advancement, the political status of black Brooklyn remained nearly as limited in 1940 as in 1900. Negro attempts to secure elective office all fared poorly during this period. No candidate seriously approached victory despite occasionally sanguine indications. From a representational perspective blacks did not exist in Kings County. The major reason for this situation was the attitude and practice of the major political parties, which simply refused to nominate blacks between 1900 and 1941. The Democrats proved as little responsive to their growing black constituency during the 1930s as had the Republicans, the traditional home of black politicians, in the earlier period. When in the early 1940s both parties acknowledged the mounting black population of Brooklyn, they did so without sincerity and for self-serving ends. Neither party provided adequate support for their black candidates, who were allowed to drown in a sea of apathy or even hostility. The alternative course of political independency inevitably foundered upon a combination of voter loyalty to the two major parties and an as yet insufficiently large and concentrated black power base. Some developments did auger well for future black political strength, however. Baker's organization was a definite advance beyond the traditional segregated, individual, white-selected leadership of the Wesley Young variety. It had its roots in both the official Democratic organization and the expanding black community. Residential segregation provided "concentrated voting strength," perhaps its only advantage. The sheer weight of numbers might yet force a reassessment of the status of blacks in Brooklyn politics. In 1940, however, the Brooklyn Negro remained, as the *Eagle* had observed in 1860, essentially a "political pariah."

## NOTES

1. Interview with Bertram Baker, July 29, 1970; interview with Norman Johnson, Aug. 13, 1970; interview with Lewis Flagg, July 24, 1970. These three gentlemen were all personally involved in Brooklyn politics beginning about 1930.

2. *New York Age*, May 30, 1907, Oct. 24, 1907, Jan. 4, 1912, Sept. 20, 1919.

3. *Brooklyn Daily Eagle*, July 2, 1920, Sept. 15, 1920, Oct. 3, 1920, Nov. 3, 1920; interview with the Hon. Franklin Morton, son of the candidate, July 24, 1970. Harlem had elected Edward Johnson to the assembly in 1917 as the first black representative.

4. *Age*, July 8, 1922, Nov. 22, 1930, July 16, 1932; *Amsterdam News*, July 14, 1926, Aug. 8, 1928, Oct. 30, 1929, Nov. 13, 1929, Nov. 20, 1929; *Eagle*, May 28, 1922, June 27, 1922, May 14, 1925, Sept. 30, 1925, Nov. 5, 1930, July 7, 1932, July 16, 1932.

5. *Age*, Jan. 6, 1923, April 19, 1924, April 2, 1938, April 8, 1939, April 22, 1944; *Amsterdam News*, Aug. 21, 1929, June 11, 1938, May 11, 1940, May 25, 1940, June 15, 1940, Feb. 19, 1944; *Eagle*, March 16, 1924, Aug. 19, 1929, Aug. 20, 1936, Dec. 30, 1939, April 12, 1944, Aug. 25, 1945; *New York Times*, Dec. 31, 1922, March 16, 1924.

6. Interview with Flagg; interview with Johnson; *Age*, Jan. 25, 1936, Feb. 15, 1936, Aug. 1, 1936, Aug. 13, 1938, May 13, 1939, July 29, 1939, Feb. 10, 1940; *Amsterdam News*, May 2, 1936, June 25, 1938, Aug. 6, 1938, July 29, 1939, Feb. 17, 1940; *Eagle*, June 25, 1938.

7. Miller received 3,140 votes out of the total of 61,495 cast (*The Brooklyn Daily Eagle Almanac, 1919*, p. 382); *Amsterdam News*, Sept. 21, 1927, Nov. 2, 1927, Oct. 31, 1928, Feb. 29, 1936. In 1927 Perry received 22,500 votes to his fellow Socialist's 19,640. In the Seven-

teenth AD, the district with the largest black population, Perry outpolled the other Socialist candidate for judge 1,139 to 446, thus indicating the existence of some degree of racial consciousness in voting.

8. Black candidates ran for the assembly in 1932, 1933, 1935, 1937, 1938, and 1944; they sought the city council in 1937, 1939, 1941, 1943, and 1945.

9. Interview with Flagg; *Age*, Feb. 6, 1932, Oct. 1, 1932, July 22, 1933; *Amsterdam News*, March 9. 1932, Sept. 28, 1932, July 19, 1933. Election returns for all elections are drawn from New York City's annual *Official Canvass of Voters*.

10. *Age*, Aug. 17, 1935, Aug. 27, 1938; *Amsterdam News*, July 27, 1935, Oct. 15, 1938; *Eagle*, Sept. 18, 1938. George argued that since it was "impossible for a white man to conscientiously represent the interest of the Negro," blacks should vote for him. He performed creditably, polling over 2,000 votes. Alcantara likewise advanced a forthrightly racial stand. "I shall be the Assemblyman-at-Large for the Negroes of Brooklyn, that is my first aim," he stated. He received 2,398 votes, approximately 12 percent of the total vote cast in the Seventeenth AD.

11. *Age*, Sept. 18, 1937; *Amsterdam News*, Sept. 25, 1937, Oct. 30, 1937, Nov. 6, 1937.

12. A number of books and articles have supported the view that at large election systems are "institutional barriers to Black political representation," including: Stokely Carmichael and Charles Hamilton, *Black Power* (New York, 1967); Clinton B. Jones, "The Impact of Local Election Systems on Black Political Representation," *Urban Affairs Quarterly*, 11 (March 1976): 345-56; R.H. Lineberry and E. F. Fowler, "Reformism and Public Policies in American Cities," *American Political Science Review* 61 (September 1967): 701-16; and R. Hofferbert and I. Sharkansky, eds., *State and Urban Politics* (Boston, 1971).

13. Under PR a voter marked a "1" on his ballot next to his first choice, a "2" next to his second, etc. All first-choice ballots were initially tabulated. The candidate with the fewest first-choice votes was then eliminated and his votes distributed among the other candidates according to the second choices. This process was repeated for each subsequent count. A candidate receiving 75,000 votes was automatically elected. Other councilmen were chosen on the basis of total votes received with one selected for every 75,000 votes cast. This cumbersome system was in effect from the election of 1937 to the election of 1945. The term of office was two years until 1945, when it was extended to four years. In 1949, PR was replaced by district elections based on state senate boundaries.

14. *Age*, Oct. 30, 1937, Dec. 4, 1937.

15. Both Bertram Baker and Lewis Flagg commented on Butler's "Irish" heritage as a significant factor in his 1937 total.

16. Interview with the Reverend George W. Thomas, Aug. 13, 1970; interview with Baker; *Age*, Aug. 30, 1941, Oct. 25, 1941; *Amsterdam News*, June 28, 1941, July 5, 1941, Oct. 4, 1941, Nov. 22, 1941. On the first ballot Baker received 17,913, Wibecan 13,877, and Thomas 13,394. Baker was the last of these three to be eliminated, bowing out with 23,061 votes, in sixteenth position.

17. Interview with Johnson; interview with Baker; *Amsterdam News*, June 19, 1943, Sept. 4, 1943, Sept. 11, 1943, Nov. 13, 1943. Johnson received 18,698 initial votes and exited with 22,008 votes, in twelfth place.

18. Interview with Baker; *Amsterdam News*, April 28, 1945, July 7, 1945, July 21, 1945, Aug. 16, 1945. The first tally gave Baker 18,993 votes and Richardson 12,174. Baker was eliminated with 28,945 votes.

19. *Age*, Jan. 18, 1936, Jan. 25, 1936, Feb. 29, 1936, March 7, 1936, March 14, 1936, April 4, 1936; *Amsterdam News*, Feb. 15, 1936, March 28, 1936, April 11, 1936; *Eagle*, April 3, 1936.

20. *Age*, May 2, 1936, March 13, 1937, May 21, 1937, June 19, 1937, Sept. 25, 1937; *Amsterdam News*, July 17, 1937; *Eagle*, June 9, 1937, Sept. 17, 1937.

21. *Age*, Jan. 20, 1940, March 30, 1940; *Amsterdam News*, Aug. 13, 1938, Sept. 3, 1938; *Eagle*, Feb. 22, 1938, Sept. 21, 1938, Oct. 28, 1938, Jan. 12, 1940.

# CHAPTER 6

# Socioeconomic Conditions

## EMPLOYMENT

The economic condition of any people is crucial to their well-being. Throughout the period between 1900 and 1940 blacks moved on the fringe of the New York City economy, working at low-paying, menial, laboring or service jobs, work left over after whites had been employed or that whites had abandoned for more lucrative opportunities.

"The great majority of the Negroes of New York live in poverty," commented Mary White Ovington in 1905.[1] What Ovington observed for the city at large applied equally to its parts. The rapid expansion of Brooklyn's black institutional life and population had little real impact upon local socioeconomic conditions. The segmentation of the local labor market by race persisted as it had in previous decades. For blacks it remained a period of restricted economic opportunity. The occupational distribution of Brooklyn blacks continued to differ markedly from that of foreign-born or native whites. The immigrants continued to fill the factories of New

113

York City; native-born white males were also extensively engaged in industrial work, but were especially prominent in trade and clerical pursuits; the modal form of black employment, male and female, was in domestic and personal service.

In 1910 well over half of all Negro males and females were still employed in domestic and personal service, occupations that whites had increasingly deserted. Those blacks who did labor in manufacturing and mechanical industries rarely advanced beyond the level of unskilled laborer. Negro professionals were considerably more likely to be musicians, actors, clergymen, and teachers than doctors, lawyers, or dentists. Public-service positions for blacks were limited to doormen, watchmen, and laborers; they were virtually excluded from being officials, policemen, or firemen.[2] The economic impact and dislocation caused by World War I propelled numerous blacks into the mainstream of American industry for the first time, as discussed in Chapter 3. Brooklyn blacks, men and women, entered manufacturing employment at this time in unprecedented numbers. By 1920 nearly a quarter of black males and a fifth of black women so labored. The clothing and textile industry especially employed the women, while black men became semiskilled operatives and longshoremen. These advances were primarily at the expense of personal- and domestic-service employment. Indeed, the gainful employment of nearly a quarter of black women in nondomestic work represented a major departure from the past.[3]

Black employment in manufacturing, however, remained novel, segmented, and precarious during the 1920s. The Urban League's placement program only occasionally succeeded in securing work opportunities beyond the traditional range of "Negro" jobs as domestics, janitors, laborers, messengers, chauffeurs, and so on. A survey of 106 industrial establishments in 1928 revealed widespread discrimination, with nearly half the firms not employing any blacks. Some encouragement was drawn from the recent employment of blacks by a number of companies, thus indicating a growing willingness or necessity for industry to use black workers in some instances. A subsequent League study, however, indicated the continued low status of most male Negro workers. Only 20 out of the 1,534 black men surveyed labored in a skilled trade; 80 percent were simply lumped as unskilled workers. Nor did these men anticipate future advancement. Their average weekly wage of $19.72 produced an annual income of $1,025 if no lapses in employment intervened.[4]

Given the marginality and insecurity of their employment, even the minor economic tremors that preceded the Great Depression could endanger black workers. The Depression itself brought widespread unemployment and eradicated previous black occupational advances, particularly those achieved by black women. Black men continued to seek and obtain industrial work, especially as laborers, but the availability of jobs sharply contracted. Faced with a disintegrating labor market, the Brooklyn Urban League's statements during the 1930s were consistently pessimistic, and not without justification. In 1931 the League reported the availability of only "emergency work" and "regular routine" jobs and even these only in "diminished numbers." Such reemployment as had reached Brooklyn by 1936 had "passed the Negro by." With opportunities nonexistent, the primary and "rather desperate" task confronting the League was simply finding jobs for men, and not vice versa. Work for black men proved especially difficult to procure; of the 496 placements made by the League in 1939, over 90 percent went to females, primarily in domestic and personal service. Despite an increase of over 10,000 in the number of working-age black males between 1930 and 1940, the number of males employed in non-relief work actually decreased by 1,393; these figures suggest the profound crisis in black male employment.[5]

Hostile employer attitudes, embodied in the acceptance of racial stereotypes and the outright refusal to hire blacks, contributed to this black economic and occupational deficit. Hearings in 1937 before the New York State Temporary Commission on the Condition of the Urban Colored Population revealed, for example, that the BMT subway employed 339 Negroes, 70 percent of them porters. There was not a single white porter, and blacks were completely absent from the most prestigious jobs of motorman and conductor. All but a handful of Brooklyn Edison's 250 Negroes worked as menials. The New York Telephone Company refused to hire Negroes because, its spokesman alleged, white girls did not wish to work in offices with blacks. Without ever having consulted Negro girls about the validity of her own beliefs, the superintendent of nurses at Kings County Hospital asserted that "there are other fields of work in which these people [black girls] are happier and enjoy ... they do not care to be nurses.... The average Negro girl does [not] want to make those personal contacts which a nurse must make—she must work very hard, she must serve—a nurse must sometimes get down on her hands and knees...." The commonly accepted inferiority of the Negro that was revealed in such attitudes and practices assured the continued relegation of blacks to the bottom stratum of the economic structure.[6]

As the Depression worsened, any job, however menial and poorly paying, seemed preferable to none. In the traditional black female occupation of household employment, for example, conditions of work deteriorated. Nevertheless, many Negro women resorted to seeking day work in modern-day "slave markets" that developed in various white neighborhoods along Eastern Parkway, in Flatbush, or Brighton Beach. To these unofficial, open-air hiring halls came unemployed black domestics unable to find regular work through employment agencies or newspaper advertisements. Carrying their work clothes, they advertised themselves as available for day-work employment. White housewives selected a likely prospect on the outward appearance of a strong body, sometimes even pinching a prospective victim to determine if muscle or fat was beneath her clothes. Wages for scrubbing, washing, ironing, dusting, ranged from twenty to thirty-five cents per hour, although most offers rarely exceeded a quarter. A full day's work would thus net a worker two dollars on the average. Many employers, however, preferred to limit such employment to fewer than eight hours, and it was not unusual for a "slave" to work two hours for a total wage of forty cents. While such treatment could scarcely be accepted cheerfully, an air of resignation pervaded the scene. As one victim explained, "If they don't hire us, who would?" A person had to pay rent and eat, explained another. These "slave markets" continued to exist until wartime employment absorbed the unemployed.[7]

The Brooklyn chapter of the National Negro Congress attempted to alleviate these conditions by supporting the establishment of a Domestic Workers' Association. In addition to better working conditions, this fledgling union recommended an "existence wage" of fifty cents per hour for day workers. It further proposed wage scales and conditions of employment for live-in maids and cooks. While some placements were made through the association, the continued presence of "slave markets" allowed most housewives to ignore such inflated demands. "They [the housewives] have been used to doing as they please and don't want to change," complained one union official. The houseworker continued to be devoid of protection, the employer paying what she pleased.[8]

The first report of the New York State Temporary Commission on the Condition of the Urban Colored Population ascribed a salient role to this dismal economic situation: "Most of the problems confronting the colored population arise primarily out of inadequate incomes." Until this basic handicap was remedied no effective attack on related social and cultural problems could be made. The Depression, however, guaranteed that this disability would not be lifted from the Negro; nor would he receive sufficient wage and employment opportunities to outpace his endemic poverty.[9]

## HOUSING

In every housing survey or statistical study between 1900 and 1940, the inferior status, absolute and relative, of black-occupied housing in Brooklyn was documented. Commenting on the scene in 1903, William H. Baldwin, Jr., the president of the Long Island Railroad, a founder of the Committee for

Improving the Industrial Condition of Negroes in New York, and a Brooklyn resident, observed that a landlord only rented to blacks after he "gets as much use as possible out of his property from the Irish, when he can no longer rent his tenement house to the Italians." One large black community lived in an area that was "dark and filled with rooming houses of a cheap and rather disreputable nature." A racially dual rental market existed; blacks were charged higher rents than whites for equal or inferior housing. During World War I the Brooklyn Urban League reported, "The houses in which the great bulk of colored people are forced to live are totally unsatisfactory as houses in which to bring up healthy, moral families." Many wooden tenement buildings provided inadequate protection against fire, halls were unsanitary, and the average apartment contained at least one interior room. Most living was done in the kitchen, usually the largest and only heated room in the apartment. The Urban League expressed little confidence in the effectiveness of the filtering process: it feared that Negroes would be "forced to take inferior houses vacated by their white neighbors for better homes instead of getting their fair share of ... new homes...." Housing conditions for Brooklyn blacks were described as being worse than those in Harlem, a significant change from twenty or thirty years previous. At the time this might have been true. Offered reasonably new and decent living accommodations after the collapse of the Harlem real estate boom in the early years of the century, blacks had flocked there and filled recently constructed houses "as fast as they were opened to them." Knowledge of such disreputable conditions in Brooklyn did not breed relief, however; these unfit homes were not vacated by order of the law since "there are no other places to which the tenants can go. The congestion is already shameful enough." [10]

A 1929 Welfare Council study related the Negro's economic status to his inadequate housing conditions. The dual pressure of low wages and the high cost of decent living "often forces colored families to live in quarters too small and congested to make normal home life possible." Housing conditions in the immediate vicinity of the Urban League building remained desperate. The frame structures lacked fire escapes. Many buildings had been converted into furnished, single-room-occupancy dwellings, with all the attendant evils of over-crowding, overutilization, and fire danger. In some houses toilet facilities were in the yard, though generally they were available communally in the hall with as many as four families sharing one toilet. Bathrooms were virtually nonexistent. Few rooms had illumination other than oil lamps. The structures were valued at as little as $500. It is scarcely surprising that Negroes fled such conditions in the downtown area when they could. The buildings in Bedford-Stuyvesant offered more substantial construction and better living conditions initially, just as Harlem had provided better housing for Manhattan blacks in an earlier time.[11]

The Depression decimated the housing construction industry, of course, but the beginnings of the federal public housing program in 1934 seemed to offer some hope for the needy poor. Yet in scope it proved of limited impact; officially enunciated guidelines accepted and then concretized existing racial attitudes and distribution. The initial Brooklyn projects were situated in predominantly Jewish Williamsburg and predominantly Italian Red Hook, areas where few blacks resided and fewer still could anticipate admission to the apartments. Only one black family reportedly resided in the Williamsburg project soon after its completion in 1938. Faced with this near-total exclusion, blacks were forced to accentuate their demands for "Negro" public housing and muffle, if not entirely stifle, their demands for integrated housing.[12]

In 1938 two black housing organizations merged to form the Brooklyn Federation for Better Housing in order to document the need for and demand the construction of public housing for blacks. Fortunately the federation possessed the skilled and dedicated services of Albert L. Clarke, whose intensive study of two neighboring but racially dissimilar areas documented the deplorable living conditions of blacks living in a part of Bedford-Stuyvesant. The 4,807 families living in the predominantly black area occupied 3,421 dwelling units, indicating a high degree of doubling up and overcrowding. Facilities in these old-law tenements offered only minimal amenities—91 percent lacked central heating; 85 percent were without hot water; 26 percent lacked a tub or shower; 16 percent lacked indoor sanitary facilities; 15 percent required major repairs or were judged unfit for habitation. The buildings were owned extensively by absentee landlords exacting maximum profit from these minimum apartments. Death by fire represented an "ever present danger, resultant from the conditions of these out-moded tinder boxes." The Reverend Theophilus Alcantara, another member of the federation, acerbically commented that the animals in the various city zoos "are living in much better condition than the colored." In contrast, housing in the neighboring, predominantly white area was of significantly better quality with sufficient dwelling units for every family, modern conveniences, yet monthly rents similar to those charged in the black section.[13]

The Brooklyn Housing Federation sponsored mass meetings demanding a "just share" of the low-cost public housing appropriations for Bedford-Stuyvesant. Clarke cited health disparities, juvenile-delinquency rates, and incidences of fire to prove that Bedford-Stuyvesant needed new housing even more than Williamsburg and Red Hook at the time their projects were constructed. His persistent badgering of officials no doubt contributed to the federal government's decision in 1939 to approve the construction of a project in the Bedford-Stuyvesant vicinity. The initial assumption that this development would be "solely Negro" evoked little black criticism.[14]

A major diversionary controversy immediately developed about the naming of the proposed project. Following in the tradition of naming projects after their general geographic location (e.g., Williamsburg and Red Hook), initial plans had simply spoken of the "Bedford-Stuyvesant Slum Clearance Project." Neighborhood groups and leaders, mostly white, objected vociferously to this designation, especially in view of the expected racial composition of the project and the obvious implication that Bedford-Stuyvesant was a slum. Local real estate brokers, both white and black, feared that such a connotation would seriously depreciate realty values. Bedford-

Stuyvesant, they argued, "is and always has been one of the finest residential sections of the community," populated with people "of the character which distinguished the early settlers of our borough." The New York City Council requested government officials to discontinue using the name "Bedford-Stuyvesant." Suggestions for a more appropriate designation abounded in the local press. Some favored the rather unimaginative and confusing use of the bordering cross streets (Buffalo-Rochester); others opted for some patriotic name "symbolic of what America means to its people"; another urged the memorialization of Henry Ward Beecher. Since Bedford-Stuyvesant lacked any specified boundaries sanctioned by law, the argument degenerated into geographic semantics. It was resolved by adopting the amorphous and inoffensive "Kingsborough." The good name of Bedford-Stuyvesant had been preserved.[15]

Contrary to preliminary expectations of black preponderance and in spite of the black majority living on the site previously, a majority of the project's initial tenantry was white. The black press sanguinely rationalized that such integration might serve to "break down the unwritten law that Negroes can only live in certain sections (and housing projects) of the city." What it really meant was that since the houses were located in a still racially heterogeneous neighborhood and not in the midst of a solid black ghetto, whites could preempt Negroes in new housing that was constructed there. This partial victory was especially galling since black initiative and persistence had played such a critical role in demonstrating the need for the project. Symbolic of the white preemption of this black project was the general failure to include Negroes in the public dedicatory ceremonies of Kingsborough Houses.[16]

Wherever large numbers of blacks lived in Brooklyn—Bedford-Stuyvesant, Brownsville, Fort Greene—their housing plight was similar. The New York City Planning Commission characterized that zone in Brownsville where most of that section's blacks lived as a blighted, decaying area. A local community study echoed this evaluation: "The needs of the

Negro families are admittedly the greatest because they now occupy the worst slum houses in excessively disproportionate numbers to their total population." Some blacks still resided in the Fort Greene-Navy Yard section, as they long had. In a kind of inverse, even perverse, form of boosterism, officials of that locality's division of the Brooklyn Committee for Better Housing claimed that "there is no area in Brooklyn that needs cleaning up more than [this] section." An intensive study of a heavily black five-block area known as "the Jungle" revealed the highest tuberculosis and infant mortality rates in the county. Furthermore, not one building complied fully with the city building code.[17]

The 1940 census provided some aggregate data on the magnitude of black housing deprivation in Brooklyn. Over one-third of black-occupied housing units needed major repairs or lacked some plumbing amenity, as contrasted to only one in eight white-occupied units. Nearly one-fifth of white housing was owner-occupied, but only 6.8 percent of black housing was. Furthermore, Negro-owned housing was of lower value than that belonging to whites. Only in the degree of overcrowding did whites approach blacks, with 20 percent of the former and 26 percent of the latter living in units with more than one person per room.[18]

Indications of the institutional racism practiced by the financial and real estate communities are usually evident impressionistically or belatedly in their functional results, but only rarely in published form. Often they are hidden behind an array of involved transactions difficult to get access to, understood only by experts, and obfuscated by public-relations statements. A rare public insight into the financial community's attitude toward blacks and the resultant availability of mortgage money for black neighborhoods was provided in a survey prepared by the Mortgage Conference of New York in 1941. Brooklyn was divided block by block into the most basic racial categories, indicating simply whether or not blacks resided there. This information was undoubtedly intended for use in determining the wisdom and terms for making mortgage loans. While the report never openly admitted prejudice,

the implications were obvious. The limited choice of character-
izations signified that to mortgagers, race was a salient factor
in realty transactions.[19]

Into whatever area one peered, the condition of blacks in
Brooklyn in 1940 was distressing. While they constituted a
still minimal percentage of the borough's total population,
blacks lived concentratedly within clear geographic constraints. More critically, the nucleus of what was to evolve into
the slum-ghetto of Bedford-Stuyvesant was well established
territorially and numerically. Furthermore, blacks usually
remained beyond the pale of local structural existence. Politically they were unrepresented and manipulated by white
politicians. With the Depression still lingering on in 1940,
Brooklyn blacks, not surprisingly, remained an economically
depressed people. Their housing was frequently only marginally sound, if not in a state of outright dilapidation. When
possible, Brooklyn blacks were ignored by local residents and
politicians; when proximity made such ignorance unfeasible,
they could anticipate hostility. They had indeed become a
troublesome presence to those whites who dwelled near them.
The one partial exception to this general negative perspective
was the internal organizational structure of the black community, which, for all its limitations and its racial isolation,
persisted and in the religious sphere actually expanded with
the founding of new churches.

## NOTES

1. Mary White Ovington, "The Negro Home in New York," *The
Negro in the Cities of the North* (New York, 1905), p. 25.
2. United States Census Bureau, *Thirteenth Census, 1910, Population, vol. 4, Occupations* (Washington, 1914), pp. 579-81.
3. United States Census Bureau, *Fourteenth Census, 1920, Population, vol. 4, Occupations* (Washington, 1923), pp. 1165-69.
4. *New York Age*, Jan. 28, 1928; *Amsterdam News*, Jan. 25, 1928,
Feb. 6, 1929.
5. United States Census Bureau, *Fifteenth Census, 1930, Population, vol. 4, Occupations* (Washington, 1933), pp. 1137-40, 1162;

United States Census Bureau, *Sixteenth Census, 1940, Population* (Washington, 1943), 3: 462-63; United States Census Bureau, *Sixteenth Census, 1940, Population and Housing, Statistics for Health Areas, New York City* (Washington, 1942), pp. 67, 87-88; Brooklyn Urban League, *Annual Report*, 1931, p. 10; 1936, pp. 9, 14; 1939, p. 10.

6. *Second Report of the New York State Temporary Commission on the Condition of the Urban Colored Population* (Albany, 1939), pp. 111-12; New York State Temporary Commission, *Public Hearings*, 8: 1420-32; *Age*, Nov. 12, 1938; *Amsterdam News*, Nov. 12, 1938, Nov. 19, 1938.

7. *Second Report*, p. 37; *Age*, Aug. 5, 1939; *Amsterdam News*, May 10, 1941; *Brooklyn Daily Eagle*, May 19, 1938, May 20, 1938, May 2, 1941.

8. Wesley Curtwright, "Brief History of the Domestic Workers' Association, Brooklyn Local" (WPA research papers, Schomburg Collection); *Amsterdam News*, Oct. 17, 1936, Feb. 13, 1937, May 13, 1939.

9. *Report of the New York State Temporary Commission on the Condition of the Urban Colored Population* (Albany, 1938), p. 14.

10. Seth Scheiner, *Negro Mecca: A History of the Negro in New York City, 1865-1920* (New York, 1965), p. 29; Clinton Avenue Congregational Church, "Community Study," pp. 35, 56; Brooklyn Urban League, *Annual Report*, 1919, pp. 2-3; *Eagle*, July 12, 1923, Nov. 22, 1923. The Baldwin family was active among those groups that eventually coalesced to form the National Urban League. William Baldwin, Jr., died in 1906 at the age of forty-two. His wife, Ruth Standish Baldwin served as chairman of the National League for the Protection of Colored Women and later, between 1913 and 1915, as chairman of the National League on Urban Conditions Among Negroes. Their son, William Baldwin, III, served as secretary of the National Urban League board and then as its president (1941-45). Guichard Parris and Lester Brooks, *Blacks in the City: A History of the National Urban League* (Boston, 1971), pp. 11, 16, 21, 70, 285.

11. Brooklyn Urban League, *Annual Report*, 1929, pp. 12-13. Compared with black Manhattan, Negroes in Brooklyn fared somewhat better in the quality of their housing, despite obvious deficiencies. Between 1900 and 1930, the proportion of black families owning their homes increased from 5.7 percent to 9 percent. Rents for blacks in Brooklyn averaged more than one-third less than Manhattan's. Brooklyn was less afflicted by the lodger problem, with 24 percent of Negro families there engaging in this practice in contrast to 40 percent in Manhattan (United States Census Bureau, *Negroes in the United States, 1920-1932* [Washington, 1935], pp. 277-85).

12. *Amsterdam News*, Oct. 23, 1937, April 30, 1938, July 16, 1938, Aug. 26, 1939.

13. *Age*, Aug. 27, 1938, Feb. 4, 1939; *Amsterdam News*, Aug. 20, 1938, Oct. 15, 1938; *Eagle*, Oct. 13, 1938.

14. *Age*, April 8, 1939, May 20, 1939;*Amsterdam News*, Nov. 12, 1938, April 8, 1939, Sept. 2, 1939, Sept. 16, 1939, Dec. 9, 1939, Dec. 16, 1939; *Eagle*, April 2, 1939, May 9, 1939, Sept. 14, 1939. The campaign for a public housing project in Bedford-Stuyvesant was opposed by advocates of such projects elsewhere in Brooklyn. Robert Moses preferred developments in the Navy Yard or Brownsville area. Milton Goell vigorously pressed for a Brownsville project. Mrs. Tempie Burge of the Brooklyn Urban League urged construction of a Negro project near the Navy Yard and the League building.

15. Arthur Smith Levy, "A Study of Some Considerations Which Influenced New York City Housing Authority Site Selection: 1934-1941" (Master of planning thesis, New York University, 1964), pp. 286-89; *Age*, Oct. 21, 1939, Feb. 10, 1940; *Amsterdam News*, Dec. 30, 1939, Jan. 6, 1940, Jan. 13, 1940; *Eagle*, Oct. 13, 1939, Oct. 16, 1939, Nov. 3, 1939, Dec. 15, 1939, Dec. 17, 1939, Jan. 4, 1940, Jan. 26, 1940, Feb. 3, 1940. The project also became the storm-center of a policy controversy between Nathan Straus, chairman of the United States Housing Authority, and Alfred Rheinstein, chairman of the New York City Housing Authority. For a time this conflict threatened federal approval of the plan, but Rheinstein's forced resignation eased the way to its acceptance (see Levy's study for more details).

16. *Age*, Nov. 18, 1939, July 6, 1940, Sept. 13, 1941; *Amsterdam News*, Aug. 30, 1941, Sept. 20, 1941; *Eagle*, Sept. 10, 1941.

17. Milton J. Goell, "Brownsville Must Have Public Housing" (Brownsville Neighborhood Council and Brooklyn Federation for Better Housing, 1940), pp. 7, 16-19, 26; Brooklyn Urban League, *Annual Report*, 1936, p. 14; Levy, "Site Selection," p. 313; *Age*, Dec. 17, 1938; *Amsterdam News*, Oct. 19, 1940; *Eagle*, June 11, 1934, July 21, 1935, July 28, 1937, Nov. 20, 1937, March 17, 1939, April 13, 1939, June 13, 1939, Aug. 21, 1939, Nov. 21, 1939, May 6, 1940, July 14, 1940, Oct. 13, 1940.

18. Census Bureau, *Sixteenth Census, 1940, Census Tract Data; New York City* (New York, 1942).

19. The Mortgage Conference of New York, *Population Survey Number 3-A, Concentration of Negroes* (New York, 1941). This document is in the collection of the Long Island Historical Society.

# PART III

# A Ghetto Grows and Grows and Grows: 1940 to the Present

# CHAPTER 7

# Demography and Popular Perceptions

## GROWTH OF THE GHETTO

The growth of Brooklyn's black population, which had moderated somewhat during the Depression, surged forward during and after World War II. A revitalized economy encouraged interregional migration from the South to the North and West. In New York City the black saturation of Harlem and increased subway convenience encouraged inter-borough movement and the dispersion of the city's black population. In 1940 nearly two-thirds of New York City blacks resided in Manhattan and only 23 percent in Brooklyn. By 1950 the Manhattan proportion had diminished to about half and the Brooklyn share had risen modestly to 28 percent. Between 1940 and 1950 Brooklyn's Negro population nearly doubled from 108,263 to 208,478. Equally portentous for Brooklyn's demographic future was a modest 50,000 decline in the number of its white residents, the first such decrease since the eighteenth century.[1] Within the boundaries of Bedford-Stuyvesant as defined by the Community Council of Greater

New York the black population more than doubled during the 1940s from 65,166 to 137,436. Blacks came to constitute over half the section's population, and 61 percent of borough blacks were concentrated in Bedford-Stuyvesant. In 1940 only 7.5 percent of the borough's black population resided in census tracts over 80 percent Negro, but by 1950 the proportion had increased nearly fivefold. It was during this decade that Bedford-Stuyvesant as a large, impacted, overwhelmingly black ghetto was forged. Subsequent developments represented an intensification and expansion of the population and ghetto boundaries in the execution of what has seemed to be an immutable law of American urban dynamics. Sections with significant black populations became totally black and areas contiguous to the ghetto invariably were annexed to this spatial entity, that is, they were incorporated into an ever greater Bedford-Stuyvesant, a name that decreased in specificity while developing an elasticity of geographic definition that utilized the presence of blacks as the primary definitional criterion.[2]

The classic urban demographic pattern of black growth and white decline accelerated during the 1950s. For the first time since the eighteenth century the total population of Kings County declined. This decrease, a modest 4 percent or 110,856, reflected a national trend away from large central cities. More significant were the component parts that made up this aggregate shift. The black population continued its vigorous growth, increasing 78 percent to 371,405 in 1960 or 14 percent of the borough's total population. This total represented virtual numerical parity with Manhattan, with each borough containing slightly more than one-third of the city's total black population. Even more startling than the high growth rate of blacks was the near quintupling of the number of Puerto Ricans in Brooklyn, from 40,199 to 180,114. By 1960 these two minority groups represented in excess of half a million persons and formed over one-fifth of the county's population as contrasted to less than one in ten in 1950. Meanwhile, Brooklyn's non-Puerto Rican white population decreased by 415,994 or 17 percent. While Brooklyn still

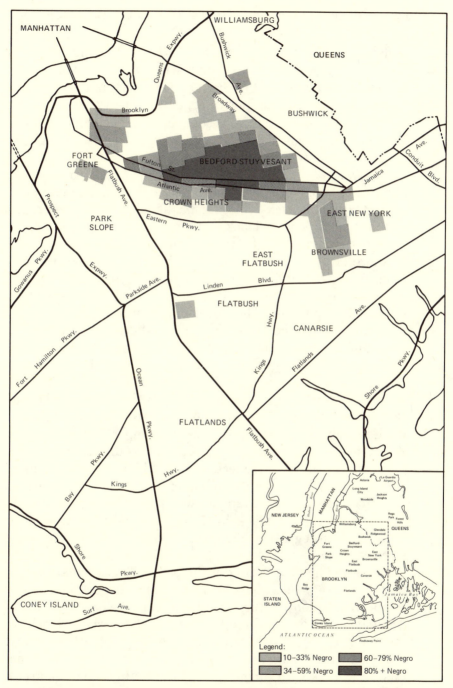

Map 4. Concentration of Black Population in Brooklyn, 1950.

remained nearly 80 percent non-Puerto Rican white, clearly the intensifying and self-fulfilling patterns of ghetto spread and white departure had interwined in a social pathology that assured an increasing minority population in Brooklyn.[3]

By 1960 black residential occupancy had not only engulfed Bedford-Stuyvesant but had expanded into the contiguous parts of Crown Heights and Brownsville. Relatively few blacks lived beyond the invisible but real boundaries of the ghetto in Brooklyn or elsewhere in the North. The essential characteristic of black demographic distribution was segregation.[4] Small pockets of black settlement did occasionally exist beyond this primary ghetto, but they usually reflected the presence of a low-income housing project. A number of such projects constructed during the 1950s soon became mini-ghettos surrounded by a predominantly white and frequently unfriendly population. The Cooper Park project, for example, located in the northern part of Williamsburg, an area almost devoid of blacks in 1950, was nearly 60 percent black in 1960 with resulting racial strife. Constructed in 1952 on mostly deserted land near Jamaica Bay, Breuckelen Houses in 1960 contained over 3,000 blacks, 45 percent of its total population. Boulevard, Cypress Hills, and Louis Heaton Pink projects in the East New York-New Lots sections and Gravesend Houses near Coney Island exhibited similar if less dramatic tendencies. Some of the older projects that had been overwhelmingly white in their origins also underwent racial transformation. Red Hook Houses, for example, where few blacks resided in 1950, was over half black by 1960. Such projects were less symbols of integration than minority islands in a hostile environment.[5]

There was no moderating in the pace of black expansion in Brooklyn after 1960. The addition of some 286,000 blacks, an amount equivalent to the fiftieth largest city in the country, demanded a correspondingly extensive territorial growth of the ghetto. Thrusting south and east, the ghetto totally absorbed Brownsville as well as most of Crown Heights and East New York with further penetration into the fringe areas of Bushwick and East Flatbush. The speed of some of these

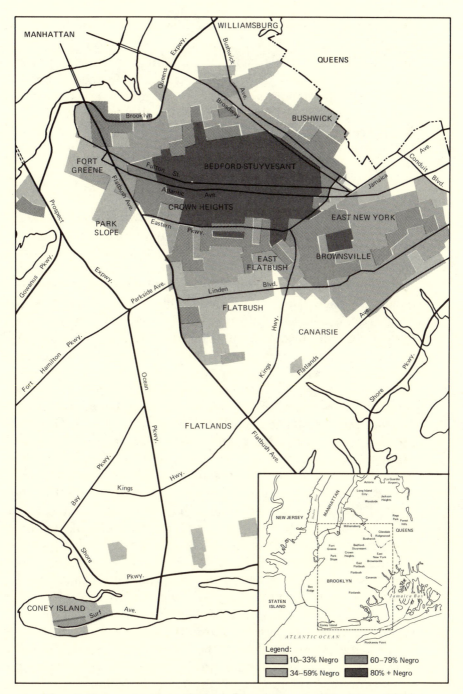

Map 5. Concentration of Black Population in Brooklyn, 1970.

neighborhood reversals could be blinding. In less than ten years much of East New York was transformed from a comfortable, predominantly white, lower-middle-class community into an impoverished, overwhelmingly black and Puerto Rican area. East Flatbush, almost all-white in 1960, became the destination of blacks overflowing Brownsville or seeking to escape beyond the ghetto. By the mid-1960s parts of Bushwick were threatening to become the "first cousin to Bedford-Stuyvesant which blends into Bushwick." [6]

Such neighborhood transition was not always accomplished with tranquillity. Most whites had psychologically if not physically abandoned Bedford-Stuyvesant by the mid-1940s, although some conflicts did develop between Orthodox Jewish sects that for a time remained in Bedford-Stuyvesant and the dominant black population. Similar black-Jewish confrontations also developed in Crown Heights, where a Hasidic Jewish vigilante organization, the Maccabees, was formed in 1964 to supplement and aid the police. It functioned for a few years before relations improved and the group disbanded. Faced with probably the most sudden population reversal, some residents of East New York resisted more vigorously. By the mid-1960s racial tension had become extreme among the area's Italian, Puerto Rican, and Negro populations. A dispute between Italian and black youths over control of a neighborhood playground led to the vandalism of a black grocery store and a black realty office. Signs in local stores and houses warned "Niggers" to keep out: "You may take Watts, but you'll never take New Lots," warned one piece of defiant doggerel. Racial violence also flared in parts of Bushwick, Flatbush, and Coney Island. Such conflict, however, was merely a required overture to an unvarying ritual that ended with black occupation of a deteriorating neighborhood.[7]

One spatially distinct black and Puerto Rican community, separated from Bedford-Stuyvesant by Brooklyn's still vast white belt, did develop during the 1960s. The ghettoization of a segment of Coney Island represented a classic example in miniature of exploitation, neglect, and deliberate official efforts to foster segregation. Capitalizing on the severe housing shortage immediately after World War II, owners of wooden summer bungalows had winterized them and rented them to veterans and others who were not notably dissimilar from the year-round residents of the section. The increasing availability of housing in the suburbs and the subsequent construction of new apartments in other parts of Coney Island reduced the demand for these converted bungalows. Excessive vacancy rates, deterioration, and difficulty in renting to anyone else generated a willingness to rent these flimsily constructed houses to welfare families who were disproportionately black and Puerto Rican. What resulted was a microcosmic slum-ghetto that manifested in miniature all the pathologies of Bedford-Stuyvesant from welfarism to subemployment; from increasingly dilapidated and abandoned housing to the concentration of public and publicly assisted housing projects in the ghetto area; from segregated schools to official fear of additional white flight. Though physically separated from the central ghetto and much smaller in population, the Coney Island black section reflected the ghetto far more than it did the proximate, predominantly white sections of Gravesend, Sea Gate, or even white Coney Island.[8]

By 1970 Greater Bedford-Stuyvesant had developed into the largest black community in New York City. Nearly 40 percent of city blacks made their home in Brooklyn in 1970. They constituted a quarter of the borough's total population, and, in conjunction with local Puerto Ricans, over a third. Migration from the South had of course contributed to this growth, but the bulk of the expansion resulted from natural increase, an increasingly common reality in northern urban demography, with a boost from West Indian migration after 1965.[9] With over half of Brooklyn's black population born in the North, it was no longer valid, if indeed it ever had been, to blame migration from the South for local ills.[10] Wherever their source, local or distant, Brooklyn blacks lived in an all-too-constricted world geographically and economically.

In 1970 well over half a million blacks, with a substantial admixture of Puerto Ricans, especially in Bushwick and Brownsville-East New York, occupied a vast area that sprawled across central Brooklyn and constituted possibly the largest contiguous black and brown ghetto in the country.[11] Between 1940 and 1970 Brooklyn blacks had increased by well in excess of 500,000 persons. What had been a modest, ignorable (at least for most Brooklynites) minority community in 1940, had burgeoned into a ghetto of overwhelming proportions. Indicative of this tremendous growth was the rise of Brooklyn, considered as an independent entity, in the ranking of cities by the number of black residents. In 1940 Brooklyn had trailed ten other cities in black population. It had moved up to seventh in 1950 and sixth in 1960. By 1970 only New York City, Chicago, and Detroit contained larger black populations than Brooklyn. The Bedford-Stuyvesant ghetto, with roots in the 1920s, had evolved into a monstrous reality during and after World War II. By 1970 Bedford-Stuyvesant had become a code word, still somewhat less universally evocative than Harlem, but nonetheless real, for America's unresolved urban and race problems.

## STIGMATIZATION: THE GRAND JURY INVESTIGATION

Coincidental with black succession to a neighborhood there often occurs a loss of status and reputation for that area. The stigmatization of Bedford-Stuyvesant had been desperately resisted by white groups in the late 1930s in their successful opposition to the designation of a local public housing project as Bedford-Stuyvesant Houses. This preservation of the area's sound reputation was seriously jeopardized in 1943 when the August grand jury of Kings County investigated charges of rampant hoodlumism in Bedford-Stuyvesant. For well over a month the investigation, report, and subsequent reverberations produced front-page headlines in the local press so that few citizens were likely to remain unaware of Bedford-Stuyvesant's evolving demography and problems. While this scarcely sealed the area's fate, the publicity no doubt assisted the development of a public perception of Bedford-Stuyvesant as a black ghetto.

After hearing more than 100 predominantly white wit-
nesses, the all-white grand jury in its presentment painted a
grim picture of Bedford-Stuyvesant.[12] "A most unusual and
extremely deplorable state of lawlessness exists in this area
and has existed for some years past." School children had been
robbed and mistreated; churches had curtailed or eliminated
their evening services since citizens considered it too dangerous to traverse the streets after dark. "Gangs of hoodlums"
armed with knives and other weapons had assaulted, robbed,
insulted, and murdered innocent, law-abiding people. A part
of the section was rife with prostitution and had become "a
cesspool of filth and venereal disease." Many local residents
were on relief illegally. Hundreds of "formerly very fine one-
family homes" had been converted to multiple family usage.
In short, Bedford-Stuyvesant was becoming a dangerous slum.

The report bemoaned the "appallingly insufficient number
of patrolmen" assigned to the area, the lack of enough
"centers for spiritual and moral training of the young," the
absence of "parental supervision," and the "lax attitude" of
proper authorities toward the congregation of persons near
bars and poolrooms. To remedy the situation, the grand jury
offered the forthright solution of saturating the area with
police, and, if need be, state troopers and national guardsmen.
The mayor could add to this occupying force special auxiliary
patrolmen drawn from the law-abiding citizens of the area,
"many of whom would be happy to perform such service." To
this end the Colored State Guard in Brooklyn could be
enlarged from a battalion of 250 to full regimental strength of
3,000. The second set of remedies demanded vigorous and
dutiful performances from city and state regulatory and
administrative agencies. The department of welfare should
root out fraudulent recipients of relief; the tenement house,
fire, and health departments should rigorously enforce building and sanitary codes; the Alcoholic Beverage Control Board
should police rowdy bars more diligently. Such recommendations were at best anachronistic in 1943. Wartime employment
and the draft had virtually eliminated the welfare component
of the economy. Code enforcement was unrealistic in a tight

housing market with a vacancy rate hovering near zero and no relief possible before the end of the war. Moreover, a vigorous campaign in one area would only disperse the evicted population to other congested quarters, a remedy no other section was enthusiastic about. Additional suggestions included expanded recreation facilities, special cultural activities, the formation of "centers ... for spiritual and moral training," and a 9:00 P.M. radio reminder to parents on the whereabouts of their children.

The growing slum conditions and changing racial character of Bedford-Stuyvesant received but passing notice. The grand jury vehemently denied that the problem presented to it was in any sense racial, insisting instead on its purely law-enforcement character. In its tunnel vision, the jury analyzed and proposed solutions to one external manifestation of a broad social and demographic development but failed to grapple with or understand the underlying dynamics that were creating tension and confrontation. Not surprisingly blacks perceived the presentment as blatantly racial in character, denouncing its "strong anti-Negro bias" and "witch-hunting" flavor. Owing to the "enforced" residential segregation of Brooklyn blacks in Bedford-Stuyvesant, the labeling of that section as unsafe and crime-ridden tended to paint all Negroes as such. In addition, they argued, the report failed to "take into consideration the underlying social and economic causes giving rise to such conditions as they describe." Any section of the city in which "the population is forced to stew in its own juices of economic, social and civic frustration is bound to collapse morally and otherwise." Poor economic conditions, unemployment, segregation, substandard housing, exorbitant rents, lack of education were all cited as factors producing a "lack of hope—which is no more than the result of frustration in the efforts of people to better themselves." [13]

Since the recommendations of the grand jury were not pursued, the only enduring legacy of the hearings was undoubtedly that left in popular perceptions of Bedford-Stuyvesant. Lengthy front-page attention expanded people's awareness of the area's problems and character. If whites did not consciously do so already, they now increasingly identified Bedford-Stuyvesant as a Negro slum. This simple equation undoubtedly contributed to continued black growth in the area, although the direction, if not the magnitude, of Bedford-Stuyvesant's demographic destiny was probably already established. By 1943, the black presence in central Brooklyn was a commanding reality that could not be destroyed or wished away. With the establishment of a sufficient population base in the section, the dynamics of ghettoization required continuation and expansion. The demographic germs of the ghetto in Bedford-Stuyvesant had by then metastasized. Symbolizing this new reality was the final meeting of the Gates Avenue Association in 1944. While there still seemed a possibility of preserving the racial integrity of the area, whites had schemed, protested, and lobbied. Once the transformation became inevitable, whites withdrew and fled. Only six members attended the meeting to disburse the remaining treasury among the Red Cross, the Hopewell Society, and Monsignor Belford and the Reverend Mr. McCaul, neither of whom was noted for his compassion for blacks.[14]

## CRISIS GHETTOS

Following the grand jury investigation general socio-economic conditions in Bedford-Stuyvesant did not improve markedly. By the mid-1960s, however, that area was being surpassed by its more recent offspring, East New York and especially Brownsville, as the epitome of urban decay, as examples of what Arthur Solomon calls "crisis ghettos." A politician's visit to New York City at that time was not complete without a tour of this area or the South Bronx, complete with appropriate expressions of dismay. It was not sufficient nor did it connote the enormity of the decay to refer to Brownsville merely as a "disaster area." The only imagery that carried sufficiently powerful connotations drew its inspiration from wartime destruction. Brownsville was compared to a "ravaged, bombed-out German city." Block fronts looked like "they had been shelled by heavy artillery." The ultimate analogy, not surprisingly, was to Hiroshima. Except for the public housing projects, local housing was "indescribably bad" and services "intolerably poor." Residents of the section were merely "going through the motions of existing because they have long ceased to live. Each time one visits Brownsville, more and more homes, stores, and buildings have been gutted by the torch, or torn down by vandals." According to then (1970) Assemblyman Sam Wright, "our community is dying. It has become the refuge of those without hope, the land of the frustrated and a symbol of decadence." Adding to this grim picture, one recent prognostication anticipated "little hope" for the improvement during the next thirty years of such "badly deteriorated and socially unwholesome" areas as Brownsville.[15]

East New York inspired somewhat fewer wartime metaphors. A 1968 Housing and Development Administration study simply stated that parts of the section "suggest death." The New York City Planning Commission pictured much of the area as a "ghost town." "Accumulated debris lay untouched. Disemboweled cars and shattered glass blanketed the streets. There were dozens of vacated, burned out and destroyed homes and stores." The commission labeled the section a "crisis area." [16]

Despite dilapidated housing, employment deficiencies, a high crime rate, and poor health indices, Bedford-Stuyvesant did not rate the extreme judgmental assessments attached to Brownsville and East New York. In comparison, Bedford-Stuyvesant seemed almost sound and prosperous; references were not uncommonly made to the middle-class, homeowning character of parts of the area, to block-association activities, to the successful endeavors of the Bedford-Stuyvesant Restoration Corporation. While containing a modicum of truth, such a focus neglected obvious and serious deficiencies. This attitude toward evident but less total deterioration indicates to some extent the normative acceptance of Bedford-Stuyvesant's decay.[17]

What existed in classic form in central Brooklyn in the mid-twentieth century was a slum ghetto of vast territorial extent that showed little indication of mitigating, let alone dissolving. Between 1940 and the mid-1970s the black population of Brooklyn had increased by approximately 600,000, a rate more rapid than that of any other city with a black population in excess of 100,000 in 1940. Were one to add the Puerto Rican component, which often tended to live on the fringe of black areas or interspersed with blacks, the aggregate increment in minority population was fast approaching 1 million. Such a demographic tidal wave was bound to have significant repercussions in other areas, occasionally beneficial (increased political representation, for example), more usually malignant (poverty, poor education, collapsing family structure). These specific topics will be dealt with in detail in the following chapters.

## NOTES

1. United States Census Bureau, *Sixteenth Census, 1940, Census Tract Data on Population and Housing, New York City* (New York, 1942), pp. 52-70; United States Census Bureau, *Seventeenth Census, 1950, Population*, 3: ch. 37; *Census Tract Statistics for New York City* (Washington, 1953), pp. 34-84. The demographic data for Brooklyn between 1940 and 1970 were:

| Year | Total Population | Negro Population | Percentage Negro | Puerto Rican Population | Percentage Puerto Rican |
|------|------------------|------------------|------------------|-------------------------|-------------------------|
| 1940 | 2,698,285 | 107,263 | 4.0 | N.A. | N.A |
| 1950 | 2,738,175 | 208,478 | 7.6 | 40,299 | 1.4 |
| 1960 | 2,627,319 | 371,405 | 14.1 | 180,114 | 6.9 |
| 1970 | 2,602,012 | 656,194 | 25.2 | 271,769 | 10.4 |

A related population measure also indicates the expansion of Brooklyn's black population:

*Proportion of New York City's Black Population by Borough*

| Year | Bronx | Brooklyn | Manhattan | Queens | Staten Island |
|------|-------|----------|-----------|--------|---------------|
| 1940 | 5  | 23 | 65 | 6  | 1 |
| 1950 | 13 | 28 | 51 | 7  | 1 |
| 1960 | 15 | 34 | 37 | 13 | 1 |
| 1970 | 21 | 39 | 23 | 15 | 1 |

It was estimated that by mid-1975 the population of Brooklyn had declined 6.4 percent, from 2,602,000 in 1970 to 2,435,600 in 1975. The net outmigration in this five-year period totaled over 250,000, the largest absolute and proportionate decrease in any county in New York State. United States Census Bureau, "Estimates of the Population of New York Counties and Metropolitan Areas," *Current Population Reports* P-25, No. 631 (July 1976). By the mid-1970s Brooklyn's black population was probably in the vicinity of 700,000 (*New York Times*, Dec. 19, 1976).

2. Robert C. Weaver, *The Negro Ghetto* (New York, 1948), p. 105; Community Council of Greater New York, *Brooklyn Communities: Population Characteristics and Neighborhood Social Resources* (2 vols.; New York, 1959), 1: 100.

3. United States Census Bureau, *Eighteenth Census, 1960, Population, Census Tracts, New York City* (Washington, 1961), pp. 54-112. Brooklyn accounted for nearly half of the city's white exodus during the 1950s.

4. Karl E. Taeuber and Alma F. Taeuber, *Negroes in Cities: Residential Segregation and Neighborhood Change* (New York, 1969); Annemette Sorensen, Karl E. Taeuber, and Leslie J. Hollingsworth, Jr., "Indexes of Racial Residential Segregation for 109 Cities in the United States, 1940 to 1970," *Institute for Research on Poverty* (February 1974). The Taeubers have computed an index of residential segregation that ranges from zero to 100. The former represents perfect integration, the latter total segregation; hence the higher the number, the greater the degree of racial separation. Brooklyn's index in 1960 was 80.0, compared with other such eastern cities as Boston (83.9), Newark (71.6), New York (79.3), and Philadelphia (87.1). In 1970, Brooklyn's index of 79.9 compared with Boston's 84.3, Newark's 76.4, New York's 77.3, and Philadelphia's 84.4. The indices, all clustering around 80, indicate the pervasive character of racial segregation. Brooklyn's segregation index for 1940 was 82.1 and for 1950 it was 85.7.

5. *Amsterdam News*, Dec. 17, 1960.

6. United States Census Bureau, *Census of Population and Housing: 1970, Census Tracts, New York, New York SMSA* (Washington, 1972), tables P-1, P-2, P-5; New York City Planning Commission, *Plan for New York, 1969: A Proposal,* vol. 3, *Brooklyn* (New York, 1969), p. 62; *Amsterdam News,* July 23, 1966.

7. *Amsterdam News,* July 23, 1966, Aug. 6, 1966, Aug, 20, 1966, June 17, 1967; *New York Times,* July 21, 1966, July 23, 1966, June 15, 1967, Feb. 2, 1968, July 15, 1969, June 29, 1970, Sept. 11, 1970, Sept. 12, 1970, June 15, 1973, Aug. 1, 1974. Following the outbreak of violence in East New York in the summer of 1966, the *Amsterdam News* editorialized at some length on the city's failure to prevent the clash. "The basic cause of the riot was classic insofar as race riots in the United States go. Negroes and Puerto Ricans moved near or into a white section of East New York. Bad blood ensued, because the whites resented them. The police were run ragged for years, trying to keep the peace between the white, Negro and Puerto Rican groups.... The East New York blow-up was the first true race riot in the city, probably in more than a century, or since the draft riots during the War of the Rebellion (Civil War) in 1863. The one in Harlem in 1964 was strictly an affair between Negroes and the police, not Negro and white."
During the 1960s New York City generally avoided the ghetto violence that characterized such cities as Los Angeles, Detroit, Newark, or Washington, D.C. In July 1964 some rioting did occur in Harlem and Bedford-Stuyvesant, but in overall perspective Brooklyn's riot was quite modest. Fred C. Shapiro and James W. Sullivan, *Race Riot: New York 1964* (New York, 1964).

8. Planning Commission, *Brooklyn,* p. 138; Jack Weinstein, decision in *Hart* v. *the Community School Board of Brooklyn, New York School District #21* (Jan. 28, 1974), pp. 10-15.

9. West Indian migration to the United States is discussed and calculated in: R. W. Palmer, "A Decade of West Indian Migration to the United States, 1962-1972: An Economic Analysis," *Social and Economic Studies* 23 (December 1974): 571-87; United States Census Bureau, "Estimate of the Population of the United States and Components of Change: 1930 to 1975," *Current Population Reports* P-25, No. 632 (July 1976); Kenneth Wheeler, "West Indians in Brooklyn," Brooklyn Studies Seminar (February 17, 1977).
Brooklyn, long a center of West Indian settlement, undoubtedly contains the largest such community in the country. The removal in 1965 of the country-of-origin restrictions for immigration enabled a larger number of blacks to enter the United States than could do so previously. In 1970, there were 36,712 black residents of Brooklyn who had been living abroad in 1965.
Official statistics on West Indian migration, however, are undoubtedly underestimates due to the large number of illegal aliens

in this country. The Roman Catholic Diocese of Brooklyn, for example, has estimated that there may be between 100,000 and 250,000 illegal Haitian aliens in Brooklyn (Wheeler).

10. Recent studies have indicated that southern-born blacks who migrate to the North are as economically successful, if not more so, than northern-born blacks. Phillips Cutright, "Region, Migration and the Earnings of White and Black Men," *Social Forces* 53 (October 1974): 297-305; Larry H. Long and Lynne R. Heltman, "Migration and Income Differences Between Black and White Men in the North," *American Journal of Sociology* 80 (May 1975): 1391-1409; Larry Long, "The Migration Experience of Blacks," *Integrated Education* 13 (May/June 1975): 28-31; Stanley H. Masters, "Are Black Migrants from the South to Northern Cities Worse off than Blacks Already There?" *Journal of Human Resources* 7 (Fall 1972): 411-23.

11. The pattern of Puerto Rican settlement on the fringe of the black area has been commented upon by Nathan Kantrowitz, *Negro and Puerto Rican Population of New York City in the Twentieth Century* (New York, 1969); Nathan Kantrowitz, *Ethnic and Racial Segregation in the New York Metropolis: Residential Patterns among White Ethnic Groups, Blacks, and Puerto Ricans* (New York, 1973); James Beshers, "Demographic Perspective on Brooklyn," *Brooklyn 1976: A Social Science Seminar* (December 8, 1976).

12. On November 15, 1943, the *Brooklyn Daily Eagle* published the complete text of the grand jury presentment. All the quotations from this document are drawn from this source.

13. *New York Age*, Nov. 27, 1943, Dec. 4, 1943, Dec. 18, 1943; *Amsterdam News*, Nov. 20, 1943, Nov. 27, 1943, Dec. 18, 1943; *Eagle*, Nov. 16, 1943, Nov. 17, 1943, Nov. 18, 1943, Nov. 19, 1943, Nov. 22, 1943, Nov. 23, 1943, Nov. 24, 1943, Nov. 26, 1943, Nov. 27, 1943, Nov. 30, 1943, Dec. 2, 1943, Dec. 4, 1943, Dec. 6, 1943, Dec. 7, 1943, Dec. 8, 1943.

14. Gates Avenue Association, *Minute Book* (Long Island Historical Society Collection).

15. Planning Commission, *Brooklyn*, pp. 166-70; Peter D. Salins, "New York in the Year 2000," *New York Affairs* 1(Spring 1974): 18; *Amsterdam News*, Feb. 28, 1970, July 25, 1970, Oct. 3, 1970, May 15, 1971, Sept. 18, 1971. *The Tablet*, the paper of the Roman Catholic Archdiocese of Brooklyn, referred to Brownsville as a "Local Death Valley" and even more dramatically, a "Second Hiroshima."

16. Planning Commission, *Brooklyn*, pp. 62-65; *Amsterdam News*, April 25, 1970, May 29, 1971, Sept. 11, 1971.

17. Planning Commission, *Brooklyn*, pp. 40-44.

# CHAPTER 8

# Changing Institutional Patterns

## INSTITUTIONAL SEGREGATION

Black institutional life in 1940 was racially separate, and, outside church-related organizations, limited in scope. Such long-established groups as the Urban League, the "colored" YMCA and YWCA, and the NAACP, along with the Elks and other such social organizations, constituted the hub of this activity. Rarely was a black individual honored in the broader community except in his distinct relationship to other blacks. Shortly after the outbreak of World War II, black Brooklynites were forcefully reminded that racial separation remained the functionally dominant ideology even during a war to extirpate racism. In 1942 prominent Brooklyn Negroes requested the establishment of a local black regiment of the New York State National Guard. Several units did, of course, exist in Kings County, but local black patriots were forced to travel to Harlem to join the only black unit in the city. A number of black leaders, including Justice Myles Paige, politicians Bertram Baker, George Wibecan, and Clarence

145

Wilson, Herbert Miller, executive director of the Carlton Y, and the Reverend George S. Starke of Siloam Presbyterian Church endorsed the plan.[1]

This suggestion of a separate black institution inevitably presented its proposed beneficiaries with a fundamental dilemma. Integration certainly remained the ideal toward which to strive ultimately, but in the practical world blacks could not expect to receive benefits except on a segregated basis. The underlying question was whether it was ever proper to accept official segregation in order to attain a desirable end. Elmer A. Carter, a former editor of *Opportunity* magazine, questioned the logic of demanding integration in defense and industrial jobs while accepting "the very opposite of integration in our military forces." The national office of the NAACP likewise protested the creation of such a unit. Apologists for the plan countered by citing the improbability of any other scheme being accepted. Clarence Wilson doubted that the public was yet "fully prepared for complete integration." Myles Paige expressed well the dilemma: "I agree in principle with the idea against imposing segregation in any form, but there are extenuating circumstances on the part of our groups in some instances accepting, without approving, certain positions or appointments for the purpose of preparing a firmer ground work for later establishing the genuine principle of non-segregation." Governor Herbert Lehman approved the proposal in late 1942 and a black unit was created with Myles Paige as commander.[2]

## INSTITUTIONAL DESEGREGATION

Yet the times were indeed changing. On July 1, 1943 the Brooklyn YWCA departed from its traditional policy of providing a separate structure for blacks. It opened the facilities of its central building to all members and moved the staff and program of the Negro Ashland Place Branch to the headquarters office. The Ashland Place building did remain a black residence hall. A Y official exuberantly claimed that as a result of this "experiment in integration," Brooklyn now stood "in the national limelight." The YWCA broadened its desegregation policy in 1950 by completely closing the Ashland Place branch and accommodating its residents in other Y facilities. By 1952, in a further effort to eliminate all vestiges of racial distinction, the interracial education committee was disbanded. In addition, the Brooklyn YWCA employed blacks in staff and executive positions.[3]

The corresponding male facility, the Carlton Avenue YMCA, shifted toward desegregation more slowly. As the black population had increasingly concentrated in Bedford-Stuyvesant, the Carlton Y, located amid the vestiges of an earlier black settlement nearer downtown Brooklyn, became increasingly remote from the majority of persons it was intended to serve. This physical divorce was early recognized, but the means and will to rectify it were lacking. Extension efforts provided some services in Bedford-Stuyvesant but were limited by the absence of a fully equipped building. Adding to Carlton's difficulties were its "antiquated, drab and dingy" facilities. Initially it was suggested that a replacement Carlton Y simply be constructed in Bedford-Stuyvesant. Such plans, however, mandated needless duplication, since the Bedford branch of the YMCA already served the area. By 1950 the Bedford Y did allow black youths to use the pool and the gymnasium, but it refused to admit blacks to full membership or permit them to reside there. Local blacks were thus confronted with the same dilemma they had faced in the early 1940s when they had sought a segregated National Guard regiment. While not necessarily desirous of a separate branch, the pressing requirements of the immediate situation outweighed the resultant imposed segregation. If the Bedford Y would not desegregate, then, demanded blacks, build a new and similar facility for blacks. "Separate but equal" had long been a philosophy of necessity imposed upon blacks.[4]

Under pressure from the Brooklyn-Queens YMCA, which lacked sufficient funds to construct a new segregated unit, and facing undeniable demographic realities, the Bedford branch formally agreed in 1951 to desegregate all its facilities, including the dormitory. Black complaints, however, did persist, especially about lengthy and unusual procedures for their admission. As the black population in Bedford-Stuyvesant increased, it became inevitable, as earlier in the case of some church properties, that institutional racial succession would occur. Increasingly programs were oriented to fit the needs of the black constituency. Symbolic of this shift in emphasis and clientele were the appointment in 1960 of Russell N. Service, a black, as executive director of the Bedford Y and the election the following year of Judge O. D. Williams to head its board of managers. This branch had been the most prestigious in Brooklyn during the 1920s and 1930s when the Reverend S. Parkes Cadman had preached his Sunday afternoon radio sermons from its auditorium, but it had lost some of its glitter in subsequent decades. To Service in 1960 it appeared "drab" and in need of sprucing up—another example of black inheritance of secondhand facilities.[5]

The Carlton Y continued to function even after the Bedford Y desegregated its building and programs. The rationale for its existence had, however, been negated by both the new Bedford Y policy and the expansion of more conveniently located community centers and Police Athletic League facilities in Bedford-Stuyvesant. Lacking adequate funds either to relocate the Carlton Y or to revitalize the existing building and program, the Brooklyn-Queens YMCA finally decided in late 1954 to abandon the old "colored" branch entirely. Coincidentally it adopted a policy that officially opened all branches to anyone regardless of race, color, or national origin. While Carlton had outlived its usefulness by 1954, it had for many years offered to Brooklyn blacks recreational and social facilities unavailable elsewhere in the borough. While not condoning such segregation, black leaders had recognized and accepted their inability to demand or force racial integration prior to the 1940s. The Carlton Y had long been a focus of black pride, with prominent Negro civic leaders serving on its board of managers.

During the 1940s and 1950s the most blatant forms of racial exclusion and separation in Brooklyn's institutional life were increasingly leavened with a degree of individual acceptance and recognition. Blacks were admitted to membership and even positions of leadership in previously all-white organizations so that, by the mid-1950s such developments were no longer exceptional or newsworthy. Much of this early recognition focused on church-related groups. Thus, in the early 1940s a Brooklyn chapter of the Catholic Interracial Council was established. The Bedford Protestant Ministers Association, which had long ignored that section's Negro ministers, finally realized in 1944 that local problems were "common to all" and could only be "solved in a spirit of cooperation," and hence opened its membership to blacks. In the same year the Long Island Baptist Association elected the Reverend James B. Adams of Concord Baptist Church as its moderator. In 1948 the Reverend William O. Carrington, pastor of the First AME Zion Church, became the first black elected to head the Brooklyn Church and Mission Federation and the Brooklyn Division of the Protestant Council. This same office went to the Reverend Gardner C. Taylor of Concord Baptist Church in 1952. Taylor later was elected president of the citywide Protestant Council. A black was appointed district lay leader of the Brooklyn South district of the Methodist church in 1960.[6]

Elsewhere in the institutional world blacks also achieved recognition. In 1942 the Brooklyn Red Cross named Dr. William R. Granger as the first black member of its board of directors. The Brooklyn Bureau of Charities accorded a similar honor in 1943 to Richard C. White. In 1944 Herbert Miller, secretary of the Carlton Y, became the first Negro to head a Brooklyn grand jury. The Brooklyn Real Estate Board admitted its first black associates in 1945. Oliver D. Williams chaired the 1952 Brooklyn financial campaign of the Brooklyn-Queens YMCA. Judge Clarence Wilson became the first black appointee to the lay advisory board of Kings County Hospital. One Negro was chosen grand knight of a local Knights of Columbus council; another was elected president of the otherwise all-white 230-member Inter-County Paint Dealers and Wallpaper Association of Brooklyn and Long Island; another became the first black bail bondsman in Brooklyn. The Pratt Institute Alumni Association elected a black woman president. Three black women from Brooklyn were included in the *Who's Who of American Women.* Much of this recognition was undoubtedly token and superficial, certainly not affecting the mass of Brooklyn blacks, yet it did represent a significant departure from the past practice of almost automatically and pervasively rejecting all blacks except in their relationship to other blacks.[7]

## PROTEST AND ADVANCEMENT GROUPS

This gradual desegregation left only a few organizations, the traditional protest and advancement groups like the NAACP and Urban League, officially and exclusively committed to black-oriented programs. The Brooklyn Urban League merged with the New York branch in 1944 to form the Greater New York Urban League. The Brooklyn branch continued to operate from its antiquated building in the downtown area until 1949, when the League purchased and renovated a brownstone in Bedford-Stuyvesant. The broad spectrum of settlement activities that had characterized the old Brooklyn League under Robert Elzy yielded increasingly to an emphasis on employment opportunities and job placement. Under League auspices some advances were achieved during the 1950s in the brewery and longshoring unions.[8]

The Brooklyn NAACP suffered from chronic financial disability and was frequently rent by internal factionalism caused by and resulting in bitter election struggles and recriminations. The local branch continued to function after the war in its traditional role of a black legal-aid society, defending blacks against various forms of discrimination, especially examples of "police brutality." Following the 1949 police killing of two black youths in separate incidents, the NAACP denounced the "brutal inhuman practices" of "police lawlessness." It distributed leaflets with pictures of the two dead youths "murdered" by the cops. Similar protests were mounted with regularity during the 1950s. A 1959 shooting of a black in a Brooklyn police station, for example, was compared with a recent Mississippi lynching.[9]

For a brief period in the late 1950s the Brooklyn NAACP expanded its protest role to encompass broader and more explosive social issues, most notably the desegregation of local schools. Central to this activist stance was the Reverend Milton A. Galamison, pastor of Siloam Presbyterian Church, who headed the group's education committee and subsequently was elected president of the Brooklyn NAACP. Galamison was the borough's most vocal black spokesman in a series of confrontations between advocates of integrated public education and the New York City Board of Education. This policy of direct social involvement and Galamison's "militant" statements were not universally applauded by fellow NAACP members and they prompted some prominent, long-standing members to resign from the organization. After Galamison demanded the resignation of Superintendent of Schools William Jansen during the bitter JHS 258 dispute in 1956, Justice Myles Paige expressed a lack of confidence in him. The Reverend Archibald McLees, white pastor of Holy Rosary Roman Catholic Church and chaplain of the local Catholic Interracial Council, referred to Galamison and his supporters as "false friends who are invading our branch." Nevertheless, Galamison was twice reelected president before choosing to devote more time to his own education-oriented organization.[10] (See Chapter 11 for a fuller account of the school-integration controversy.)

During the 1960s the most persistently aggressive and imaginative campaigns aimed at achieving general civil rights goals and expanding opportunities for blacks in Brooklyn specifically were mounted by the local chapter of the Congress of Racial Equality (CORE). Established in 1960, Brooklyn CORE immediately attacked examples of institutional and individual racism in housing, employment, and education. Its diversified arsenal of tactics encompassed negotiation and confrontation, protest meetings, sit-ins, and picketing. CORE's initial target was the normative pattern of segregated housing that blocked blacks from renting or buying housing beyond the ghetto. After a black applicant was denied available housing and the existence of racial discrimination was verified by subsequent white checkers who were offered the same unit, CORE would attempt to negotiate with the owner or agent. Where remedy of the grievance was not forthcoming, it would then initiate a direct-action campaign, including a series of sleep-ins at real estate offices and a model home.[11]

In the employment sphere, Brooklyn CORE initiated or supported demonstrations aimed at expanding black job opportunities. It participated in the coalition of civil rights groups that protested hiring inequities at the Sealtest Dairy in Bedford-Stuyvesant in 1961, and later in 1963 demanded more black construction workers at the Downstate Medical Center project.[12] In education, Brooklyn CORE pressed for the general integration of New York City's schools and supported the efforts of individual black parents to obtain integrated education for their children. It sat in at the board of education to protest high school zoning practices that tended to perpetuate segregation. During the efforts of civil rights groups to obtain an integrated educational park in the Canarsie-Brownsville-East Flatbush area, it picketed City Hall to show its support. When the Reverend Milton Galamison and the citywide Committee for Integrated Schools sponsored two pupil boycotts of classes in 1964, Brooklyn CORE wholeheartedly supported the action, although the national office of CORE exhibited no enthusiasm.[13] In all these specific areas the essential concern was integration and equal opportunity. In some instances, as a result of CORE's actions, blacks did attend integrated schools, obtained housing outside the ghetto, and found employment. Such benefits, however, tended to be divisible—that is, applicable to an individual, or at best a small group of blacks, but leaving essentially unbreached the overall pattern of institutional discrimination and segregation.

To dramatize the persistence of other local and national inequities, Brooklyn CORE sponsored imaginative protests that focused publicity on both the demands and the tactics. Under the slogan, "Taxation without Sanitation Is Tyranny," CORE dumped three carloads of garbage on the steps of

Brooklyn's Borough Hall to protest inadequate services in black Brooklyn. Its most flamboyant and publicized protest involved the opening day of the 1964 World's Fair in New York City. To protest continued discrimination against blacks and Puerto Ricans in the city, Brooklyn CORE, in conjunction with the local Bronx and Manhattan chapters, proposed to snarl city traffic generally and specifically to block visitors to the fair by means of a "stall-in" on New York City parkways. This plan produced an enormous volume of publicity and nearly universal condemnation, including censure by the national office of CORE, which suspended the sponsors of the stall-in from the organization. Mayor Robert Wagner, Senator Robert Kennedy, and President Johnson deplored the proposed tie-up and warned of its possible damaging effect on the civil rights movement. The proposed massive disruption of vehicular traffic on April 20, 1964 never did materialize.[14]

After spending the first part of the 1960s protesting segregation and discrimination locally and nationally, Brooklyn CORE began in 1965 to move into the political arena. CORE and Galamison formed the Brooklyn Freedom Democratic Party "to channel and give identity to the growing Negro vote" in the borough. James Farmer, the national director of CORE, bestowed his blessing: "Many of the changes we want to see can come only from political decisions, and we intend to be in a position to help make those decisions." Major Owens, chairman of Brooklyn CORE, ran unsuccessfully for the city council in 1965. In 1968 CORE again named candidates for office, including James Farmer himself, who ran against Shirley Chisholm for the newly delineated "black" congressional district in Brooklyn, but to no avail. By the mid-1970s CORE still existed but functioned less visibly and actively.[15]

## THE ANTIPOVERTY INSTITUTIONAL NETWORK

During the 1960s the traditional black organizations continued to function, but a new layer of agencies, both rivals and complementary to one another, was superimposed upon the existing structure. These institutions had as their unifying theme their relationship to, or more accurately their dependence upon, Washington, D.C. These new groups represented the various progeny of the war on poverty. They managed to achieve a somewhat imperfectly guaranteed and unstable lease on institutional life that has nevertheless sustained them for the past decade. They were ostensibly intended to counter the poverty of dollars and/or services that traditionally characterized impoverished ghetto areas. Their strength, but also a source of weakness and instability, was their access to the Washington pipeline from which flowed jobs, money, power, and annual uncertainty.

In early 1963 the Central Brooklyn Coordinating Council (CBCC) appealed to Mayor Wagner to do something about the high level of unemployment among Bedford-Stuyvesant youth. As a result of the wastage of this "good youthful fibre ... which could be turned into vital citizenry," the CBCC warned, the area was becoming "a powderkeg that can blow up anytime." It urged the establishment of a local agency similar to the Mobilization For Youth project which had studied the problems of youth and poverty on the Lower East Side and suggested remedies. Consequently, Bedford-Stuyvesant Youth In Action was incorporated on July 1, 1964 with a budget of $223,000 for the purpose of conducting a research study of the needs and problems of the community in order to develop a comprehensive antipoverty program. In 1965, as the war on poverty escalated and became institutionalized, Youth In Action became the officially sanctioned local (Bedford-Stuyvesant) community action program. Similar agencies were established in Brownsville, Williamsburg, and Crown Heights.[16]

In their birth and subsequent development, Youth In Action and the other Brooklyn antipoverty groups experienced all the pains that characterized most such agencies, including recurrent leadership struggles and changes in top personnel; ethnic and racial factionalism; low voter participation in local poverty elections; "pitifully insufficient" funding for the needed tasks; and accounting irregularities.[17] Amidst the problems, programs nevertheless developed and were funded. Youth In Action offered a broad array of youth-oriented services not previously available or available only on a small scale. Among the shotgun array of programs were Headstart for preschool children, an after school study center, a youth leadership institute, family life services, a young and unwed mothers program, adult job training, an apprenticeship training program, an emergency home repair service, a consumer education and action program, a legal services office, and the administration of the Neighborhood Youth Corps. The other neighborhood community action programs offered similar services, but Youth In Action was the largest and most generously funded, and as of 1977 was the single largest such program in the country with an annual budget of about $6 million.[18]

In addition to providing jobs and services, the local anti-poverty agencies also offered a new alternative road to political prominence and success. Previous black elected officials had had their roots in traditional political organizations. Assemblyman Bertram Baker and Councilman J. Daniel Diggs were founders of the United Action Democratic Association in the mid-1930s; Assemblyman Thomas Jones had been one of the initiators of the Unity Democratic Club in 1960; Shirley Chisholm had been an officer of the Bedford-Stuyvesant Political League in the late 1950s. Employment in a prominent position in these new and, by local standards, well-funded organizations gave a person visibility, patronage, and power. Waldaba Stewart and Calvin Williams both held positions in Youth In Action before winning elective office. In 1968 Williams defeated Baker for the leadership of his district, a position he had held without serious opposition since 1954. He then succeeded to Baker's assembly seat when the latter retired in 1970. Stewart was elected in 1968 to the state senate from Brooklyn. Thomas Fortune, who had been elected to the assembly in 1964 without such institutional connections, recognized their potential strength. In 1970 he stood for election to Youth In Action's community board, was one of the seventy-five elected, and was then chosen chairman of its board. Major Owens, who headed the Brownsville Community Council, that section's antipoverty agency, became commissioner of the city's community development agency in 1968 and in 1974 was elected to the state senate.[19]

Another offspring of the community concern exhibited by the CBCC was the Bedford-Stuyvesant Restoration Corporation, the largest community development corporation in the country. In February 1966, Senator Robert F. Kennedy accepted a CBCC invitation to tour the community. Impressed by the magnitude of the problems he observed and challenged to do something about them, yet also convinced that government alone would and could never provide sufficient funds for amelioration, Kennedy, supported by Senator Jacob Javits, introduced legislation in Congress that allowed for the creation of local development corporations. Under the program as enacted, a group of local citizens would form a corporation and then seek appropriate funding from various governmental agencies, private foundations, and the business community. "The basic purpose of the program," according to Senator Kennedy, "is to create jobs. There isn't enough [government] money to solve the problems of the ghettos. Private enterprise must be brought into the area." It was hoped that this public-private-sector corporation would become a kind of local "economic development conglomerate." [20]

By the end of 1966 developments in Brooklyn were proceeding satisfactorily toward the goal of a community development corporation. Bedford-Stuyvesant was selected as the first slum area to participate in this new program. In December, two corporations were formed—one consisting of community leaders, the other of prominent businessmen—to cooperate in redeveloping Bedford-Stuyvesant. The Bedford-Stuyvesant Renewal and Rehabilitation Corporation, the community group, was headed by Civil Court Judge Thomas R. Jones. This nonprofit corporation, it was expected, would canvass the section, and draft and implement appropriate plans for remedying local housing, health, recreational, employment, and business deficiencies. The Development and Services Corporation, which included such impressive names as Douglas Dillon, secretary of the treasury under President Kennedy; William Paley of the Columbia Broadcasting System; Thomas Watson, Jr., of IBM; and Andre Meyer, the local corporation's chairman, of the investment-banking firm Lazard Frères and Company; was expected to provide expert managerial advice and to persuade private capital to invest in Bedford-Stuyvesant. Grants from the Edgar M. Stern Family Fund ($15,000) and the Ford Foundation ($25,000) primed the pump.[21]

Internal factionalism on the renewal and rehabilitation board over a proposed expansion of its membership temporarily imperiled the operation and led to the secession of Judge Jones and the formation in April 1967, with Senator Kennedy's blessing, of the Bedford-Stuyvesant Restoration Corporation, which then became the recognized community corporation. Shortly thereafter the leadership of the corporation was established when Deputy Police Commissioner Franklin A. Thomas resigned his position to become president of Restoration. Whatever struggle for power and control might have developed between the rival groups was rendered moot with the announcement that Restoration would receive a federal grant of $7 million to create new jobs and train local youths to fill them. Additional grants from the Ford Foundation ($750,000) and the Vincent Astor Foundation ($1 million) assured Restoration of visibility and impact. Both in its initial development and funding, and continuing thereafter, Restoration enjoyed this kind of "energetic political and business support." Between fiscal years 1968 and 1973 it received over one-third of the $90 million expended by the federal government under the Special Impact Program. Not surprisingly, it became the nation's "largest, and ... most technically sophisticated" community development corporation.[22]

Restoration generally established as its primary goals "physical asset development" and the creation of jobs. "Our intention," stated Frank Thomas, "is to create employment and ownership opportunities for local residents and thereby aid in the creation of a healthy viable community." The initial project undertaken by Restoration in 1967 combined these goals. Local craftsmen and youths rehabilitated the exteriors of houses on ten blocks in Bedford-Stuyvesant. This emphasis on substantial and visible endeavors was evident in many of the other projects undertaken by Restoration, including the conversion of the former Sheffield Dairy to office, retail, and community uses; the formation of a $65 million home-mortgage fund; large-scale business loans to establish enterprises of a size sufficient to make a significant employment impact; the luring to Bedford-Stuyvesant of an IBM branch plant; and apartment house construction. Additionally, though definitely secondary to economic and physical development, Restoration supported such community services as an ex-offender program, day-care and senior-citizen facilities, four outreach centers to disseminate information about the community, and the Billie Holiday Theatre. By 1977 Restoration's activities in Bedford-Stuyvesant had included over 1,000 mortgage loans averaging about $20,000; financing for nearly 125 businesses at over $100,000 per venture; 7,500 workers placed in jobs developed in the private sector; exterior renovation of over 3,800 houses; 1,280 new, rehabilitatated, or under-construction dwelling units. Taken in total, this represented a not unimpressive array of physical and manpower accomplishments. A 1972 study of a number of community development corporations ranked Restoration "lowest ... as a mechanism for community control of development." The same evaluation, however, ranked Restoration first in four vital economic categories: job creation; human capital development; physical asset development; and the generation of private-sector resources. Restoration itself constituted a major local employer with some 250 workers on its payroll.[23]

Such a brief institutional history is both personal and selective. It would require an extensive book unto itself simply to list, catalogue, and define all the organizations that function in black Brooklyn. We have concentrated on the major civil rights and antipoverty agencies without any attempt to be comprehensive. These institutions, individually and collectively, have developed and provided jobs, services, and vehicles for protest. As valuable as they have no doubt been, they ultimately were limited in what they could accomplish. In recent years the most visible and probably most effective organizations (Restoration, Youth In Action) have depended on soft-money financing, either from the federal or the foundation till. They have developed no sustained economic base beyond the periodic grants to operate their programs. They were, in effect, examples of what Charles Hamilton called "public-sector organizations operating in low-income, public-sector communities." As such, their vulnerability is obvious, their existence always precarious, and their expansion doubtful.

## NOTES

1. *Amsterdam News*, Aug. 8, 1942, Sept. 19, 1942; *Brooklyn Daily Eagle*, Sept. 7, 1942.

2. *New York Age*, Oct. 31,1942; *Amsterdam News*, Sept. 19, 1942, Nov. 7, 1942, Dec. 19, 1942; *Eagle*, Oct. 23, 1942.

3. *Age*, Oct. 30, 1943, Oct. 28, 1944; *Amsterdam News*, Oct. 7, 1950, April 12, 1952.

4. *Age*, Oct. 21, 1944, Jan. 5, 1946, Aug. 24, 1946, June 30, 1951; *Amsterdam News*, Oct. 21, 1944, Nov. 16, 1946, Dec. 16, 1946, Oct. 22, 1949.

5. *Age*, March 27, 1954, June 12, 1959; *Amsterdam News*, Dec. 15, 1951, June 27, 1953, Dec. 4, 1954, Dec. 26, 1959.

6. *Interracial Review*, 15 (December 1942): 181, 187; *Age*, Oct. 27, 1944, Feb. l4, 1948; *Amsterdam News*, Dec. 9, 1944, Feb. 9, 1952, Feb. 15, 1958, June 25, 1960; *Eagle*, Dec. 3, 1944, Feb. 4, 1948, Feb. 7, 1948.

7. *The Open Door*, 19 (May-June 1943): 2; *Interracial Review*, 31 (July 1958): 123; *Age*, Jan. 9, 1943, July 3, 1943, May 7, 1955; *Amsterdam News*, Jan. 8, 1944, May 19, 1945, July 28, 1945, Jan. 19, 1952, Dec. 13, 1952, July 5, 1958, Jan. 31, 1959, Feb. 7, 1959, Feb. 28, 1959, May 9, 1959; *Eagle*, Jan. 3, 1944, Sept. 26, 1944, Nov. 2, 1952. The three Brooklyn women in *Who's Who* were author Pauli Murray, politician Dollie Robinson, and businesswoman Carmel Carrington Marr.

8. Greater New York Urban League, *Annual Report*, 1955-1956.

9. *Age*, Sept. 29, 1945, July 9, 1949, May 23, 1959; *Amsterdam News*, April 6, 1946, Sept. 14, 1946, Aug. 14, 1948, March 12, 1949, March 26, 1949, June 25, 1949, April 1, 1950, June 2, 1951, Oct. 27, 1951, March 8,

1952, April 26, 1952, Aug. 23, 1952, May 9, 1953, May 15, 1954, Jan. 1, 1955, April 27, 1957, June 29, 1957, March 29, 1958, April 25, 1959, May 16, 1959, June 6, 1959; *Eagle*, April 26, 1949, June 28, 1949, Aug. 12, 1949. The leaflets are in the vertical file of the Schomburg Collection.

10. *Amsterdam News*, Dec. 22, 1956, Jan. 19, 1957. Galamison's expressed belief in a "social ministry" makes his activism predictable. He had refused to allow his church, Siloam Presbyterian Church, to pay a tax to the Brooklyn-Nassau Presbytery to assist the construction of a Presbyterian church in Levittown, Long Island because of this development's discriminatory policies. Galamison served as president of the Stuyford Community Center, and as a member of the lay advisory board of Cumberland Hospital. His church building served as the home of the Stuyvesant Center for Older People (*Amsterdam News*, Jan. 28, 1950, July 30, 1955).

11. *Amsterdam News*, Oct. 14, 1961, Nov. 25, 1961, Dec. 22, 1962, Dec. 29, 1962.

12. *Amsterdam News*, April 1, 1961, Nov. 25, 1961, Aug. 11, 1962, Aug. 18, 1962, Aug. 25, 1962, July 6, 1963, July 20, 1963, Aug. 17, 1963.

13. *Amsterdam News*, Sept. 9, 1962, Sept. 22, 1962, Feb. 2, 1963, July 13, 1963, Oct. 12, 1963, Dec. 21, 1963, Jan. 4, 1964, Dec. 19, 1964; *New York Times*, Dec. 18, 1963, April 11, 1964.

14. *Amsterdam News*, Sept. 22, 1962, April 18, 1964; *New York Times*, April 11, 1964, April 17, 1964, April 18, 1964, April 20, 1964.

15. *Amsterdam News*, Aug. 3, 1968; *New York Times*, April 17, 1965. In discussing Brooklyn CORE during the late 1960's mention at least should be made of the controversial and militant Sonny Carson, who achieved a certain notoriety at the time, especially during the Ocean Hill-Brownsville school confrontation. Mwlina Imiri Abubadika (Robert "Sonny" Carson), *The Education of Sonny Carson* (New York, 1972).

16. *Amsterdam News*, Feb. 9, 1963, Feb. 16, 1963, Aug. 10 1963, Aug. 1, 1964, July 31, 1965. The Central Brooklyn Coordinating Council was founded in 1958 with Maude B. Richardson as its first president. It was a voluntary association of community agencies and organizations concerned with the socioeconomic state of the citizens of Bedford-Stuyvesant. Its initial focus on juvenile delinquency was broadened to encompass the total spectrum of social welfare problems in the community. The generative role it played in the creation of the two major local anti-poverty agencies—Bedford Stuyvesant Youth In Action and the Bedford-Stuyvesant Restoration Corporation—should be examined in detail by some serious community researcher.

17. *Amsterdam News*, Jan 2, 1965, April 3, 1965, April 9, 1966, Oct. 1, 1966, Dec. 10, 1966, April 26, 1969, June 7, 1969, Sept. 12, 1969, April 11, 1970, Feb. 12, 1971, Sept. 11, 1971.

18. *Amsterdam News*, July 31, 1965, Dec. 25, 1965, Jan. 1, 1966, Jan. 15, 1966, Jan. 29, 1966, Feb. 5, 1966, Feb. 12, 1966, June 18, 1966.

19. *Amsterdam News*, Dec. 10, 1966, Oct. 7, 1967, July 20, 1968, March 28, 1970.

20. *Amsterdam News*, Feb. 5, 1966, Feb. 12, 1966, Oct. 22, 1966; *New York Times*, Oct. 17, 1966, Oct. 18, 1966. On the history of community development corporations, see the extensive pamphlet literature of the Center for Community Economic Development, including Barry Stein, "Rebuilding Bedford-Stuyvesant" (1975), and Matthew Edel, "Development or Dispersal? Approaches to Ghetto Poverty" (1970); also Geoffrey Faux, *CDCs: New Hope for the Inner City* (New York, 1971), and Jack Newfield, *Robert Kennedy: A Memoir* (New York, 1970).

21. *Amsterdam News*, Dec. 17, 1966; *New York Times*, Dec. 11, 1966. The *Times* editorialized that the new community corporation could become "the country's most exciting endeavor to give the people in racial ghettos meaningful participation in reviving their decaying neighborhoods" (Dec. 12, 1966).

22. Stewart E. Perry, "Federal Support for CDCs: Some of the History and Issues of Community Control" (Cambridge, Mass.: Center for Community Economic Development, 1973), pp. 12-13; National Center for Urban Ethnic Affairs, "Community Development Corporations: A Review of Their Experiences" (Washington, 1973), p. 46; *Amsterdam News*, April 8, 1967, April 15, 1967, April 22, 1967, May 13, 1967, July 1, 1967; *New York Times*, April 2, 1967, April 6, 1967, April 7, 1967, April 8, 1967, May 11, 1967, June 25, 1967.

23. Abt Associates, *An Evaluation of the Special Impact Program* (4 vols.; Cambridge, Mass., 1972); *Amsterdam News*, April 6, 1968, April 20, 1968, Aug. 3, 1968, Aug. 10, 1968. Statistics are taken from the *Restoration Newsletter*, a regular publication of the Bedford-Stuyvesant Restoration Corporation.

CHAPTER 9

# The Politics of Success?

## THE FIRST BLACK ELECTED OFFICIAL

In contrast to previous years, primary efforts in politics from 1944 on aimed at electing a black to the state assembly rather than the city council. Given black geographic segregation and the relatively small size of assembly districts, which rendered racial gerrymandering more difficult, this represented a logical political decision. The proximate road to black elected representation began in 1944 when Fred Moritt resigned as assemblyman from the Seventeenth AD, which encompassed much of the emerging Bedford-Stuyvesant ghetto and was the most concentrated black political subdivision in Brooklyn, to seek advancement to the state senate. Both the Republican and American Labor parties seized the opportunity and nominated Negro candidates both in deference to the increasing blackness of the area and as a dramatic ploy to wrest control of the district from the Democrats, who had held uninterrupted sway there since 1931. The Republicans selected Louis Johnson Warner, a city employee, while the ALP nominated Ada B. Jackson, a longtime civic activist. Moritt's withdrawal had, of course, created an unanticipated opportunity for the Democrats also to name a black and thus guarantee a Negro assemblyman. Instead they nominated John Walsh, a white.

The presence of two blacks in the race diminished the slim chance of either for victory since both could be expected to draw their core strength from the same black constituency. Efforts to have Mrs. Jackson, as the representative of the lesser party, withdraw in favor of Warner failed. "She [Mrs. Jackson] could perform a far better job for the community by refusing to run than to continue in the race and split our vote," argued the *Amsterdam News.* Assisted by this division, John Walsh won with a substantial plurality. "Colored people are not yet prepared to put the interest and welfare of the group ahead of the personal ambition of the individual," observed the *Amsterdam News* bitterly.[1]

The assumption that a single black could have won with united community support rested on the combined Warner-Jackson total of 18,059 votes contrasted to Walsh's 14,756. Yet black victory might not have resulted even if only one black had run. If, using the 1940 census data, one divides the Seventeenth AD into its predominantly black and white components, it is possible to focus upon the racial factor in the voting tally. The combined vote of Warner and Jackson in the black area far exceeded Walsh's total, but Walsh did exhibit good strength there too. By polling approximately the same number of votes as Warner, his primary black opponent, Walsh was able to neutralize any possible black advantage in the black part of the district. Thus, he was ideally situated to capitalize on white voting strength without having to overcome any deficit resulting from a solid black front. To win, Walsh had but to attract one-quarter of Mrs. Jackson's total vote, a not unlikely occurrence given her electoral strength in some overwhelmingly white areas where racial bonds would not have united her supporters with Warner's. More likely, these white voters would have switched to the Democratic column because of the greater harmony in social, political, economic, and philosophic attitudes between the ALP and the Democrats. One heavily white district, for example, which gave Mrs. Jackson 313 votes out of a total of 797, virtually ignored Warner, who received a paltry 28 votes. Such Jackson supporters would probably have switched to Walsh in the absence of an ALP nominee. The only arrangement that might have produced a black victory required a joint Republican-ALP endorsement, an improbable alliance.[2]

The election of 1946 virtually replicated the preceding race. The ALP again selected Mrs. Jackson; the Republicans nominated Mrs. Maude B. Richardson, who had run for city council the previous year; the Democrats renamed the incumbent Walsh. The specter of a divided black vote again haunted the Negro community, with efforts to have Mrs. Jackson withdraw in the interests of race unity-proving fruitless. The election results were more frustrating than those of 1944 because of their closeness—Walsh eased in by a narrow 77 votes. The *Amsterdam News* blamed Mrs. Jackson for this defeat, castigated Bert Baker for not pressing the Democrats to select a black candidate, and warned the Democrats to realize that they were "losing ground in the area because of their 'lily white' candidate list." [3]

Voter attitudes had shifted perceptibly in two years; the dichotomy between white and black was more sharply drawn. Whereas Walsh had gained a respectable portion of the black vote in 1944, both he and Mrs. Jackson lost a considerable proportion of votes in the black part of the district. Mrs. Richardson was clearly perceived as the "black" candidate and received a clear majority, more than double Walsh's tally, in the black election districts. In almost symmetrical contrast, Walsh reversed these totals in the predominantly white districts, polling more votes than his black rivals combined.

Despite the closeness of the contest, the probability of a black victory without Jackson's presence remained debatable at least. Mrs. Jackson's proportion of the total vote declined from 1944, but her proportion in the white districts actually increased. Simultaneously she lost 25 percent of her black proportion. She was apparently perceived much less as a race candidate than as a representative of a particular leftist ideology; on this premise she was accepted by many radical white voters. Thus, while Mrs. Richardson might have secured the necessary votes from Mrs. Jackson's totals to overtake Walsh had Mrs. Jackson not run, the geographic distribution of American Laborite voting strength renders this hypothetical result at least problematic. Indeed, Mrs. Jackson may actually have siphoned off more votes from Walsh than from Mrs. Richardson. Had the ALP supported a black Republican, the probability of a black assemblyman would have been enhanced, if not assured. An additional critical element, to which we shall return in the future, was the relatively lower voter turnout in the predominantly black areas. In those election districts giving Walsh a majority vote, the average number of votes cast equaled 633 compared to 521 in those districts supporting Mrs. Richardson. Since election officials attempted to maintain a relatively equal population in each election district, the disparity seemingly resulted from a less active electorate in the black area.

In the year following Mrs. Richardson's defeat, fate seemed about to intervene and to bestow some political good fortune upon Brooklyn blacks. Councilman Anthony DiGiovanna planned to resign his post to accept a judicial position; Borough President John Cashmore would then appoint a successor. Since this temporary designee would undoubtedly receive the Democratic nomination for the special election in November to fill the seat permanently, Cashmore's decision assumed some significance. According to law Cashmore could appoint anyone; the tradition that had evolved, however, favored the selection of that member of the borough president's party whose vote total in the previous council election placed him next on the proportional representation list. Such a procedure would have designated Rita Casey, but she had already been rewarded with a lucrative city position. The next Democrat on the list was Bertram Baker. Supported by a vigorous mail campaign, Baker laid claim to the office. This forced Cashmore into an unwelcome position, since DiGiovanna was the only Italian among Brooklyn's councilmanic delegation. While the black population exceeded 150,000 and was increasing rapidly, the borough's Italian-born and Italian-American population represented a significantly more potent voting bloc. Thus it became politically more expedient to satisfy Italian expectations and offend Negro sensibilities. The black press bitterly castigated such a solution, but to no avail as Cashmore appointed Thomas Mirabile.[4]

The black press and local politicians viewed the impending election of 1948 with resigned pessimism. Although over half the population of the Seventeenth AD was black, recurrent defeat had dulled the enthusiasm and optimism expressed so easily in previous campaigns. While urging Democratic boss Cashmore to select a black candidate for the district, the black press viewed such an eventuality as "unlikely," given recent Democratic history "which left the Negro 'out in the cold.' " As had become traditional and opportune, the Republicans designated a black, Mrs. Maude B. Richardson. Still maintaining its independence, the ALP planned to run its own black candidate. The Democrats meanwhile circulated nominating petitions on behalf of Walsh, who duly received the Democratic designation. Without warning, Walsh announced his voluntary withdrawal from the race owing to the pressure of his private law practice. Steve Carney, Democratic leader of the Seventeenth, promptly substituted Bert Baker, thus guaranteeing an all-black contest and Brooklyn's first black elected official.[5]

Such political machinations smelled of clever maneuverings by Carney. It seems reasonable that an astute, practical politician like Carney, after analyzing the 1946 results, clearly foresaw a Democratic defeat if blacks were not recognized with a nomination. However, while black voting strength had increased locally, the substantial white minority still residing in the district might oppose a petition drive for a black designee thus spawning a primary contest, something no entrenched politician relished. Carney therefore devised a delicate stratagem intended to finesse whites, who would sign petitions on behalf of Walsh, to avoid a black rebellion, and to assure a Democratic victory. Walsh's withdrawal neatly com-

pleted this gambit. It would appear from subsequent developments that Walsh expected future considerations for his
"voluntary" declination. That Carney planned this outcome
from the beginning in recognition of the voting strength of an
expanding black community seems probable. Baker himself
expressed surprise at his selection. He had benefited from
Carney's political realism and the clear threat expressed in
recent elections that normally Democratic black voters would
elect a black Republican. Although Baker also received ALP
backing, the official Democratic designation assured his election as Brooklyn's first black elected official.[6]

## CHALLENGING THE ORGANIZATION

Baker's election was to some extent the fortuitous result of
white maneuverings. The events of 1953, though, signaled the
beginning of a vigorous, indigenous black political movement.
For the first time in Brooklyn history a black dared to
challenge the Democratic organization in a primary contest.
Equally significant, this insurgent group remained intact and
active, functioning as a political catalyst among Brooklyn
blacks. This energizing event centered somewhat improbably
upon a judicial contest in the Second Municipal Court District,
which encompassed most of Bedford-Stuyvesant plus contiguous areas. Although the district's population was substantially Negro and over half the court's business involved blacks,
the three judges remained white. In early 1953 one of these
justices, Edward Wynne, died. While the appointment of a
black to succeed Wynne seemed appropriate, bungling and
callous county politicians managed not merely to select a
white man, Benjamin Schor, for the interim appointment until
the November election, but also to import him from outside
the district, finding him a room within its confines so that he
could fulfill the residence requirement. Local politicians, black
and white, were incensed at this gratuitous insult, yet their
anger might have dissipated but for a subsequent confrontation between Schor and Lewis S. Flagg at the black Brooklyn

and Long Island Lawyers Association annual dinner. Speaking before the judge-designate, Flagg criticized the appointment as an "affront" to the local voters. Schor replied in kind, claiming the office as both a legal resident of the district and a deserving, loyal party worker and challenging the black group to take it away from him since he did not intend to step aside voluntarily. Stung and spurred by this challenge, the black lawyers' group determined to oppose Schor in the Democratic primary. Lewis Flagg, who had reentered local politics in 1949 running under the ALP banner in this same municipal court district and who had precipitated the immediate confrontation with his remarks, emerged as the insurgent candidate. Adding diversity, a still disgruntled John Walsh also entered the primary.[7]

Ably supported by a campaign organization headed by Wesley McDonald Holder and expertly exploiting the carpetbagging issue, Flagg vigorously campaigned throughout the entire district. Local Democratic politicians, black and white, were united in their distaste for the selection of a nonresident. Many of these men, including Vincent Carney and Bert Baker, adopted a passive attitude toward Schor's candidacy. While they did not openly oppose the organization's choice, their support did not exceed the perfunctory. To most everyone's surprise, Flagg outpolled Schor 4,503 to 4,365. With the essential primary victory secured, Flagg's election in November as the first Brooklyn black elected to a New York City office proved considerably simpler.[8]

Although this judicial district would eventually have elected a black, given demographic realities, Flagg's success in 1953 resulted at least in part from a unique convergence of forces over which he and the black electorate possessed no control. Schor's appointment itself was an egregious blunder by the county Democratic organization. The selection of a white already residing in the district would have deprived Flagg of his most effective issue and would not have alienated local politicians. Flagg's insistent exploitation of Schor's political change of address did impact upon white registrants so that his victory was by no means fashioned by black votes alone. Equally crucial was the candidacy of John Walsh, who received 2,339 votes and siphoned off much of the Irish vote that probably would have otherwise supported the organization's choice. Nevertheless, local political history had been made in Brooklyn with this first successful black primary challenge of the regular machine. Never again would Bedford-Stuyvesant politics be quite so perfunctory and white-dominated, although the changes were laborious and slow in gestation. Not until nine years later was there another successful black primary campaign against a white incumbent.[9]

The organization fashioned by Wesley Holder to elect Flagg continued to function after its primary purpose was accomplished. Christened the Bedford-Stuyvesant Political League, it regularly offered primary challenges to Bert Baker and local white politicians, bargained with the power structure, and, although it won no electoral victories, succeeded in extracting some concessions for blacks. In 1954 the league opposed the Democratic organization's white choices in the new Seventeenth AD and the Eleventh SD.[10] Anxious to avoid a primary confrontation, Vincent Carney, white district leader of the Seventeenth and brother of the late Steve Carney, promised to support a black in the next city council election in 1957 as well as to integrate his own organization. In return, the league withdrew its opposition candidates in the district (who had little chance of victory anyway). The league repeated this ploy the following year in the Second Municipal Court District. Holder threatened to enter an insurgent candidate against the incumbent, Milton M. Wecht. Again desirous of avoiding a primary squabble and perhaps recognizing the impending black takeover of the district, the Democratic hierarchy met with local black and white leaders. As a result, the league withdrew its opposition on the promise that one of the current white judges would be transferred to another court and a black appointed as his successor. According to Holder, the "extension of Negro representation" could be achieved by two methods—"negotiation and fighting." Being realistic about its chances of unseating Wecht, the league chose negotiation. Shortly after the election, the agreement was consummated as Oliver D. Williams replaced Justice Lloyd Herzka. Subsequently, in 1957, Carney supported Baker in the nomination of Baker's longtime friend and political associate, J. Daniel Diggs, for the city council.[11]

Baker's election and Flagg's rousing success signaled an end both to local politics as usual and to white political domination. As blacks became sufficiently numerous and concentrated they took over the local party governance of the Seventeenth AD (subsequently the Sixth AD). In 1952 Republican Herbert R. Hurd became the first borough black elected to a national convention. With the appointment of Lawrence Pierce in 1955 to join Franklin W. Morton, the Kings County district attorney's office had two blacks on its professional staff for the first time. In 1950 Brooklyn's 210,000 blacks were still represented by a single judicial figure, Myles Paige. In 1951 Mayor Vincent Impellitteri appointed Assistant District Attorney Clarence Wilson a magistrate. Subsequently Wilson moved to the domestic relations court. Upon Wilson's death in 1958, Paige was transferred from special sessions court to succeed him. Moreover, by 1958 blacks had secured all three judgeships in the Second Municipal Court District.[12]

In 1960, blacks represented over 14 percent of Brooklyn's population; however, they still remained grossly underrepresented politically, despite their rising population and the concomitant white flight from Kings County. Baker and Diggs were the only black legislators at any level of government. Negro political influence was confined almost exclusively to the totally segregated Sixth AD. In surrounding districts white politicians still clung to control despite black majorities. In the Kings County judiciary a mere four positions out of a total of eighty-nine were allotted to blacks. Patronage was limited to minor non-policy-making positions. Thus black voters and black politicians still remained virtual ciphers in Brooklyn political life.

## EXCLUSIONARY TACTICS

While blacks had lacked numerical strength they could be treated as political nonentities with impunity. The growth of Brooklyn's black population in the 1940s and 1950s threatened this political arrangement generally and rendered any rearrangement of political boundaries a matter of racial concern. By the early 1950s the various patterns of official response to black political and demographic pressure were already established. Prior to the 1952 election new congressional boundaries sliced Bedford-Stuyvesant into shreds, making it part of four predominantly white districts. This illustrated the first technique of preserving the status quo, which by definition excluded black representation—that of fragmenting the black vote among a number of white districts. The new 1954 assembly district boundaries illustrated the alternate approach to restricting black elective possibilities. The successes of Baker and Flagg had demonstrated that some accommodation was inevitable; blacks could no longer be totally excluded from the political arena and its rewards. The newly drawn Sixth AD created an overwhelmingly (90 percent) black district that obviously assured the continued election of a Negro to the state legislature and black control of the local party leadership and patronage, but it also siphoned off as many of the troublesome ingredients as possible from the surrounding districts. The two districts embracing the Sixth AD contained substantial and expanding black populations but remained sufficiently white to assure continued white leadership and assemblymen for nearly another decade. In the mid-1950s the Sixth AD was over 90 percent black, while the surrounding Seventeenth AD and Tenth AD were 60 percent and 38 percent black, respectively. These three districts constituted the Eleventh SD, with a 62 percent black population. Negro demographic pressure might eventually force a shift in the racial control of these districts, but local white politicians had no intention of yielding such power graciously: only an unsurmountable black influx would cause such a transformation. Meanwhile, the status quo would prevail. This method of creating a "reservation" where blacks could play politics among themselves while keeping proximate areas for whites was a not uncommon tactic of Kings County politicians during the next twenty years. These two restrictive techniques proved effective indeed. Although blacks did challenge white Democratic organization candidates in assembly, senate, and congressional districts beyond the reservation in both primary and general elections, not until the 1960s did they achieve any success. These seemingly contradictory tactics of fragmentation and concentration were functionally synonymous in slowing black elective advancement and perpetuating white political control.

## EXPANDING BLACK REPRESENTATION

During the 1960s, first as a result of the demographic and geographic pressures detailed previously, and later assisted by the law as interpreted by the judiciary which mandated a more equitable apportioning arithmetic in drawing district lines, black elective representation expanded with regularity. Each two-year period brought at least one additional black elected legislative official. In 1962, for example, there was added a second assemblyman, in 1964 the first state senator, and in 1968 a congresswoman. In 1960 only two of Brooklyn's city, state, and federal legislators were black; by 1977 ten seats were held by blacks of the borough's total of forty-seven.

In 1962 Thomas Jones, leader of the Unity Democratic Club, challenged the incumbent assemblyman and district leader Samuel Berman for both honors in the Seventeenth AD Democratic primary. Berman attempted to diffuse black opposition and maintain some control in this two-thirds black district by putting up Wesley Holder for assemblyman while retaining the local party leadership position for himself. The strategy failed, and Tom Jones swept to a double victory and inevitable election in November. A simultaneous attempt to unseat Walter Cooke in the Eleventh SD by Al Grant failed, but Democratic politicians had apparently received the message. The Brooklyn Democratic leadership reportedly agreed to support a black state senator in 1964 if Cooke were reelected in 1962. Cooke did not seek reelection in 1964, and Risley Dent, with the support of Baker and Jones, defeated Wes Holder in an all-black Democratic primary contest that would undoubtedly determine Cooke's successor. Within a week Dent died unexpectedly, and William Thompson, who had managed Dent's recent campaign, succeeded to the nomination and subsequent election. Tom Jones, meanwhile, moved from one branch of government to another, yielding his assembly seat to become a judge in the municipal court. His Albany position fell to Brooklyn's first black female legislator, Shirley Chisholm. Thus by 1964, at least one Brooklyn black sat in the various state and city legislatures; only national representation for Bedford-Stuyvesant was still wanting.[13]

Racial gerrymandering continued to obstruct the election of a black congressman. Reminiscent of 1952, the 1962 redistricting plan carved up Bedford-Stuyvesant and distributed the carcass among five congressional districts with blacks constituting between 10 and 40 percent of any district. In 1964 there was formed the Bedford-Stuyvesant Committee for a Representative Congressman, led by Harold Brady, which proposed to end the gerrymander of Bedford-Stuyvesant at the next state legislative session. State Senator William Thompson did introduce such legislation in 1965 but to no avail. In 1966 Ray Williams ran unsuccessfully against incumbent Joseph Brasco in the Democratic primary in the Eleventh CD.[14]

Despite rising black dissatisfaction and mounting demographic pressure, the true catalyst in accomplishing the goal of a black congressman from Brooklyn was the federal judiciary in its insistence upon the one-man, one-vote principle and its opposition to the more blatant forms of racial gerrymandering. In 1966 disgruntled Brooklyn blacks filed suit in federal district court demanding judicial remedy to the deliberate gerrymandering that allowed five districts to "snake into Bedford-Stuyvesant, thus fragmenting the Negro vote so that it is helpless to elect or defeat any congressional candidate." In a supporting affidavit Roy Wilkins argued that the "obviously irrational districts there were in fact set up along racial lines—for the purpose of diluting the political strength of the Negro inhabitants of the Bedford-Stuyvesant ghetto." Floyd McKissick, national director of CORE, denounced the perpetrators of the gerrymander as "racists" and compared those who intentionally divided black communities electorally to white Mississippians who simply resorted to less sophisticated forms of violence. "The result in both cases is that black men are governed by white men." Mayor John Lindsay of New York supported the suit in an *amicus curiae* brief. Paul O'Dwyer expressed the seriousness of the case: "At stake is the right of 500,000 Negro residents of Brooklyn who are locked in a ghetto by public attitudes and then gerrymandered out of their right to Congressional representation." The decision, handed down in early 1967, directed that new districts be drawn without consideration of race but with equal population and "reasonably compact and contiguous" bounds.[15]

In eager anticipation of the forthcoming redistricting and to thwart the white machine bosses from choosing for black people, the Committee for a Negro Congressman from Brooklyn designated Assemblywoman Shirley Chisholm as its candidate even before the district lines were established. This preemptory decision by no means assured her the Democratic nomination. Such prominent local male politicians as Judge Thomas Jones, State Senator William Thompson, Assemblyman Sam Wright, Rev. William Jones of Bethany Baptist Church, and Rev. Gardner C. Taylor of Concord Baptist Church all expressed interest or were actively advanced by local supporters in the scramble to become the first black congressman from Brooklyn. Meanwhile the Liberal party seized the spotlight and nominated James Farmer, the nationally recognized civil rights leader, for the new Twelfth CD. In a closely contested three-person Democratic primary contest, Shirley Chisholm received 5,431 votes to 4,643 for Thompson and 1,751 for Dollie Robinson.[16] In securing the Democratic nomination in an overwhelmingly black and Democratic area, Chisholm would normally have been assured automatic victory in November. The Liberal party, in selecting Farmer, however, had created an unexpected situation. Recognizing the impossibility of success if they nominated a party functionary, the Republicans cast aside ideology and joined the Liberals in supporting Farmer. Not unexpectedly, given his national prominence, Farmer received far more visibility than a local Republican party regular would have and hence posed a real electoral threat to Chisholm. Farmer, however, was not without handicaps. While Shirley Chisholm was probably not well known beyond Brooklyn and Albany, she did have strong roots in the local Democratic party structure and local black club life. She was indigenous to the Bedford-Stuyvesant community and had been nominated in an open primary by the people of the district. Farmer, contrariwise, was labeled a "carpetbagger," "imposed" on local blacks "from the outside." Yet he could attract publicity and star endorsements. A benefit performance at the Brooklyn Academy of Music for Farmer's campaign fund was headlined by actors Sidney Poitier and Brock Peters, jazzman Lionel Hampton, singers Mahalia Jackson and Nina Simone, and Richard Hatcher, mayor of Gary, Indiana, and attracted 1,400 persons. For the first time in its organizational history the national office of CORE endorsed a candidate, Farmer, for Congress. The walls of Bedford-Stuyvesant were plastered with Farmer posters. Yet local black Democratic politicians and political columnists remained unconvinced. "The face ... of Jim Farmer pops out of posters plus billboards, and the face of ... Shirley Chisholm pops up at luncheons, dinners, etc." The overwhelming Democratic registration of the district; Mr. Farmer's roots outside Brooklyn; and Mrs. Chisholm's solid, local organizational structure enabled her to defeat her more famous, elaborately packaged opponent by a two to one margin. She polled her heaviest support in the predominantly black areas of the district, while Farmer garnered the bulk of his support from the whiter sections. Shirley Chisholm clearly represented the people for whom the new Twelfth CD had been created. With her election blacks had achieved electoral success at every legislative level from City Council to Congress.[17]

## THE PROBLEM OF NONPARTICIPATION

Since the late 1960s the number of black elected officials nationally has expanded substantially, although they still constitute less than 1 percent of the total.[18] This growth has been especially rapid in the South but has not bypassed the North. However, the developments in the two sections have been shaped by somewhat different forces. The federal enforcement of black political rights in the South, which was institutionalized in the Voting Rights Act of 1965, effectively enfranchised the southern black who had previously been obstructed by law, custom, or force from voting. The subsequent election of blacks to office in the South flowed from this legislative-judicial action. Black representation in the North no doubt benefited from the general ethos and specific acts of the 1960s; but the critical elements there were demographic and a somewhat different judicial perspective. The concentration of large numbers of urban blacks in segregated communities made some political representation inevitable. The courts' insistence upon the one-man, one-vote principle and its rejection of the grosser forms of racial gerrymandering assisted the creation of legislative districts either open to black challenge or consciously intended for black representation. Such political advancement as was achieved, however, trailed behind demographic growth. A major reason for this lag was the low incidence of voter participation by residents of northern urban ghettos. Had one relied upon black use of the ballot, as in the South, black representation would not have expanded nearly so rapidly.

This franchise failure was long recognized and lamented in Brooklyn, but with the creation of the all-black Sixth AD in

1954, the dimensions of this phenomenon became manifest. In the presidential and gubernatorial elections between 1954 and 1960, fewer votes were cast in this district than in any other district in Kings County, and by a wide margin. Furthermore, residents of the neighboring Tenth and Seventeenth ADs, which contained large black populations, voted with only marginally higher frequency. This clearly facilitated continued white control of these districts long after the racial composition of their population had shifted. Thomas Booker of the *Amsterdam News* estimated that less than 30 percent of eligible Brooklyn blacks were registered in 1959.[19]

Local black leaders repeatedly deplored this fact. In 1957 Risley Dent, president of the Brooklyn NAACP, attributed many of the blacks' local problems to this failure to consolidate their voting strength. "Other groups can influence officials through the ballot. This is where we must concentrate." The Reverend Gardner Taylor advised local residents in 1959 that "we have no right to better housing, to better sanitation, to better bus service, to better schools, until we use the weight of our numbers at the polls to express our strength, our indignation and our determination." "Every citizen who was not registered, or who failed to vote," he added, "helped to fasten the handcuffs of second-class citizenship on Stuyfordites." What made such voter apathy even more disturbing were the coincidental voter-registration drives in the South, where blacks were struggling and even dying in an effort to obtain the franchise; northern blacks faced no such formidable opposition.[20]

This self-critical theme persisted explicitly in public statements and implicitly in the perennial announcements of still another voter-registration drive, which were ritualistically mounted under political, community, civic, church, poverty, and labor-group sponsorship. A flurry of activity, for example, focused on the 1960 election, one of high national salience.[21] All the presumed activity had no impact whatsoever on local black participation. In fact, nearly 10 percent fewer persons voted in 1960 in the Sixth AD than in 1956. Throughout the 1960s the rhetoric of voter registration was pursued but to

apparently little effect. The legislative districts, at whatever
governmental level, with the highest percentage of minority
population coincided with the districts with the lowest voter
turnout. As in the 1950s, it was estimated in 1971 that only 30
percent of those eligible to vote in Bedford-Stuyvesant or
Brownsville were registered. Phrased in related statistical
terms, minorities constituted 30 percent of Brooklyn's adult
population but only 15 percent of registered voters. Congresswoman Chisholm denounced the "lethargic, apathetic
character" of black voting patterns in Bedford-Stuyvesant.
"Before the black vote becomes the power that it can be, there
must be a black vote," she admonished. An inevitable result of
this nonparticipation was delayed black representation. Not
until 1970, for example, when the district was 70 percent
black, was a black finally elected in the Fifty-fourth AD.[22]

One might argue that since blacks received few rewards
from the political system, their participation was futile. White
politicians, of course, could simply invert the terms of this
logic and justify continued nonrecognition on the basis of
their failure to vote. Such thinking generated a kind of self-
fulfilling negative prophecy. Moreover, while the rhetoric of
participation and registration might prevail in public, few of
the established local political leaders or organizations found it
in their interests to advocate too strenuously or implement too
effectively voter-registration drives. "The politicians in the
Bedford-Stuyvesant area are not interested in a larger registration," observed the politically sagacious Wesley Holder.
The Republicans, quite correctly equating potential black
voters with Democratic proclivities, preferred to minimize the
extent of their annual electoral defeat by restricting the
franchise. The locally dominant Democratic organizations
already controlled district offices and patronage. Additional
voters might only prove difficult to control, or, even worse, fall
prey to insurgency and thus adversely affect the established
power realities.

This pattern of low black voter participation has persisted
as a constant feature of much northern urban politics, but it
has been more extreme in parts of New York City than

elsewhere. So extensive had it become in Kings County that after the extension of the Voting Rights Act in 1970, Brooklyn, along with Manhattan and the Bronx, fell within its purview, since more than half its voting-age population failed to vote in the 1968 presidential election.[23] In response to federal pressure, New York redrew Brooklyn congressional districts before the 1974 elections, creating two districts with black and/or Puerto Rican majorities. The federal intervention was in response to previous redistrictings in 1970 and 1972 that had increasingly concentrated blacks and Puerto Ricans in Chisholm's district while dispersing the balance of the minority population among a number of surrounding districts. In 1968 when the new black Twelfth CD was created, it was 70 percent minority, but subsequent boundary modifications increased the proportion to 90 percent by 1972. This reservation tactic was reminiscent of the mid-1950s when blacks were initially securing elective office. The new plan combined two previous districts, the Twelfth CD, which had been 90 percent minority, and the Fourteenth CD, which had been 46 percent minority, and drew a north-south boundary line instead of an east-west one. The resultant Twelfth CD was three-fourths minority and the new Fourteenth District nearly two-thirds so. Shirley Chisholm, incumbent in the Twelfth District, was reelected handily. In the other district, which had presumably been created for a minority representative, this tradition of low black participation engendered an apprehension that minority voters could not translate their demographic majority into an electoral majority. Councilman Sam Wright, already a prominent local black politician and an obvious candidate for the position, declined to yield his councilmanic position and seek election for this very reason. Since the minority areas of the district were so impoverished and disorganized politically, and voting turnout there was insignificant compared with the more organized white part of the district, a black candidate could not win, argued Wright.[24] In the Democratic primary contest, the two leading candidates were white, with a Puerto Rican and a black trailing behind. Frederick W. Richmond, the primary victor, was subsequently elected with ease to Congress and reelected in 1976.[25]

One of the few benefits of black ghettoization (territorial occupation of a large contiguous geographic area) has been the succession of blacks to locally elective political offices. Since victory has generally been predicated upon the absence of white voters, this success has been primarily limited to positions at the most local level, to positions chosen from well-defined limited geographic areas (assembly, state senate, and congressional districts). Owing especially to a rather inert black electorate, Brooklyn blacks have rarely broadened their power base to the more extensive realms of county or citywide elective office. Thus one can certainly point to elements of success; but success has by no means been proportional to blacks' numbers in the population, or even in the voting-age population. In 1976 blacks held only ten of the forty-seven elective legislative positions from Brooklyn. Underrepresentation was even more severe in the locally elected judiciary where blacks occupied only five of the forty-four seats in the second judicial district (Brooklyn and Staten Island) of the New York State Supreme Court and three of twenty-eight in the Kings County branch of the New York City Civil Court.[26]

## NOTES

1. *Amsterdam News*, Feb. 19, 1944, April 29, 1944, May 27, 1944, June 3, 1944, Aug. 12, 1944, Aug. 26, 1944, Oct. 28, 1944, Nov. 18, 1944, Nov. 25, 1944; *Brooklyn Daily Eagle*, May 19, 1944, May 28, 1944, July 1, 1944. Mrs. Jackson had been active in local movements to better neighborhood conditions. She served as chairman of the Brooklyn Inter-Racial Assembly and headed the PTA at PS 35.

2. Election returns up to 1960 are taken from New York City's annual *Official Canvass of Voters*. Subsequent to 1960, the *New York Times* is the primary source. The detailed results of the 1944 election were:

|  | *Walsh* | *Warner* | *Jackson* |
|---|---|---|---|
| Votes–Black Area | 5,035 | 5,091 | 3,299 |
| Votes–Mixed Area | 2,216 | 1,448 | 1,299 |
| Votes–White Area | 7,505 | 4,349 | 2,643 |
| Total Votes | 14,756 | 10,888 | 7,171 |

3. *Amsterdam News*, June 8, 1946, Aug. 24, 1946, Aug. 31, 1946, Oct. 5, 1946, Nov. 16, 1946. The election results in 1946 were:

|  | *Walsh* | *Richardson* | *Jackson* |
|---|---|---|---|
| Votes–Black Area | 2,093 | 4,302 | 1,402 |
| Votes–Mixed Area | 3,044 | 2,909 | 1,089 |
| Votes–White Area | 4,554 | 2,403 | 1,708 |
| Total Votes | 9,691 | 9,614 | 4,199 |

4. Interview with Bertram Baker, July 29, 1970; *New York Age*, May 24, 1947; *Amsterdam News*, May 17, 1947, May 31, 1947, June 7, 1947. In the special election held in November 1947 to fill this council seat permanently, Mrs. Jackson received 135,957 votes as the ALP candidate, the highest total ever for a Brooklyn black. Her total was fewer than 4,000 votes below that of the Republican candidate. In the Seventeenth AD she trailed Mirabile, the Democratic victor, by only twenty-six votes.

5. Interview with Baker; *Age*, April 10, 1948, June 12, 1948; *Amsterdam News*, Jan. 17, 1948, March 6, 1948, July 3, 1948; *Eagle*, July 21, 1948, July 23, 1948. A detailed rendering of Baker's lengthy career in Albany (1948-70) is not within the purview of this book but certainly constitutes a worthwhile topic for investigation.

6. Interview with Baker; *Amsterdam News*, July 24, 1948. The political columnist of the *Eagle* reinforced this notion of political dealings. He noted that Walsh had stepped aside at considerable sacrifice and was becoming impatient for some compensatory position. When no reward was forthcoming, the disgruntled Walsh returned to the local political arena to challenge for office. In 1949 he unsuccessfully sought the Democratic nomination for the Second Municipal Court District. He unsuccessfully challenged Baker for the assembly in the 1952 primary. Walsh's presence in the 1953 Democratic primary for the municipal court was a crucial element in deciding its outcome *(Eagle*, Jan. 31, 1949, June 20, 1949, June 28, 1949, July 8, 1949, June 10, 1952, July 16, 1952, Aug. 20, 1952).

7. Interview with Lewis Flagg, July 24, 1970; *Amsterdam News*, March 28, 1953, April 11, 1953, April 25, 1953, July 14, 1953; *Eagle*, Aug. 4, 1953. In 1953 there were no blacks among Brooklyn's elected judiciary.

8. Interview with Franklin W. Morton, a local black politician in 1953, subsequently also elected to a judgeship; interview with Baker; interview with Flagg; *Eagle*, Sept. 4, 1953.

9. Interview with Norman Johnson, Aug. 13, 1970; *Amsterdam News*, Sept. 26, 1953; *Eagle*, Sept. 16, 1953, Nov. 4, 1953.

10. Between the 1952 and 1954 elections the Brooklyn assembly districts were redrawn and renumbered. Thus, Baker's district changed from the Seventeenth AD to the Sixth AD. It was surrounded by the new Eleventh and Seventeenth ADs.

11. *Age*, July 10, 1954, June 4, 1955, July 9, 1955; *Amsterdam News*, Jan. 2, 1954, May 29, 1954, July 24, 1954, Aug. 7, 1954, Aug. 21, 1954, Aug. 28, 1954, May 14, 1955, May 28, 1955, June 11, 1955, July 9, 1955, Dec. 3, 1955, Jan. 5, 1957; *Eagle*, May 24, 1954, July 15, 1954, July 20, 1954, Aug. 21, 1954, Sept. 15, 1954, Sept. 20, 1954.

12. *Amsterdam News*, Feb. 4, 1950, Aug. 5, 1950, Sept. 9, 1950, May 19, 1951, April 26, 1952, March 21, 1953, Jan. 8, 1955, May 21, 1955, May 3, 1958; *Eagle*, Feb. 19, 1950, July 19, 1950, May 16, 1951. In 1958 Franklin Morton joined Flagg and Williams in the Second Municipal Court District.

After Flagg's victory, blacks did challenge white candidates either in Democratic primaries or as Republicans in the general election. In 1954 William Chisholm and Oliver D. Williams opposed incumbent Walter Cooke in the Democratic primary in the 11th S.D. as did Winston Craig two years later. The Republican party occasionally sought to woo black Democratic voters by running a black candidate against a white Democrat. Thus, in 1952, the Rev. George Thomas opposed Edna Kelly in the 10th C.D. In 1956 Thomas ran in the 11th S.D. against Cooke and in 1960 Charles Greene similarly opposed Cooke. None of these black challenges proved successful.

13. *Amsterdam News*, June 16, 1962, June 23, 1962, Aug. 11, 1962, Aug. 18, 1962, Sept. 15, 1962, March 14, 1964, May 8, 1964, June 13, 1964, July 18, 1964, Nov. 7, 1964.

14. *Amsterdam News*, Nov. 25, 1961, March 7, 1964, Dec. 26, 1964, May 29, 1965, Feb. 26, 1966.

15. *Amsterdam News*, June 25, 1966, March 25, 1967, April 1, 1967, May 20, 1967, Dec. 23, 1967.

16. *Amsterdam News*, Dec. 30, 1967, Jan. 13, 1968, Jan. 27, 1968, Feb. 17, 1968, Feb. 24, 1968, March 2, 1968, March 9, 1968, March 30, 1968, April 20, 1968, June 29, 1968; *New York Times*, Feb. 26, 1968, June 19, 1968.

17. *Amsterdam News*, March 9, 1968, May 25, 1968, Aug. 24, 1968,

Sept. 28, 1968, Oct. 5, 1968, Oct. 26, 1968, Nov. 9, 1968; *New York Times*, May 20, 1968, Oct. 26, 1968, Nov. 6, 1968. Chisholm received 34,885 votes to Farmer's 13,777. Shirley Chisholm has told her own story in: *Unbought and Unbossed* (Boston, 1970); and *The Good Fight* (New York, 1973).

18. A complete listing of all black elected officials is published annually by the Joint Center for Political Studies.

19. *Amsterdam News*, Feb. 7, 1959, Jan. 23, 1960.

20. *Age*, Oct. 25, 1958; *Amsterdam News*, June 29, 1957, Nov. 21, 1959.

21. *Amsterdam News*, Feb. 20, 1960, March 26, 1960, Oct. 1, 1960.

22. *Amsterdam News*, Jan. 10, 1970, July 24, 1971, Oct. 2, 1971. Voter-registration drives were undertaken in 1961 by the NAACP *(Amsterdam News*, Oct. 14, 1961), in 1963 by Concord Baptist Church and the Kings County Democratic Organization *(Amsterdam News*, May 4, 1963, Aug. 10, 1963), in 1964 by the NAACP *(Amsterdam News*, July 25, 1964), in 1966 and 1968 by Youth In Action *(Amsterdam News*, Aug. 13, 1966, Aug. 10, 1968).

23. United States Civil Rights Commission, *The Voting Rights Act: Ten Years After* (January 1975), pp. 220-30. In the 1972 presidential election, Brooklyn and the Bronx were the only counties in New York State in which less than half the voting age population voted. United States Census Bureau, "Language Minority, Illiteracy, and Voting Data Used in Making Determinations for the Voting Rights Act Amendments of 1975," *Current Population Reports* P-25, No. 627 (June 1976).

24. Civil Rights Commission, pp. 225-28; *New York Times*, July 2, 1974, Sept. 12, 1974, Nov. 7, 1974. The Justice Department rejected the objections that the new Fourteenth CD was not sufficiently minority: "Whether or not these minorities choose to exercise their right by registering and voting is obviously a matter of great concern, but as a matter of law, it is not one upon which the Attorney General can base an objection." Charles V. Hamilton similarly expressed criticism of black politicians' objections: "At some point, local black and Puerto Rican politicians must assume the responsibility for their own political mobilization. The courts should not be asked to require district lines predicated on turnout. If the minority voters are not prone to turn out, this is not, in this instance, a legal problem, but a political one. This situation calls for the skills of precinct captains, not plaintiffs" *(New York Times*, July 11, 1974).

25. Returns for the 1974 primary election were Frederick W. Richmond (9,317), Donald Elliott (5,985), Cesar Perales (4,178), and David Billings (2,637) *(New York Times*, Sept. 12, 1974).

26. William Doyle and Arlene Kurtis, eds., *The City of New York Official Directory* (New York, 1976).

# CHAPTER 10

# An Aura of Progress

## ECONOMICS

### Employment Advances, 1940-70

The coming of war in Europe and the resulting stimulation of American industry created renewed employment opportunities for all unemployed and underemployed workers. Unemployment, which afflicted 17 percent of Brooklyn blacks in 1940, was virtually nonexistent within a few years. To assure local black representation in this burgeoning defense industry, representatives of the Urban League, Carlton and Ashland Ys, National Negro Congress, and other groups joined to form the Brooklyn Joint Committee on Employment for National Defense. The program registered borough blacks and their particular skills, provided information on where jobs and training were available, encouraged Negroes to avail themselves of this training to prepare themselves for skilled positions, and kept industry informed of qualified and available Negroes. The integration of blacks into Brooklyn's industrial plants, however, represented a formidable task. A 1941 Urban League survey of 72 borough defense plants indicated that only 234 Negroes were employed in a total work force of 13,840. Almost half of the responding firms excluded blacks entirely; those that did employ blacks usually relegated them to maintenance positions.[1]

After United States involvement in the war passed from that of an indirect participant to that of an active combatant, the manpower squeeze became acute. Those who did not enlist or were not drafted into the armed forces could find some form of employment. The problem thus shifted from finding employment for blacks to obtaining better-paying jobs for them. Despite the creation of both national and state fair employment practices commissions to assure, at least on the surface, equal opportunity in hiring, blacks were still not readily accepted "when they offered their labor at the gates of Defense Factories." Robert Washburn, executive secretary of the Governor's Committee on Discrimination in Employment, condemned Brooklyn as the least progressive center in New York State in the reduction of job discrimination against Negroes, Jews, and Italians. The Arma Corporation of Brooklyn, for example, repeatedly rejected potential nonwhite referrals from the United States Employment Service, except for menial positions. The Brooklyn Navy Yard systematically denied the upgrading of blacks to supervisory positions except under severe pressure. It was "not uncommon" for the entire porter and maintenance staff in a defense plant to be black because of a company policy of hiring Negroes only in those categories.[2]

Most of the stream of black employment, however, was absorbed by the nondefense sector of the economy, which was losing its regular employees to more lucrative defense work. "We are not in war work but we are taking the place of those who are going into war work," commented the Urban League. Though such plants recruited black labor for low-wage jobs, black workers were thereby advancing into positions formerly closed to them. American Telephone and Telegraph (AT&T)

hired its first black clericals; telegraph and messenger services utilized Negroes; blacks became subway and trolley motormen, clerks, salesgirls, and waitresses.[3] Much of this advancement accrued to black women, who increasingly deserted domestic and personal service for better-paying factory jobs. Especially eager to employ these women were the traditionally low-paying garment trades: the radio, electronics, and aircraft industries also sought them. Black women, moreover, "surpassed Negro men in obtaining white collar office and professional positions." [4] Blacks were better off than they had been during the previous ten or fifteen years, but so too were millions of white workers who had likewise suffered through the Depression.

As during World War I, blacks had capitalized on a tight labor market and advanced their occupational and economic status. The employment gains made by blacks during the First World War, however, had not proven to be permanent and were especially eroded by the Depression. Following World War II, despite occasional recessions, the American economy entered a period of unprecedented, continuous prosperity, fueled in part by substantial government expenditures, a military draft that artificially restricted the labor pool of young males, and periodic military adventures abroad. Abetted by this general prosperity and a relatively tight labor market throughout much of the postwar period and further assisted by antidiscrimination statutes, affirmative-action decrees, and corporate concern, blacks were able to solidify and even expand their improved occupational status.

Between 1940 and 1970 the occupational distribution of Brooklyn blacks changed significantly. In 1940 only 14 percent were employed in white-collar positions. This increased to 18 percent in 1950 and to 43 percent by 1970. Much of this movement into the white-collar field resulted from black female abandonment of domestic service and their coincidental acceptance into clerical jobs. In 1940 nearly two-thirds of employed black women worked as domestics. This proportion declined precipitously, to one-third in 1950, to one-fifth in 1960 and to less than one in ten by 1970. The proportion of Brooklyn blacks employed at professional and managerial levels nearly doubled between 1940 and 1970. In the blue collar area, black males in 1970 were more likely to be craftsmen or foremen than in 1940, and less likely to be unskilled laborers. As a result of such overall black occupational upgrading, the occupational distribution of Brooklyn blacks and whites was significantly more similar in 1970 than in 1940. As such, this development constituted an impressive accomplishment.[5]

Significant as was this black advancement, it was often halting and certainly did not bring job or income parity with whites in Brooklyn or nationally. In 1950, over half of Brooklyn whites worked in white-collar positions, while only about one in six blacks was so employed. Blacks were heavily concentrated in the lower-paying, less secure, dirtier types of employment as semiskilled factory operatives, private house-hold workers, service workers, and laborers. Black unemployment, especially among males, remained severe—more than one in eight adult black males in 1950 was unemployed as contrasted to a white rate of 7.5 percent. As an inevitable consequence of these statistics, median income for nonwhite families and unrelated individuals in 1949 amounted to less than $2,000, or only about 60 percent of the Brooklyn white figure.[6]

During the 1950s, black women continued to achieve occupational mobility, especially into clerical positions. The proportion of employed black women in such work doubled from 9 percent to 19 percent between 1950 and 1960. The black male unemployment rate in 1960 (6.4 percent) was half that for 1950. The black borough unemployment rate exceeded that for whites by only 1.5 times, well below the national ratio of 2.1. Among both black males and females the level of labor-force participation increased modestly during the decade. Although interracial equality in income was far from approximated, the gap was markedly diminished. Black median family income in 1959 was $4,349, or 72 percent of the white figure of $6,025. Altogether the local picture was sanguine if not ideal.[7]

Economic Betterment Endeavors of the 1960s

The 1960s were marked by extensive internal and external efforts to improve further the economic status of the ghetto and its residents. An early vehicle to achieve this economic betterment was rooted tactically in the black civil rights movement. Various groups including the Brooklyn chapter of CORE, the Parents Workshop for Equality in New York Schools, the Unity Democratic Club, and the Ministers Movement protested, boycotted, picketed, and negotiated with major local employers to demand that they hire additional blacks. The Sealtest-Sheffield Farms milk plant, located in the heart of the ghetto but with only seven blacks in a work force of 367, was denounced as a "monstrous illegal insult to Bedford-Stuyvesant." Picketing of the plant led Sealtest to negotiate and agree to hire additional blacks. Other targets included Ebinger's Bakery, Bond Bread, and A&P, all of whom expanded their minority hiring practices.[8] During the summer of 1963 black groups attempted to halt construction at the Downstate Medical Center to force the hiring of additional black construction workers. The confrontation produced picketing, arrests, bitterness and a few minority hirings.[9] Later in the 1960s the New York branch of Operation Breadbasket, the economic arm of the Southern Christian Leadership Conference, revived these direct confrontation and negotiation tactics. Under the leadership of the Reverend William Jones, pastor of Brooklyn's Bethany Baptist Church, it reached agreements with Taystee Bread, Continental Bakeries, Robert Hall, Coca-Cola, and Pepsi-Cola to hire more blacks and to deposit some of their funds in black financial institutions.[10]

During the early 1960s, economists and manpower professionals adopted a new labor market strategy designed to have a direct impact upon the "structural unemployment" of ghetto residents. This approach rested on the assumption that the primary obstacle to an individual's employment was his lack of education and/or skills. Unemployment and poverty could therefore be reduced by "raising everyone's marginal product to the level where [they] would be able to earn an acceptable income." Hence education and training programs were enthusiastically and broadly embraced.[11]

The federal government consequently funded a number of often cleverly acronymic programs in Brooklyn such as JOIN (Job Orientation in Neighborhoods), TRY (Training Resources for Youth), and OIC (Opportunities Industrialization Centers). Additionally such broad-gauged socioeconomic institutions as the Bedford-Stuyvesant Restoration Corporation, Bedford-Stuyvesant Youth In Action, and Central Brooklyn Model Cities offered training programs as one of their many ameliorative functions. Lending official support service to these manpower programs were city- and state-sponsored employment offices located in the ghetto.[12]

The previous schemes of protest and manpower training concentrated on locating and/or opening jobs already existent in the city's economic structure and placing ghetto residents in them. Beginning in the mid-1960s internal ghetto economic development as a remedy for black pennilessness and powerlessness emerged as a new public policy.[13] It functioned under various guises, including black capitalism, location in the ghetto of branch plants of major corporations, and community economic development corporations.

Historically, ghetto enterprise has been divided into what might be called a dual retail market: a primary, profitable, large, white-dominated component and a black business sector that was small, frequently service-oriented, and marginally profitable. Black capitalism aimed ostensibly at remedying this imbalance and even facilitating black business succession to complement previous black residential succession.[14] In 1964 the Small Business Administration opened an office in Bedford-Stuyvesant for the purpose of providing loans up to $6,000, as well as business counseling and management training, to help persons start or improve a business. A related federally funded program, the Brooklyn Small Business Development Opportunities Corporation, operated briefly in 1966 and 1967, granting forty-eight loans to minority businessmen before a cost-effectiveness study led to a decision by the

Federal Office of Economic Opportunity not to re-fund the program. This role of stimulating local business development was inherited by the multipurpose Bedford-Stuyvesant Restoration Corporation and the more narrowly focused Brooklyn Local Economic Development Corporation (BLEDCO). Between its establishment in 1966 and 1977, Restoration helped finance nearly 125 business ventures— including the first black new-car franchise in New York State—at a total investment of more than $17 million. Founded in 1967 for the purpose of creating, saving, and expanding minority businesses, BLEDCO offered its clients technical expertise and assistance as well as direction and aid in securing financing. By 1977 it had helped over 250 ventures to obtain loans totaling $20 million thereby creating or saving an estimated 3,600 jobs.[15]

The economic impact of these entrepreneurial creations, however, was often quite limited because of their smallness, their limited ability to create linkages with the larger economic system, and the lack of local employment opportunities generated. According to the Census Bureau's 1972 *Survey of Minority-Owned Business Enterprises*, there were approximately 3,300 black-owned firms in Brooklyn. All but 400 of these did not have any paid employees, and among those that did, the total payroll encompassed fewer than 2,000 persons.[16]

Following the ghetto riots of the mid-1960s, some large corporations sought to discharge their social obligations by locating branch plants in ghetto neighborhoods. These facilities were designed to provide locally available employment opportunities and to pump additional money indirectly into the ghetto economy. One of the most publicized ventures in social capitalism has been IBM's Bedford-Stuyvesant cable-manufacturing plant, which employs more than 400 persons and is managed by a black. It stands as Restoration's single notable success in luring branch plants to the area. IBM certainly derived sufficient public-relations payment to justify its decision, but received additionally the bonus of an efficient profitable plant, something not anticipated initially. No other major corporation, however, followed IBM's initiative, and it remains an isolated example of a previous era's concern for and fear about the ghetto.[17]

Another form of ghetto economic betterment was the community development corporation (CDC), exemplified by such institutions as the Bedford-Stuyvesant Restoration Corporation (see also Chapter 8), Harlem Commonwealth Council, or Hough Area Development Corporation. These community-oriented corporations provided a multitude of services and types of investment, including direct business investments or loans, organization of mortgage pools, housing renovation, technical assistance to local entrepreneurs, bonding for local contractors, and loans to local pharmacies awaiting delayed Medicaid payments. Profits were viewed as but one of several desirable ends which also included manpower training, consumer education, reduction of anomie, and development of political strength. Some of Restoration's economic activities have been detailed already, but they do not illustrate the organization's diversity. Between 1967 and 1977 Restoration provided exterior renovation for more than 3,700 houses; organized a $65 million home-mortgage pool that has granted more than 1,000 loans; built, rehabilitated, or was constructing 1,280 housing units; sponsored four local outreach centers staffed by neighborhood residents and focusing on social-service needs; made summer-camp placements; constructed a community center, theater, and office building complex; and placed nearly 7,500 local residents in jobs and training programs.[18]

In spite of the surface diversity of these programs, they possessed as their unifying theme the creation of employment opportunities. In the economic sphere, Restoration's primacy among CDCs has been established (see Chapter 8). Restoration was the first CDC in the country, is the largest and most sophisticated, and has enjoyed "energetic political and business support since its inception." Between 1967 and 1974 Restoration obtained about $50 million in overall funding support from government and foundation sources. While the aggregate amount sounds impressive, it amounted to an investment of only about $125 per Bedford-Stuyvesant resident over a seven-year period.[19]

## Disturbing Statistics

Despite thirty years of occupational advances by blacks in Brooklyn; despite antidiscrimination statutes and city and state human rights commissions; and despite the special programs of the 1960s designed both to upgrade blacks for presumed employment opportunities and to open the local capitalist structure to black entrepreneurs; the economic picture of black Brooklyn remained rather bleak. On the most elementary level, black median family income in 1970 ($6,772) lagged disastrously relative to that for non-Puerto Rican whites (+$10,000). Although many upwardly mobile whites had undoubtedly left Brooklyn in the 1960s for the suburbs or Staten Island, the gap between black and white median family incomes not only increased absolutely but failed to narrow proportionately. Between 1960 and 1970 this dollar gap in Brooklyn increased from $1,675 to nearly $3,000; even more critically, the ratio of black to white median family income decreased marginally from 72.2 percent in 1960 to 71.5 percent by 1970. If one excluded Puerto Ricans from the white aggregate, the 1970 black/white ratio dropped to 67.3 percent. If one utilized per capita instead of family data, the relationship of black to non-Puerto Rican white income fell below 60 percent. Over one-fourth of black Brooklynites survived on incomes beneath the official poverty definition. Approximately half the local black families fell below the Bureau of Labor Statistics's more realistic measure of survival, its low urban family budget ($6,800 in 1969). Utilizing another definition of income adequacy, only 40 percent of borough blacks met Scammon and Wattenberg's criterion for inclusion in the black middle class ($8,000).[20] The 1960s had been a period of high expectations fueled in part by national data that indicated a narrowing of the interracial income gap; but this phenomenon primarily resulted from dramatic black economic advances in the South. In the North and West generally, and Brooklyn particularly, no relative gain occurred.

It is undeniable that some Brooklyn blacks did indeed improve their economic condition during the 1960s. According to Bedford-Stuyvesant Restoration, the proportion of black families in the area it serviced earning more than $10,000 in real dollars increased from 14 percent to 25 percent between 1960 and 1970. Simultaneously, the proportion of families earning less than $4,000 remained unchanged. Real per capita income in Bedford-Stuyvesant in 1970 did not differ from that in 1960. A number of black economists have commented concernedly on this "deepening schism" between those blacks registering significant gains and those left behind in a "residue of unemployment, underemployment, and poverty." [21]

Other evidence—unemployment and labor-force participation rates, educational attainment in relation to economic attainment, female-headed family structure, and welfarism—adds substance to this rather grim overall economic picture. Increased sophistication in analyzing employment data has led to dissatisfaction with the traditional official unemployment statistics, which mask the true severity of the problem, especially among blacks. In its tally the government counts as unemployed only those who are out of work and are actively seeking work. A more accurate index of employment *and* income deprivation would include not only the officially unemployed but also those working part-time but desiring a full-time position, those earning approximately the equivalent of the minimum wage, those who had despaired of finding work and had dropped out of the labor force, and a proportion of those "unfound males" who evaded attempts at official enumeration. According to a 1966 study, such a "subemployment rate" exceeded the official unemployment rate in most ghetto communities by a factor of three to four. In Bedford-Stuyvesant this more comprehensive index yielded an under-

employment rate of 27.6 percent in contrast to the more
benign official unemployment level of 6.3 percent. The unemployment rate in 1970-71 in the Bedford-Stuyvesant, East
New York, and Brownsville low-income area was 8.7 percent,
which, using the same enlargement formula as in 1966, would
yield an approximate subemployment rate of 33 percent. By
the mid-1970s this figure probably approached 50 percent. As a
consequence of such widespread underemployment, black
poverty was clearly both epidemic and endemic.[22]

The labor-force participation rate, which indicates to some
extent people's attachment to the work force and their
expectations for employment, declined sharply for Brooklyn
blacks between 1960 and 1970. For males the rate fell from
79.0 percent in 1960 to 72.5 percent in 1970 and for women
from 47.3 percent to 44.3 percent. The fewer people there are
participating in the labor force, the lower will be the number
of potential earners and hence potential income as well.[23]

Education, which had acted as a vehicle for upward mobility
for immigrant white groups, did not seem to exert the same
upward thrust for blacks. A 1960 Bureau of Labor Statistics
study revealed the discontinuity between Negro educational
attainment and income. While 38 percent of borough blacks
lived in census tracts in the lowest educational quartile, 85
percent languished in tracts in the lowest income quartile. By
1970 Brooklyn blacks had attained virtual parity with whites
in educational background as measured by the rather crude
criterion of the number of school years completed. Such
equality may have influenced interracial occupational distribution; yet black income relative to that for whites in 1970 was
even more depressed than a decade previous. While a number
of variables, including age, family composition, and work
experience, no doubt influenced this disheartening statistic,
one might also conclude that despite equality of length of
school experience, Negro education, either in the South or in
Brooklyn, was of such inferior quality that it failed to prepare
its students adequately for the world of work. Alternatively,
granting the equality of black and white educational experi-

ences, blacks were then broadly discriminated against in hiring and wages. Neither conclusion offered great hope for the future.[24]

It was not a matter of social and economic insignificance that over a third of black families in Brooklyn in 1970 were female-headed. This represented a substantial rise from 1960, when such families represented about a quarter of all black families. To be sure, a majority of black female-headed families were not poor, but they most definitely did form the bulk of those below the poverty threshold. Nearly two-thirds of all poor black families in Brooklyn in 1969 were female-headed. This is not to argue that the essential obstacle to nonpoverty status was female-headedness per se. There do exist in conjunction with this reality a number of related economic phenomena that restrict the level or type of jobs, income, or public support available to women heading such families. But female-headedness does present serious economic implications if for no other reason than that, by definition, it effectively limits the number of labor force participants in such a family to one.[25]

In some areas of Brooklyn during the later 1960s welfarism developed as the functional base of the local economy. Nearly a quarter of the borough's black families were receiving public assistance in 1969. Between 1965 and 1972 over three-quarters of a million persons were added to New York City's welfare rolls. In Brooklyn's ten official poverty areas the welfare population more than doubled. Whereas only 19 percent of Bedford-Stuyvesant residents in 1965 received welfare payments, 36 percent did so in 1971. In absolute terms this meant a rise from 48,000 to 84,500. In Brownsville the growth was from 23 percent to 38 percent, and in some pockets of that depressed section over half the residents were on welfare. The most rapid increase in the city (290 percent) occurred in East New York, where only 8 percent were welfare recipients in 1965 but 31 percent were in 1971. While welfare benefits in New York City were among the least ungenerous in the country, they scarcely provided more than a minimum level of subsistence at a maximum degree of dehumanization and control.[26]

## HOUSING

Since income is the single most critical variable in predicting a person's state of housing, it should not be particularly surprising that blacks in Brooklyn suffered severe and continuing housing deprivation. Indeed, black residents of Brooklyn and other northern urban ghettos have consistently perceived inadequate housing as their primary grievance, outranking other such obvious problems as uneducating schools, political impotence and exclusion, ineffective community services, and even unemployment. Shelter is a basic human requirement that becomes a fundamental grievance when inadequately provided. When the Bedford-Stuyvesant Restoration Corporation surveyed the area in 1967 and asked residents to list the three most important problems facing them, over half cited housing, considerably more than any other specific complaint.[27]

### Housing Quality and Cost

Between 1940 and 1960 the state of black housing in Brooklyn remained relatively unchanged. The proportion of nonwhite-occupied dwelling units that were dilapidated, deteriorating, or lacking some plumbing amenity increased from 34 percent in 1940 to 38.5 percent in 1960, more than double the borough white rate of approximately 17 percent. Despite the net gain of 113,000 housing units in Brooklyn during those twenty years and no increase in total population, overutilization of the housing stock remained as serious a problem among blacks in 1960 as in 1940, with slightly over one-fourth of all nonwhite units overcrowded in both years. For these qualitatively unequal facilities, blacks paid in 1960 rent approximately equal to that paid by borough whites for their superior quarters. This constituted a change from 1940, when blacks were at least compensated for their inferior housing by lower rents. Such rent parity weighed heavily on black families, absorbing nearly a quarter of their income in contrast to only 16 percent of white family income. In the only favorable development of this period, the proportion of homeowning blacks doubled from 6.8 percent to 15.3 percent of black-occupied dwelling units. This was no doubt a function of the wartime prosperity of some blacks and the white abandonment of Bedford-Stuyvesant.[28]

Since the Census Bureau deleted the assessment of housing quality from its 1970 questionnaire, direct comparisons with previous census returns are not possible. It seems probable, however, that the quality of housing available to and occupied by blacks did not improve notably during the 1960s. Horace Morancie, director of Central Brooklyn Model Cities, estimated that 60 percent of that area's 125,000 housing units were deteriorated or dilapidated in 1971. Bedford-Stuyvesant Restoration estimated in 1974 that a third of local properties required "substantial rehabilitation." Any visual inspection of Brownsville irrefutably showed that housing there consisted primarily of "decayed and crumbling three-story frame dwellings and four-story apartments." Blight had also spread to East New York where many of the nineteenth-century frame buildings were in "appalling condition." In these areas especially, landlord disinvestment in the form of housing abandonment reached epidemic proportions. Abandoned, vandalized, burned-out structures littered the streets no less than the battered, discarded hulks of automobiles. Tax arrearage, an accurate predictor of ultimate abandonment, affected anywhere from a fifth to a third of ghetto-area properties.[29]

Overcrowding remained nearly as severe in 1970 as in previous years, with over one-fifth of black-occupied housing units so classified. While 27 percent of white dwelling units were owner-occupied, black ownership was only half as likely.

The ratio of white to black owner-occupancy rates equaled 1.93, among the higher differentials for major cities in the country. Whites were four times as likely as blacks to possess air conditioning and about twice as likely to have the luxury of more than one bathroom. For their inferior housing blacks still paid rent approximately equal to that paid by whites. The combination of this equal rent for unequal housing and inadequate black income forced blacks to bear a disproportionate burden for the housing they occupied. Relative to their respective incomes, blacks paid rent 1.41 times greater than that paid by whites. The financial pressure on lower- and moderate-income families, black or white, could be severe. Over one-third of those black households with an income less than $10,000 expended over 35 percent of their income for gross rent, and an additional 18 percent paid between 25 and 35 percent of income.[30]

## Public Housing

What new housing was constructed in the ghetto after 1940 was built either through direct public funding prior to the mid-1960s or subsequently with public assistance, usually in the form of mortgage or rent subsidies. In its origins and for a time after World War II, public housing serviced the working, upwardly mobile, temporary poor, who had been spawned by the Depression decade.[31] Yet progressively from the early 1950s the character of public housing took on a different tint. Given a reasonably healthy American economy and abetted by government mortgage policy, the democratization of the suburbs proceeded apace. The upwardly mobile poor soon exceeded established administrative income limits for residency in low-income projects. The often white, "worthy," poor tenant of the 1930s and 1940s gradually yielded to the permanently poor, the welfare family, the female-headed household, the "multiproblem" family who tended disproportionately to be black or Puerto Rican. By the mid-1950s approximately 40 percent of the beneficiaries of Brooklyn's public housing were black. These Negro tenants were unevenly distributed, with projects located in ghetto areas overwhelmingly black-occupied and other projects clearly designed as white preserves. Some projects located in predominantly white areas and occupied by an interracial tenantry, represented not so much islands of integration as mini-ghettos surrounded by less than friendly neighbors. These latter projects usually evolved in the direction of black and Puerto Rican predominance. By 1973 blacks constituted 62 percent of Brooklyn's 160,000 public housing occupants. Puerto Ricans and whites each formed 19 percent. Over a third of all public housing families were receiving welfare assistance although in some specific projects the proportion exceeded one-half. Single-parent households made up over a quarter of all families and the proportion exceeded 40 percent in many individual projects.[32]

While public housing projects often provided, at least temporarily, an improved physical environment for their tenants, they by no means solved black housing deficiency. The city planning commission cited Brownsville, the area most plagued with housing deterioration and abandonment as well as the location of more public housing units than any other part of Brooklyn, as testimony that "slum clearance and massive building of low-income projects alone are no solution to problems of the slums." The new buildings may have replaced slum housing, may have represented the only sound housing in the area, but "they helped institutionalize poverty and the ghetto." However, as a local housing official stated, "If we wait until the ghettos are broken up, we would have to wait a long, long time. Meanwhile the people would be living in a social evil." [33]

## Seeking Shelter Beyond the Ghetto

Efforts to break the constrictions imposed by this residential segregation required persistence and even courage. The Brooklyn chapter of CORE, established in 1960, immediately attacked segregated housing patterns (see Chapter 8). During the early 1960s CORE conducted sit-ins and sleep-ins at real estate offices, financial institutions, and model houses to publicize discriminatory practices. In 1966 the Brooklyn Urban League opened its "Operation Open City" office, designed to locate available housing for blacks in white neighborhoods.[34]

For blacks moving beyond the ghetto, violence was a not uncommon greeting. A black woman who bought a home in South Brooklyn in the late 1950s determined to remain even after her house was stoned, her daughter abused by profanity, and rubbish piled in a lot next door and set afire. A cross was burned outside another South Brooklyn house where a black family had lived for six years. It took more than three years to resolve successfully the struggle of one black family to purchase a home in the Canarsie section. In Park Slope, following racial conflict in a local school, one black-occupied house was fire-bombed and in another the windows were broken. Less than twenty-four hours after a black couple purchased a $31,000 house in East Flatbush, an explosion and fire caused extensive damage to the structure. Racial tension remained serious in this neighborhood. In 1971 local youths chanted outside one house, "Move out by Monday, niggers, or we'll burn you out," threw garbage on the property, and caused minor damage.[35]

Far more common and functionally more effective in expanding housing opportunities for blacks than the various efforts to promote open housing was the work of blockbusters in fringe areas undergoing racial transition. Capitalizing on white fear and prejudice and black desire for housing opportunities and assisted by the reluctance of financial institutions to invest in ghetto or imminently ghetto property, these realtors bought cheaply and sold dearly. Testifying before the City Commission on Human Rights, one realtor viewed it simply as "good merchandising" to purchase a house from its white owner for $12,250 and resell it shortly to a black or Puerto Rican for $20,000. The most publicized examples of this practice occurred in East New York in the early 1960s, where it facilitated the area's rapid racial inversion, and somewhat later in East Flatbush, but no neighborhood proximate to the spreading ghetto was immune from such tactics.[36]

## HEALTH

### Infant Mortality

The deplorable state of black health in the United States has been long documented. Health status as well as the availability and quality of medical services are related to, if not entirely dependent upon, income. It has been argued that poverty (that is, poverty-related diseases) is the third highest cause of death in New York City. That ill health has persisted almost as a way of life in the black community should not therefore be shocking. Illustrative of this point, according to the 1970 *United Nations Demographic Yearbook*, the United States nonwhite infant mortality rate (31.4 per 1,000 live births) ranked twenty-ninth among countries of the world. The Kerner Commission summed up this situation well: "The residents of the racial ghetto are significantly less healthy than most other Americans. They suffer from higher mortality rates, higher incidence of major diseases, and lower availability and utilization of medical services. They also experience higher admission rates to mental hospitals." [37]

From the perspective of both availability and accuracy of data, probably the best indicator of an area's or group's health is its infant mortality rate. In Brooklyn in 1940 the nonwhite rate of 52.1 infant deaths per 1,000 live births was 1.7 times the white rate of 31.0. Between then and 1960 the rates for both racial groups declined, but the interracial disparity actually increased from a factor of 1.7 to 2.1. Subsequently, and especially after 1965, this gap has narrowed, so that by 1971 the nonwhite rate of 28.0 was only 1.6 times that for whites, an insignificant shift from the 1940 differential. In fact, not until 1971 did the nonwhite rate finally decrease below the white rate of thirty years previous. One can reasonably presume that this diminishing interracial difference reflects, in part, a rising number of Puerto Rican births and infant deaths, most of which were recorded as white. Were one able to divide the white rate into Puerto Rican and non-Puerto Rican sectors, it seems probable that the black rate would then exceed the non-Puerto Rican white rate by the traditional, normative 2.0 ratio. Thus a black baby was twice as likely as a white baby not to survive its first year of life.[38]

## Health-care Facilities in Bedford-Stuyvesant

In addition to resident poverty, such institutional factors as the lack of adequate health-care facilities serving blacks in Bedford-Stuyvesant, and hospital discrimination against black doctors and their patients contributed to the poor health of area residents. As a result of these realities a demand arose for the construction of a new local interracial hospital. Plans for a privately financed hospital never really matured, but some promise did seem to materialize when a 1949 study by the Hospital Council of the City of New York stressed the need for 300 to 500 additional general-care beds in Bedford-Stuyvesant. The council further recommended the inclusion of facilities "for the private and semi-private patients of Negro physicians in that locality." The plan had the support of Brooklyn Borough President John Cashmore and City Hospital Commissioner Marcus D. Kogel, who promised, shortly before the November mayoralty election, a municipal hospital within five years. Any black doctor with the proper qualifications would be "guaranteed" an appointment there.[39]

Within a few months, however, the promise began to fade. In its five-year plan, the Mayor's Special Committee on Hospitals made no provision for the Bedford-Stuyvesant unit. The once enthusiastic Kogel now expressed reservations about the city's immediately embarking on such a project. Since black staff appointments, he argued, could be provided through existing hospitals, private, voluntary, and municipal, there was really no need for an additional facility. Yet the proposal refused to be buried. In 1951 the board of estimate revived the idea and allowed the search for a suitable site to proceed. Long years of frustration, however, had forewarned the community to believe only when construction had begun. Such mistrust seemed well justified as the search for a proper location proceeded lackadaisically. The board of estimate was reportedly prepared to reverse its earlier approval and divert the funds from Bedford-Stuyvesant to other hospital projects. Commissioner Kogel symbolized this ambivalence: Although Bedford-Stuyvesant was "particularly poor in hospital facilities and relatively rich in tuberculosis . . ." other items in the hospital department's budget had greater urgency.[40]

The board of estimate again aroused expectation in 1953, another mayoralty election year, by appropriating for the capital budget $1,250,000 for site acquisition and architectural designs. But the city responded with nearly total inaction despite continued community pressure from the Citizens' Committee for a Bedford-Stuyvesant Hospital Site Now and from prominent Brooklyn leaders. Kogel again turned sympathetic: "I am firmly convinced that we will never completely decompress the existing hard pressed Brooklyn hospitals until we build a hospital in the Bedford-Stuyvesant area." He struck at the central problem beyond mere numbers of beds or staff appointments for black physicians when he noted that "we are dealing with an underprivileged population which by its very socio-demographic characteristics is known to require more hospital care than an average population." Intensifying community frustration with the recurrent delays was the fact that the city had reportedly decided upon a Fulton Street location for the hospital. Its purchase only awaited the release of funds by the city.[41]

Meanwhile, the hospital council, which had given impetus to this movement with its 1949 report, reversed its original position. To the consternation of Stuyfordites, it now recommended that the money voted for the Bedford-Stuyvesant hospital be diverted to the expansion of the city's Cumberland Hospital. Supporting this proposal was the new hospital commissioner, Dr. Basil C. MacLean, who had incurred no previous commitment to Bedford-Stuyvesant. Local groups bitterly protested, arguing that Cumberland Hospital was already old, obsolete, and operating at capacity and was located too far from the center of Bedford-Stuyvesant, especially for the elderly and young. Such arguments had no influence; in 1956 the board of estimate approved plans for the expansion of Cumberland Hospital.[42]

Pressure on public health facilities was intensified by the flight of private physicians from the ghetto. The median age of practicing doctors in Bedford-Stuyvesant exceeded sixty years in 1970, and almost no new medical practices were being established in the area. This situation placed a greater burden on an already overtaxed public health system. The family doctor became a large municipal hospital outpatient clinic, emergency room, or a public health department facility. To seek medical care meant much bureaucratic processing followed by long hours of waiting in a crowded, drab clinic waiting room. Not uncommonly, the wait for emergency treatment at Kings County Hospital, for example, reputedly ranged between eight and twelve hours. While new clinics and centers have been constructed in the ghetto areas of Brooklyn, and federal monies have flowed to local health-care projects, in most ghetto sections these facilities were generally described as "overcrowded," "inadequate," and "outdated." Not without reason did a 1969 report conclude that an estimated 120,000 persons in central Brooklyn, approximately one-third of the area's population, did not receive proper medical care.[43]

Were one to analyze other measures of social and economic well-being, or dislocation, in the Brooklyn black community, the overall picture would not be significantly altered. Central to any understanding of the aggregate situation in Bedford-Stuyvesant or any large, black urban slum-ghetto must be the pervasiveness of income deprivation among the area's residents. Although it offers no guarantee against poor living conditions, illness, or poor nutrition, money does provide a certain access to more adequate levels of shelter, health care, food, and, parenthetically, power. As long as blacks in Brooklyn or anywhere else continue in relative and/or absolute economic poverty, they will remain a deprived people, a people set apart. Such a description is easy to document, but curative prescriptions have proven difficult to formulate, much less to implement.

## NOTES

1. *New York Age,* Jan. 18, 1941; *Amsterdam News,* Dec. 17, 1940, March 8, 1941, April 12, 1941, May 31, 1941, July 26, 1941; *Brooklyn Daily Eagle,* June 14, 1941, Feb. 18, 1942.

2. Herman Bloch, "Social and Economic Discrimination against New York City Negroes" (Ph.D. dissertation, New School for Social Research, 1950), pp. 55-64; *The Open Door,* 17 (March 1941): 1; Brooklyn Urban League, *Annual Report,* 1942, pp. 6-7; *Age,* July 25, 1942, Dec. 12, 1942, Feb. 13, 1943; *Amsterdam News,* Dec. 25, 1943, March 4, 1944, March 25, 1944; *Eagle,* Oct. 31, 1942.

3. Brooklyn Urban League, *Annual Report,* 1942, p. 5; 1943, p. 9; *Interracial Review* 14 (July 1941): 112; *Age,* Nov. 15, 1941, July 25, 1942, Dec. 12, 1942, July 31, 1943; *Amsterdam News,* Nov. 21, 1942; *Eagle,* Oct. 31, 1942.

4. Brooklyn Urban League, *Annual Report,* 1941, p. 4; 1942, p. 6; *Age,* Nov. 15, 1941, Nov. 28, 1942, April 17, 1943; *Amsterdam News,* Sept. 12, 1942.

5. Occupational data for Brooklyn blacks in 1940 are not available in the published census material. I have assumed that the occupational distribution of blacks in the city as a whole is reasonably similar to that for Brooklyn blacks and have therefore used the citywide percentages for this year only.

6. United States Census Bureau, *Seventeenth Census, 1950, Population,* 3: ch. 37; *Census Tract Statistics for New York City,* (Washington, 1953), pp. 198, 573-78.

7. United States Census Bureau, *Eighteenth Census, 1960, Population; Census Tracts, New York City,* (Washington, 1961), pp. 23, 517, 683.

8. *Amsterdam News,* Oct. 28, 1961, Nov. 25, 1961, Dec. 2, 1961, Jan. 13, 1962, Feb. 3, 1962, Feb. 17, 1962, May 26, 1962, June 2, 1962, Aug. 11, 1962, Aug. 18, 1962, Aug. 25, 1962, June 15, 1963, Sept. 28, 1963; *New York Times,* April 1, 1962.

9. *Amsterdam News,* July 6, 1963, July 13, 1963, July 20, 1963, July 27, 1963, Aug. 3, 1963, Aug. 10, 1963, Aug. 17, 1963, Aug. 31, 1963.

10. *Amsterdam News,* Oct. 21, 1967, Dec. 23, 1967, July 13, 1968, July 26, 1969, Nov. 1, 1969, Sept. 19, 1970.

11. Lester C. Thurow, "Raising Incomes through Manpower Training Programs," in *Contributions to the Analysis of Urban Problems,* ed. Anthony H. Pascal (Santa Monica: The Rand Corporation, 1968), p. 92. The notion of structural unemployment is discussed in, among other books, August C. Bolino, *Manpower and the City*

(Cambridge, Mass., 1969); Eleanor G. Gilpatrick, *Structural Unemployment and Aggregate Demand* (Baltimore, 1969); Charles C. Holt, et al., *The Unemployment-Inflation Dilemma* (Washington, 1971).

12. *Amsterdam News*, June 15, 1963, Jan. 25, 1964, Aug. 29, 1964, March 27, 1965, Aug. 7, 1965, Aug. 6, 1966, Aug. 20, 1966, March 25, 1967, July 29, 1967, Nov. 11, 1967, Dec. 2, 1967, Dec. 9, 1967, Jan. 6, 1968, Feb. 3, 1968, Aug. 10, 1968, Oct. 19, 1968, Feb. 21, 1970, March 28, 1970, April 18, 1970, Sept. 19, 1970, June 12, 1971; *New York Times*, July 26, 1966. The employment placement services have been criticized for routing the poor "to the secondary sector of the labor market," by providing "the very same jobs which have kept them in poverty." Yeheskel Hasenfeld, "The Role of Employment Placement Services in Maintaining Poverty," *Social Service Review*, 49 (December 1975): 584-585.

13. Bennett Harrison, "Ghetto Economic Development: A Survey," *Journal of Economic Literature* 12 (March 1974): 1-37.

14. A study of Harlem concluded: "The retail economy in Harlem actually consists of two sectors—one white and one non-white—that overlap only in part and compete with each other very imperfectly." James Heilbrun and Roger R. Conant, "Profitability and Size of Firm as Evidence of Dualism in the Black Ghetto," *Urban Affairs Quarterly* 7 (March 1972): 266. On the topic of black capitalism see, for example, Theodore L. Cross, *Black Capitalism* (New York, 1969); Earl Ofari, *The Myth of Black Capitalism* (New York, 1970); Arthur I. Blaustein and Geoffrey Faux, *The Star Spangled Hustle* (New York, 1972); Andrew F. Brimmer and Henry S. Terrell, "The Economic Potential of Black Capitalism," *Public Policy* 19 (Spring 1971): 289-308; Timothy Bates, "Employment Potential of Inner City Black Enterprise," *The Review of Black Political Economy* 4 (Summer 1974): 59-67.

15. *Restoration Newsletter*, April 1977; *Amsterdam News*, Aug. 8, 1964, April 30, 1966, July 16, 1966, Sept. 17, 1966, Oct. 1, 1966, April 15, 1967, Nov. 18, 1967, Jan. 27, 1968, Feb. 10, 1968, Nov. 30, 1968, April 19, 1969, June 7, 1969, June 14, 1969, Nov. 11, 1969, July 11, 1970, Sept. 26, 1970, March 20, 1971, Jan. 15, 1972.

16. United States Census Bureau, *1972 Survey of Minority-Owned Business Enterprises*, Special Report MB 72-1 (Washington, 1974), p. 91. Comments on the limited character of black capitalism as it has been practiced can be found in Flournoy Coles, Jr., "The Unique Problems of the Black Businessman," *The Review of Black Political Economy* 5 (Fall 1974): 45-55; Neil M. Singer, "Federal Aid to Minority Business: Survey and Critique," *Social Science Quarterly* 54 (September 1973): 292-305; Timothy Bates, "Government Promotion of Minority Group Entrepreneurship: Trends and Conse-

quences," *Institute for Research on Poverty* (February 1974).

17. Robert Schrank and Susan Stein, "Industry in the Black Community: I.B.M. in Bedford-Stuyvesant," *Journal of the American Institute of Planners* 25 (September 1969): 348-51; *Amsterdam News*, April 20, 1968; *New York Times*, April 18, 1968. In 1976, IBM announced plans to construct a $10 million plant in Bedford-Stuyvesant to replace the existing facility *(Amsterdam News*, Jan. 10, 1976; *Restoration Newsletter*, Winter 1975).

18. Harrison, "Ghetto Economic Development," pp. 20-23. Restoration statistics are from *Restoration Newsletter*, April 1977.

19. Abt Associates, *An Evaluation of the Special Impact Program* (4 vols; Cambridge, Mass., 1972); The National Center for Urban Ethnic Affairs, "Community Development Corporations, A Review of Their Experiences" (Washington, 1973), p. 46; Bedford-Stuyvesant Restoration Corporation, "A Summary of Private Sector Involvement of the Bedford-Stuyvesant Restoration Corporation, June, 1974" (mimeographed).

20. United States Census Bureau, *Census of Population and Housing: 1970, Census Tracts, New York, New York SMSA* (Washington, 1972), tables P-4, P-6, P-8; Ben J. Wattenberg and Richard M. Scammon, "Black Progress and Liberal Rhetoric," *Commentary* 55 (April 1973): 35-36.

21. Bedford-Stuyvesant Restoration Corporation, "The State of the Community" (n.d.), pp. 4-6; Robert Browne, "Economics and the Black Community in America," *The Review of Black Political Economy* 5 (Spring 1975): 302-13; Bernard Anderson and Phyllis Wallace, "Public Policy and Black Economic Progress: A Review of the Evidence," *American Economic Review* 65 (May 1975): 47-52; Daniel Fusfeld "Discussion," *American Economic Review* 65 (May 1975): 60-62; Vivian W. Henderson, "Race, Economics, and Public Policy with Reflections on W.E.B. Du Bois," *Phylon* 37 (Spring 1976): 1-11.

22. Bennett Harrison, "Education and Underemployment in the Urban Ghetto," *American Economic Review* 62 (December 1972): 797; United States Department of Labor, "Sub-Employment in the Slums of New York" (n.d.); *Restoration Newsletter* (January-February 1974). In Central Harlem the 1966 unemployment rate of 8.3 percent grew to a subemployment rate of 28.6 percent; in Roxbury from 6.5 percent to 24.2 percent; and in North Philadelphia from 9.1 percent to 34.2 percent.

23. Among non-Puerto Rican whites in Brooklyn the labor force participation rate declined from 77.7 to 73.2 for males but increased from 34.5 to 38.7 for females between 1960 and 1970. This local pattern in labor force participation paralleled that for the nation.

| LABOR FORCE PARTICIPATION RATE | | | | |
| --- | --- | --- | --- | --- |
| | WHITE | | NEGRO AND OTHER RACES | |
| Year | Male | Female | Male | Female |
| 1950 | 86.4 | 32.6 | 85.9 | 46.9 |
| 1960 | 83.4 | 36.5 | 83.0 | 48.2 |
| 1970 | 80.0 | 42.6 | 76.5 | 49.5 |
| 1975 | 78.7 | 45.9 | 71.5 | 49.2 |

The rate declined for both white and black males but much more precipitously for the latter. Among black and white women the participation rate increased but much more rapidly for white females. Thus blacks were squeezed from both ends, their rate declining more rapidly on the male side and growing more slowly on the female side.

In one recent article, it was suggested that "long-term residence in urban areas may depress the level of labor force attachment among poor blacks." Sally Bould Van Til, "Race, Poverty, and Labor Force Participation," *Social Science Quarterly* 55 (December 1974): 657-669.

24. Bureau of Labor Statistics, "Income, Education, and Unemployment: New York City; Brooklyn" (1963), p. 4; Census Bureau, *Census of Population and Housing, 1970, Census Tracts*, tables P-2, P-5; *New York Times*, Oct. 26, 1963. According to Albert Niemi, Jr., the major source of interracial earning differentials in New York "may originate in the formative prelabor market years when minorities receive a low quality education which provides them with a relatively low level of embodied skill." The consequent earnings gaps, therefore, "largely reflect real skill differences rather than color based employer discrimination" ("Wage Discrimination Against Negroes and Puerto Ricans in the New York SMSA: An Assessment of Educational and Occupational Differences," *Social Science Quarterly* 55 [June 1974]: 112, 120).

25. Census Bureau, *Census of Population and Housing, 1970, Census Tracts*, tables P-5, P-6. Nationally the proportion of black female-headed households increased from 21 percent of black families in 1955 to 24 percent in 1965 and to 35 percent in 1972. United States Census Bureau, "Female Family Heads," *Current Population Reports* P-23, No. 50 (July 1974).

26. *New York Times*, April 10, 1972. The topic of welfare in New York City is extensively discussed in Miriam Ostrow and Anne B. Dutka, *Work and Welfare in New York City* (Baltimore, 1975), and

Blanche Bernstein and William Meezan, *The Impact of Welfare on Family Stability* (New York, 1975).

27. The Center for Urban Education, *Community Attitudes in Bedford-Stuyvesant: An Area Study* (New York, 1967), pp. 15-16, 22; *New York Times*, July 27, 1964. Community surveys taken in the wake of the ghetto riots of the 1960s revealed the salience of the housing issue. Blacks in Newark cited "bad housing conditions" most often when asked to choose among fifteen underlying causes of the 1967 disorders *(Report for Action,* Governor's Select Commission on Civil Disorder, February 1968, p. 55). The Kerner Commission placed "inadequate housing" in the "first level of intensity" of black grievances (p. 143).

28. United States Census Bureau, *Sixteenth Census, 1940, Census Tract Data on Population and Housing, New York City* (New York, 1942); Census Bureau, *Eighteenth Census, 1960, Population; Census Tracts, New York City,* pp. 752, 1001, 1012-23. One should note the imprecise, impressionistic, and changing character of housing data and terms. The presence or absence of plumbing amenities and overcrowding have been constant features of census publications between 1940 and 1970. More general qualitative terms have changed decennially. The 1940 census referred to houses "needing major repairs." In 1950, "dilapidated" was used, but did not necessarily equate with the 1940 phrase. The 1960 census terms offered gradations of "deteriorating" and "dilapidated." The 1970 census solved this problem of constantly shifting definitions by eliminating the qualitative evaluation of housing entirely.

29. Emanual Tobier, *Aspects of the New York City Property Market* (Citizens Housing and Planning Council of New York, 1975), pp. 4-5; New York City Planning Commission, *Plan for New York, 1969: A Proposal,* vol. 3, *Brooklyn* (New York, 1969), pp. 62, 166; *Restoration Newsletter,* March-April 1974; *Amsterdam News,* Jan. 2, 1971. According to Tobier 37 percent of the total number of residential parcels in Bedford-Stuyvesant and Fort Greene were tax delinquent in 1974. Brownsville, Bushwick, Crown Heights, and East New York had delinquency rates between 20 and 25 percent. The phenomenon of abandonment has been treated extensively in Michael A. Stegman, *Housing Investment in the Inner City: The Dynamics of Decline; A Study of Baltimore, Maryland, 1968-1970* (Cambridge, Mass., 1972); George Sternlieb, *The Tenement Landlord* (New Brunswick, N.J., 1966); George Sternlieb and Robert W. Burchell, *Residential Abandonment: The Tenement Landlord Revisited* (New Brunswick, N.J., 1973); and U.S. Department of Housing and Urban Development, *Abandoned Housing Research: A Compendium* (Washington, D.C., 1973).

30. Census Bureau, *Census of Population and Housing, 1970, Census Tracts*, tables H-1, H-2, H-3, H-4; "City Housing," *Municipal Performance Review* 1 (November 1973).

31. The story of public housing in America, past and present, is treated in Henry J. Aaron, *Shelter and Subsidies: Who Benefits from Federal Housing Policies?* (Washington, 1972); Leonard Freedman, *Public Housing: The Politics of Poverty* (New York, 1969); Joseph P. Fried, *Housing Crisis U.S.A.* (New York, 1971); Robert Taggart III, *Low-Income Housing: A Critique of Federal Aid* (Baltimore, 1970); Lawrence M. Friedman, "Public Housing and the Poor," in *Housing Urban America*, ed. Jon Pynoos, Robert Schafer, and Chester W. Hartman (Chicago, 1973), pp. 448-59.

32. New York City Housing Authority, *Tenant Data: Characteristics of Tenants as of January 1, 1973* (New York, 1973); *Amsterdam News*, June 29, 1957.

33. New York City Planning Commission, *Brooklyn*, p. 166; *New York Times*, March 13, 1962. Leonard Weller and Elmer Luchterhand support this view of the limited impact of public housing. "Large, low income families are so overburdened by their economic problems and by the degradation of identities that tend to characterize inner-city life . . ., that simply moving into better quarters, even in some cases with supportive services, will not greatly improve family functioning, at least not in the short run." Leonard Weller and Elmer Luchterhand, "Effects of Improved Housing on the Family Functioning of Large Low-Income Black Families," *Social Problems* 20 (Winter 1973): 388.

34. *Amsterdam News*, Aug. 20, 1960, Nov. 5, 1960, Nov. 19, 1960, March 25, 1961, Nov. 25, 1961, June 15, 1968.

35. *Age*, July 27, 1957; *Amsterdam News*, Nov. 19, 1960, Dec. 3, 1960, March 18, 1961, April 15, 1961, Aug. 5, 1961, March 12, 1966, Jan. 21, 1967, Aug. 21, 1971.

36. On the dynamic nature of residential succession see, for example, Otis and Beverly Duncan's classic study of Chicago, *The Negro Population of Chicago. A Study of Residential Succession* (Chicago, 1957); Howard Aldrich, "Ecological Succession in Racially Changing Neighborhoods: A Review of the Literature," *Urban Affairs Quarterly* 10 (March 1975): 327-348; R. Helper, *Racial Policies and Practices of Real Estate Brokers* (Minneapolis, 1969).

37. *Report of the National Advisory Commission on Civil Disorders* (New York, 1968), p. 269; *New York Times*, Oct. 10, 1964.

38. Health statistics are derived from the New York City Department of Health's annual *Vital Statistics by Health Areas and Health Center Districts*. Race is a factor in infant mortality largely because of the excess of low birthweight babies among nonwhites. Farida K.

Shah and Helen Abbey, "Effect of Some Factors on Neonatal and Postneonatal Mortality, *The Millbank Memorial Fund Quarterly* 49 (January 1971): Part 1, pp. 43, 54.

39. *The Bulletin of the Medical Society of the County of Kings and Academy of Medicine of Brooklyn* 28 (February 1949): 45; *Amsterdam News*, April 22, 1944, May 20, 1944, Nov. 12, 1949; *Eagle*, May 10, 1944, Nov. 4, 1949, Nov. 5, 1949, Nov. 6, 1949, Nov. 15, 1949, Dec. 6, 1949.

40. *Amsterdam News*, April 15, 1950, Oct. 28, 1950, July 28, 1951, Oct. 20, 1951, Dec. 1, 1951, Feb. 2, 1952, Aug. 30, 1952; *Eagle*, Feb. 21, 1950, Feb. 22, 1950, April 21, 1950, July 22, 1951.

41. *Age*, Nov. 26, 1955; *Amsterdam News*, Nov. 29, 1952, Aug. 26, 1953, Sept. 26, 1953, Oct. 24, 1953, Sept. 4, 1954.

42. *Amsterdam News*, Dec. 12, 1953, Sept. 4, 1954, Oct. 29, 1955, Nov. 19, 1955; *Eagle*, Aug. 15, 1954.

43. Mary Manoni, *Bedford-Stuyvesant: The Anatomy of a Central City Community* (New York, 1973), ch. 5; *Amsterdam News*, Feb. 7, 1970.

# CHAPTER 11

# Education, Separate and Inferior

The recent history of the Brooklyn public schools and their relationship with and impact upon black pupils parallels the reality of urban education throughout the North in the increasingly black and minority character of the pupil population; in the development of a separate but unequal school system; and in the failure of that system, with depressing regularity, to provide a functional education for its black pupils. Efforts to control or reverse these patterns and to attain some degree of remedy were repeatedly frustrated by official apathy or even hostility; by white flight; by white student and parent resistance; by the continuing low socioeconomic status of blacks; and by the irrelevancy of educational hardware and software to pupil outcomes. In 1940 blacks were a numerically insignificant part of the Brooklyn public schools. By the 1970s, abetted by a rapidly growing and geographically expanding black population, a rigid pattern of housing segregation that concentrated this increasing black population in Bedford-Stuyvesant and contiguous areas, an increasing proportion of whites using the nonpublic educational system, and a generally passive attitude by the New York City Board of Education toward school desegregation, blacks had become a plurality of a substantially segregated and only marginally educating Brooklyn public school system.

## EARLY COMPLAINTS

In its 1938 report the New York State Commission on the Condition of the Urban Colored Population viewed it as an "indisputable conclusion that Negroes do not ... receive equality in educational opportunities in the state—especially in districts having a predominance of Negro population." The influx of blacks into a neighborhood apparently produced a change in attitude by school officials. As an example of this phenomenon, the report cited Girls High School, located in the middle of Bedford-Stuyvesant, which possessed a history of high scholastic standards. As black attendance there increased, the traditional academic program was diluted with such industrial and appropriately "colored" subjects as homemaking, millinery, and weaving. The commission expressed concern that successful efforts to relocate the school elsewhere in Brooklyn would diminish even further the quality of education that would be offered to black girls attending high school in Bedford-Stuyvesant. Girls High was apparently too good and prestigious for blacks.[1]

Although generally more vigorous and bitter after 1954, black protests about school conditions were not uncommon in the 1940s. The School Council of Bedford-Stuyvesant and Williamsburg persistently charged the board of education with discrimination against schools in these areas. It accused the board of refusing to supply a sufficient number of teachers, to repair plumbing, or to allow blacks to attend newer schools in the area. PS 44 could not prepare hot lunches because of an unrepaired hot-water system. In PS 35 the only women's toilet in one building was broken, and even its purported repair scarcely eliminated problems. "On rainy days the ceiling of this toilet leaked so badly that teachers must use an umbrella to go into it." The council also charged that black students were "Jim-Crowed in their choice of academic high schools," being excluded from the more attractive facilities that featured pools, cafeterias, and other modern equipment.[2]

## INTEGRATION STRUGGLES

The increasing black population of Bedford-Stuyvesant, combined with the neighborhood school concept, inevitably produced educational ghettoization. Black concern with the poor quality of this segregated education, however, did not reach a sustained degree of opposition until after the Supreme Court's 1954 desegregation decision *(Brown v. Board of Education)*. This concern was complemented by official board of education pronouncements. Shortly after the *Brown* decision, in a bold statement that promised more than it could deliver, the board established as its policy the elimination of *de facto* segregated schools.[3] Almost at once this ideal conflicted with concrete reality. In September 1955, ten months after the board had pledged to prevent the further development of *de facto* segregated schools and to integrate existing schools as rapidly as practicable, newly constructed Junior High School (JHS) 258, located in the Bedford-Stuyvesant area, opened with a virtually all-black student population. Immediately the education committee of the Brooklyn chapter of the NAACP, under the leadership of the Reverend Milton A. Galamison of Siloam Presbyterian Church, expressed its public outrage at this continuation of segregated education. Galamison claimed, somewhat extravagantly given the school's location well within the ghetto, that the fate of JHS 258 was a "concrete test" of the board's integration policy and demanded that the school become a "pilot project" in integration. The education committee proposed a broad desegregation plan covering a number of junior high schools and fringe-area elementary schools. Superintendent of Schools William Jansen, a firm believer in the neighborhood school concept, and Charles Silver, president of the board of education, rejected the specific proposals for JHS 258, citing both the school's location "in the center of a large homogeneous [Negro] population" and the fear that white parents might resort to violence if their children were required to attend a school located in the heart of the ghetto. The NAACP persisted in this struggle through 1957, but Jansen refused to modify his position and JHS 258 remained an all-black school. As a consequence of this impasse, six other New York City NAACP branches joined the Brooklyn branch to form a citywide coordinating committee to work for school integration. Galamison increasingly emerged as a major spokesman for integrated education.[4]

The struggle to integrate JHS 258 represented the first of a series of confrontations between the board of education and advocates of integrated education in Brooklyn. A strikingly similar case developed shortly thereafter with the construction of PS 289 in a "racially fringe" area between Bedford-Stuyvesant and Crown Heights. John Theobald, who had succeeded Jansen as superintendent and was substantially more sympathetic to the goal of desegregated education, had pledged maximum integration even before completion of the structure. When the school opened on a limited basis in March 1959, however, the student body was nearly 90 percent black. The NAACP immediately protested this reversal of earlier promises and submitted a comprehensive plan for the integration of PS 289 and five other neighborhood schools. Four of these schools had a black and Puerto Rican registration below 40 percent. By dealing with a broader geographic area and a larger number of white families, the scheme attempted not only to solve the immediate problem of PS 289 but also to introduce some movement toward integration in other neighborhoods. The board's central zoning unit rejected the proposal, and PS 289 opened on a full-time basis in September 1959 as a segregated school and remained so.[5]

Black demographic influx into Brooklyn created a kind of moving frontier for fringe areas. Thus the locus of confrontation in the continuing struggle to effect a degree of school desegregation shifted southeastward from the Bedford-Stuyvesant and Crown Heights areas toward the confluence of the Brownsville, Canarsie, and East Flatbush sections. Brownsville in the early 1960s was in the process of evolving into Brooklyn's most deteriorated slum area, inhabited by an impoverished black and Puerto Rican population. Canarsie was a solidly white, heavily Italian area. East Flatbush, to the south of Crown Heights, was to become in the later 1960s and 1970s what is euphemistically called an "area of transition," but in the early 1960s it was attempting to retain its predominantly white, Jewish character. The initial confrontation in this convergence of neighborhoods and ethnic groups involved the siting and zoning of the new JHS 275. Integrationists favored a school located on the boundary of the black and white communities and zoned for integration. Most residents of East Flatbush and Canarsie preferred that JHS 275 be situated in Brownsville to serve "that" population. The board of education compromised, placing the school near the racial boundary but zoning it for segregation. Buffeted by both black and white community pressure, the board drew up various racial-balance proposals but finally settled on a 70-30 minority-white ratio. Contending that their children were being used to satisfy a racial quota and hence were being discriminated against as whites, some white parents resisted this arrangement and obtained a court order allowing their children to register instead at a predominantly white junior high school. Consequently JHS 275 opened in September 1963 with a black and Puerto Rican enrollment in excess of 80 percent and rapidly became a totally minority school.[6]

Not surprisingly, given such nonactions in Brooklyn and elsewhere in the city, the so-called Allen Commission concluded pessimistically in its 1964 report:

Nothing undertaken by the New York City Board of Education since 1954, and nothing proposed since 1963, has contributed or will contribute in any meaningful degree to desegregating the public schools of the city. Each past effort, each current plan, and each projected proposal is either not aimed at reducing segregation or is developed in too limited a fashion to stimulate even slight progress toward desegregation.[7]

This policy of not resisting, or even blatantly facilitating, segregation was not seriously disrupted by the Allen Commission report, by the ghetto unrest of the mid-1960s, by black protest, even by lawsuits.[8] Illustrating the pattern of calculated, official segregation more starkly than other instances, primarily because of Coney Island's physical separation from Bedford-Stuyvesant, was the fate of Mark Twain Junior High School (JHS 239). In 1962 Mark Twain had a student register of 1,933, 81 percent of whom were white, and a utilization level of 88 percent capacity. By 1973 the school's enrollment had declined precipitously to 713 pupils, 82 percent of whom were now black or Hispanic, with a scandalously low utilization rate of 41 percent.

How could such a complete reversal have occurred? Demographic shifts to be sure had contributed, but, according to Judge Jack Weinstein, "To a substantial degree the present condition at Mark Twain is attributable to decisions of school officials." During the 1960s the judicious manipulation of feeder patterns—that is, rezoning some predominantly white elementary schools that once sent their graduates to Mark Twain to other junior high schools—and zoning for new school construction, "had the natural and foreseeable effect of decreasing the white student enrollment at Mark Twain." Only two schools, both predominantly minority, were left to feed Mark Twain by 1973. Efforts by Chancellor Harvey Scribner in the late 1960s and early 1970s to eliminate this racial imbalance and improve utilization were resisted by the local community school board. The result of this impasse was the stigmatization and ghettoization of the school and the neighborhood. In his testimony before Judge Weinstein, Dan Dodson, educational consultant to the NAACP, stressed the role of the school in determining neighborhood quality: "The school comes nearer determining the housing of the neighborhood than vice versa, by far." This interaction of school and residence was highlighted by Judge Weinstein: "Housing and school patterns feed on each other. The segregated schools discourage middle class whites from moving into the area and the segregated housing patterns lead to segregated schools." Furthermore, the quality of education provided at Mark Twain was indisputably inferior. Only 14 percent of its pupils were reading at or above grade level with a majority at least two years below grade level. With care and deliberation school officials had helped to create a mini-separate school system.[9]

## CONFRONTATION IN CANARSIE

The overt educational-racial confrontations of the 1950s and 1960s usually cast blacks against the board of education, although no one could ignore the potent if not always visible reality of white parental, and hence political, resistance to the bolder integration proposals of Galamison or Commissioner Allen. Student violence did erupt at some high schools receiving black open-enrollment transfer students or schools undergoing racial transition, but it was sporadic and ineffective in reversing policy or demography.[10] The preferred white solution to a changing school population was avoidance either through flight from Brooklyn or to nonpublic education, or zoning manipulation. More recently, however, confrontation replaced avoidance. No issue has been so inflammatory of late as school desegregation, especially as achieved through the policy of "forced busing." This was symbolized for the nation in the 1974-75 South Boston impasse; but two years prior to Boston's troubles, white parents in Canarsie had demonstrated before national media the functional effectiveness of united and determined opposition to integration policies that they considered a threat to their community.

Since the opening of the low-income Tilden Houses project in Brownsville in 1961, some black and Puerto Rican children had been bused from there to various schools in Canarsie-East Flatbush. During the summer of 1972 the District 18 Community School Board, which had jurisdiction over the schools in

Canarsie and East Flatbush, and was concerned about a rising proportion of minority pupils in its schools, sought to block the future assignment of Tilden Houses children to District 18 junior high schools. District 18 was composed of two neighborhoods, East Flatbush and Canarsie. In reality, it was a biracial district, with the schools in East Flatbush overwhelmingly minority and those in Canarsie predominantly white. A majority of the locally elected school board was from Canarsie. To some extent the subsequent bitter confrontation was an attempt by Canarsie whites to preserve the ethnic-racial character of their schools irrespective of the racial composition of the minority East Flatbush schools. The actual number of pupils involved was small (about 90 in a district of over 20,000), but the issues of local power and control were significant and permitted little possible compromise.[11]

When school opened in September 1972, black parents from Tilden Houses sought to register their children at JHS 285 (43 percent white), the school the project children traditionally attended, but they were refused admission. The community school board agreed to accept the pupils if they attended JHS 252 (5 percent white). Deputy Chancellor Irving Anker reversed this ruling and ordered the children back to JHS 285, which promptly closed its doors rather than accept them in order to "avoid a very volatile situation." On October 11th, Chancellor Harvey Scribner offered a compromise proposal that divided the children among three schools, including JHS 285. He also ordered the local school board to develop a comprehensive plan for the integration of these three junior high schools. Scribner thus succeeded in broadening the controversy by drawing in JHS 211 and JHS 68, both majority white schools. Local groups succeeded in closing both schools to prevent registration efforts. On October 23rd Scribner shifted course, retracted his previous order, and reassigned the JHS 211 contingent to JHS 68. At this point the central board of education intervened, reversed Scribner's order, and shipped the "unwanted merchandise" back to JHS 211. This inevitably precipitated a white boycott of all the Canarsie schools, which ended after a week with a warning of future resistance if the final assignment plan did not accord with local wishes. Throughout these boycotts, hostile white crowds besieged the buses transporting the black pupils and taunted their occupants. At least for a while, though, formal education was allowed to proceed with some of the black Tilden Houses children attending white Canarsie schools.

On January 12, 1973 the District 18 Community School Board submitted to Chancellor Scribner its proposed rezoning plan, which scheduled the Tilden Houses pupils to be phased out of District 18 junior high schools by 1975. Scribner rejected the proposal, but the central board of education subsequently interjected itself and promised a final ruling by March 30th. Local white pressure was unremitting; to dramatize their determination and seriousness the Italian-American Civil Rights League and the Concerned Citizens of Canarsie called for and implemented a districtwide boycott. The boycott proved broadly popular and lasted for the entire month of March until the central board issued its decision, which excluded from District 18 schools *all* Tilden Houses children not already attending district schools. These children were offered the option to attend "integrated" schools in other predominantly white districts. Thus the principle of integration was formally upheld, but more significant was the power wielded by an organized and determined community in establishing its own self-defined limits to minority attendance at schools in its area.[12]

After one has catalogued the major struggles over school integration in Brooklyn, it becomes quite apparent that the New York City Board of Education was willing to promote desegregation only within the limits of political realism and power.

## A MINORITY SCHOOL SYSTEM

This segregated public school system developed in Brooklyn with startling rapidity. Between 1954 and 1960 the number of segregated (90 + percent) black and Puerto Rican schools in Brooklyn increased from nine to thirty-eight and by 1963 to sixty-one, or 22 percent of borough schools. On the elementary and junior high school levels over half the minority pupils attended minority segregated schools. Similarly, 55 percent of white pupils attended white segregated schools. By 1970 over half of Brooklyn's 310 schools were predominantly (75 + percent) minority. Indeed, by the 1970s there had developed, abetted by a pattern of rigid housing segregation, a kind of triethnic school system. In the northern tier of the borough a predominantly Puerto Rican school system existed. Stretching east and south across central Brooklyn from the Fort Greene section across Bedford-Stuyvesant to Crown Heights, Brownsville, East New York, and East Flatbush was the overwhelmingly black school system. In most of the rest of the county public school pupils were predominantly white. Non-Hispanic white pupils, however, were a rapidly diminishing commodity. By 1973 whites constituted only 29 percent of the nearly 300,000 total enrollment. Blacks then constituted 43 percent, Puerto Ricans and other Hispanics 27 percent. Adding diversity to Brooklyn's education structure was a large, predominantly white, nonpublic school system that in 1973 educated more whites (about 90,000) in the elementary and junior high school levels than the much larger public school system (about 83,000).[13]

Segregation might have seemed less destructive if ghetto schools were supplying a rudimentary education to their black pupils. Occasionally a predominantly minority school scored well on standard academic achievement tests, but the prevailing result seemed to be less compulsory education than what Du Bois once called "compulsory ignorance." According to a Bedford-Stuyvesant Restoration Corporation study, about 80 percent of that neighborhood's elementary and junior high school children were performing below national norms in reading and/or mathematics. In Community School District 23, which encompassed Brownsville, including those schools that had constituted the experimental Ocean Hill-Brownsville school district, academic achievement lagged even more disastrously. In spring 1973 only 14 percent of the pupils in this impoverished black and Hispanic district were reading at or above grade level. Fifth-graders were reading at a median of 3.8 years instead of 5.7, and the eighth-grade median of 5.3 was nearly three and one-half years below the normal score. Thus by the eighth grade many District 23 pupils suffered disastrous, irremediable academic retardation. While District 23 represented the epitome of "compulsory ignorance," other neighboring districts performed only marginally better.[14]

With even more rapidity than the overall demographic trends, the public education system in Brooklyn changed its ethnic composition. What had been a majority white (and generally segregated) system in the mid-1960s had become a predominantly minority system with a black plurality by 1970. By the mid-1970s whites constituted only about a quarter of the public school population in Brooklyn, with blacks approaching 50 percent. This shift would not have been particularly alarming except for the increasingly inferior quality of the system. As any system becomes increasingly minority, almost by definition it is inhabited by lower-status pupils. While no perfect correlation exists, socioeconomic condition has long proven a powerful predictor of educational results. Thus dismal socioeconomic data are probable indicators of inferior school results, which become in turn a serious restriction upon future human and economic potential. Thus, between the previous chapter and this one there exists a disturbing relationship that cannot help but be depressing.

## NOTES

1. *Second Report of the New York State Temporary Commission on the Condition of the Urban Colored Population* (Albany, 1939), pp. 99-103.

2. *Amsterdam News*, Feb. 3, 1945, Oct. 20, 1945; *Brooklyn Daily Eagle*, Oct. 14, 1945, Oct. 16, 1945. Protests against conditions in these schools dated back to the mid- and late-1930s *(New York Age*, Dec. 11, 1937; *Amsterdam News*, Nov. 21, 1936, April 27, 1940, Nov. 21, 1942). Max Geller ("Some Social Factors Related to the Educational Achievement of 100 Negro Secondary School Students Resid-

ing in the Bedford-Stuyvesant Area of Brooklyn, City of New York"
[Ph.D. dissertation, New York University, 1943]) had indicated low
IQ and reading scores among his sample and hence low enrollment in
academic programs.

3. Diane Ravitch, *The Great School Wars, New York City, 1805-
1973* (New York, 1974), pp. 252-53.

4. Irving Goldaber, "The Treatment by the New York Board of
Education of Problems Affecting the Negro, 1954-1965" (Ph.D.
dissertation, New York University, 1964), pp. 91-96; Ravitch, *Great
School Wars*, p. 255; *Amsterdam News*, May 26, 1956, June 2, 1956,
June 30, 1956, July 28, 1956, Aug. 11, 1956, Sept. 15, 1956, Nov. 10,
1956, May 4, 1957, June 29, 1957.

5. Goldaber, "Treatment by the Board of Education," pp. 163-67.
David Rogers, in his *110 Livingston Street: Politics and Bu-
reaucracy in the New York City School System* (New York, 1968), p.
22, attributes primary responsibility for the rejection of this broad
integrationist program to the board's central zoning office. The
white community was apparently willing to desegregate.

6. Ravitch, *Great School Wars*, p. 271; *Amsterdam News*, Feb. 2,
1963, March 2, 1963, March 16, 1963, March 23, 1963, March 30, 1963,
April 6, 1963, April 13, 1963, August 10, 1963, Sept. 14, 1963; *New
York Times*, Sept. 7, 1963; Ira Glasser and Norman Siegel, "School
Desegregation: Northern Style," *Civil Liberties in New York* (Octo-
ber 1973): 6.

7. "Desegregating the Public Schools of New York City," a report
prepared for the Board of Education of the City of New York by the
State Education Commissioner's Advisory Committee on Human
Relations and Community Tensions (May 12, 1964), p. 8. James Allen
was commissioner of education in New York State; hence the
popular name of the commission. The commission consisted of Dr.
John Fischer, president of Teachers College, Rabbi Judah Cahn, and
Dr. Kenneth B. Clark, professor of psychology at the City College of
New York.

8. The 1968 New York City teachers' strike was precipitated by
events that occurred in Brooklyn in the Ocean Hill-Brownsville
experimental school district. Because of the extensive literature that
developed on this subject, because of the complexity of the issues
involved which would require too detailed a rendering for this book,
I have not included any chronology or analysis of the subject.
Anyone interested can consult: Maurice Berube and Marilyn Gittell,
eds., *Confrontation at Ocean Hill-Brownsville: the New York School
Strikes of 1968* (New York, 1969); Mario Fantini, Marilyn Gittell, and
Richard Magat, *Community Control and the Urban School* (New
York, 1970); Naomi Levine with Richard Cohen, *Ocean Hill-
Brownsville: Schools in Crisis* (New York, 1969); and Melvin

Urofsky, *Why Teachers Strike: Teachers' Rights and Community Control* (Garden City, N.Y., 1970).

9. The story of Mark Twain is taken from Judge Jack Weinstein's decision in *Hart* v. *the Community School Board of Brooklyn, New York School District #21* (Jan. 28, 1974).

10. *Amsterdam News*, March 23, 1963, Oct. 12, 1963. Violence against blacks was reported, for example, at John Jay High School *(Amsterdam News*, March 23, 1963, Oct. 12, 1963; *New York Times*, Oct. 24, 1964, Oct. 25, 1964, Oct. 27, 1964); at Lafayette High School *(Amsterdam News*, Nov. 5, 1966), Canarsie High School *(Amsterdam News*, March 1, 1969, March 8, 1969), and South Shore High School *(Amsterdam News*, Sept. 26, 1970).

11. Glasser and Siegel, "School Desegregation," pp. 6-7; Kenneth B. Clark et al., "Analysis of the *Decision and Order* of the New York City Board of Education" (Metropolitan Applied Research Center, 1973); Diane Ravitch, "Canarsie and Fuentes: The Limits of School Decentralization," *New York Affairs* 1 (Summer 1973): 88-97. In addition, the *New York Times* provided nearly daily coverage, especially during the more controversial periods.

12. In 1975 State Commissioner of Education Ewald Nyquist ordered the local community school district to redraw school zones to achieve racial equalization in the five District 18 junior high schools. In January 1977 he rescinded this order because it would hasten white flight from the area and hence prove "counterproductive." The junior high schools at issue had by then become "well integrated," especially since the district was steadily losing white pupils *(New York Times*, Jan. 18, 1977).

13. "Desegregating the Public Schools of New York City," pp. 37-39; U.S. Department of Health, Education, and Welfare, Office of Civil Rights, *Directory of Public Elementary and Secondary Schools, Fall 1970* (Washington), pp. 973-76; Bernard Mackler, "Non-Public Schools and Racial Discrimination" (mimeographed, 1975), pp. 4, 19, 27-29. For a graphic presentation of the triethnic school system, see the Metropolitan Applied Research Center's map of the "Distribution of Black, Puerto Rican and Other Pupils in New York Public Schools 1972-73, Borough of Brooklyn," (1974). Despite the obvious segregation in the New York City school system, it was somewhat less extensive than that in other major northern cities such as Boston, Cleveland, Philadelphia, or Chicago.

Irving Anker, Chancellor of the New York City public schools, cited a variety of factors that adversely affected the city's programs for school desegregation, including segregated housing patterns within the city and between city and suburb; high unemployment rates; the influx of minority poor from other geographic areas; white attendance at non-public schools; and the exodus of white and middle class families to the suburbs. "Integration in New York City Schools," *Integrated Education* 13 (May/June 1975): 137-42. Significantly, all of these contributory factors were beyond the control of the Board of Education.

14. *Restoration Newsletter*, May-June 1974, p. 3; *New York Times*, Feb. 15, 1974.

# Conclusion: The Intensifying Ghetto

## WHAT KIND OF GHETTO?

Besides chronicling the story of an historically neglected people, what do these pages tell us about Brooklyn, about ghettoization, about cities, about race and America? What do they say about the current status and future prospects of urban Brooklyn blacks? History is a dangerous subject because we live in such a dynamic context that the past's lessons are difficult to assimilate and make relevant. How does one distinguish between eternal verities and the vagaries of current style and mores? How do you compare Babe Ruth and Willie Mays, Ty Cobb and Maury Wills? The game of baseball is still played with a bat and a ball with bases 90 feet apart, but the internal context and dynamics have constantly evolved to a point that comparisons are at best tenuous. Similarly, the urban structure of turn-of-the-century Brooklyn and that of contemporary Brooklyn are so distant that it seems somewhat foolhardy or audacious to attempt any comparative analysis. But historians and authors being human, few can resist the

226

plunge into such uncharted paths, speculations, and assessments. Nor indeed should they, since analysis is an unending process or search, and those who have examined the issues should speak, while acknowledging the fallibility and tentativeness of their conclusions.

In assessing twentieth-century urban black history it is not uncommon to speak in terms of an "enduring ghetto." This does not mean that conditions have remained stable between 1900 and the 1970s; obviously, they have not. Most of these changes, however, have been of a societal nature affecting everyone's way of life. When one utilizes the phrase "enduring ghetto," one is suggesting that blacks in Brooklyn or elsewhere were, relatively speaking, as deprived in 1977 as in 1900.

A primary source for such a view is the repetitive character of so many of the reports that depict the condition of local blacks during this lengthy period. It is certainly possible to select generalized statements from studies dating from various periods, all of which, except for style and specific names and dates, are sufficiently alike to support this view. Thus a recently released Model Cities or Bedford-Stuyvesant Restoration Corporation study seems reminiscent of some Brooklyn Urban League report of the 1930s or a Brooklyn Church and Mission Federation study of the early twentieth century. The problems—lack of employment, poor education, low income, decayed housing, poor health—seem unchanged, perennial.

While this "enduring" typology appears reasonably appropriate, it is also possible to advance, with reason, the view that there has occurred some moderating in the degree of black deprivation. Martin Kilson has suggested that city dwelling has proven "particularly favorable to the growth of the black middle class." Certainly more blacks, especially northern urban blacks, have entered the economic mainstream during the past fifteen years than ever before. Some interracial discrepancies, especially in health, have moderated. And significant changes have occurred in the realms of politics and public attitudes. It is thus not unreasonable to emphasize "how closely the sociological characteristics of blacks have begun to resemble those of whites." [1]

Hopeful as these indicators may be, however, the weight of evidence, I would hold, suggests that neither progress nor even stability has come to urban blacks during the past three-quarters of a century. Rather, they have become the victims and occupants of an "intensifying ghetto" of substantial proportions that has wrought a broad swath of destruction through the ghetto and upon its residents. Manifestations of this intensification are evident in ghetto subemployment rates of perhaps 50 percent; persistently low aggregate family income; rampant welfarism; the abandonment of entire neighborhoods and their housing stock; academic achievement scores and dropout rates that can only portend a future marginal existence for so many black youths; excessive and still-rising levels of female-headed households.[2] No doubt earlier periods exhibited some or all of these pathologies or related ones, but the demographic context has changed. At some point quantitative differences become qualitative in nature, and at some point Brooklyn crossed that threshold. There is thus a vast difference between a total black population of approximately 700,000 and that of 18,367 (1900) or even 107,263 (1940); a vast difference between the time when the black proportion of the population approaches one-third and when it constituted 1.6 percent (1900) or 4.0 percent (1940). Thus what differentiates the employment or housing deficiencies of blacks in 1975 from earlier periods is not the uniqueness of the problems but the staggering magnitude of the population at risk and in need.

Perhaps this distinction between "enduring" and "intensifying" is artificial, semantic, irrelevant, dependent upon such subjectivities as personal philosophy and temperament. What is ultimately and fundamentally disturbing, however, is the paucity of change in the black condition over time. Compared to national or local norms—and this is the central issue, change not for its own sake but toward an interracial parity of benefits and situations—conditions for urban blacks have not improved notably.

## THE URBAN/BLACK CRISIS

The existence of an urban crisis in America is scarcely new. The Brooklyn of 1900—or first-century Rome for that matter—was confronted with an array of problems, including transit difficulties, congested and deteriorated housing, noisome smells and fumes, large unassimilated immigrant populations. What has changed in more recent years is less the presence of problems than a public posture that has abandoned its laissez-faire attitudes and adopted a more activist role in an attempt to remedy urban and racial problems. During the past decade and a half, there has been a proliferation of federal programs, all with laudable purposes, but seemingly with little impact on local conditions. Antipoverty programs barely disturbed the poverty of many. Other ghetto economic development schemes scarcely developed. It was difficult to tell what cities were models of, except deterioration, after Model Cities. Special education programs only seemed to foster declining student achievement. As we have seen, Brooklyn participated fully in these betterment endeavors, but few, if any, miracles, even minor ones, were wrought.

The reasons for such limited success (or outright failure) were many and varied. Marginal funding was, of course, an important factor. More than any other federal program, the Office of Economic Opportunity (OEO) (more popularly known as the Anti-Poverty Program) symbolized the Great Society's commitment to the poor, especially the urban poor. Yet no program more blatantly and paradoxically belied the presumed profligacy of this period. Even in the halcyon years (1966-69) before the OEO was gradually dismantled, annual expenditures for programs either directly administered by OEO or delegated by it to other agencies never exceeded $2 billion. In the ten years or so of its effective existence, this most fundamental antipoverty program expended about $15 billion, a mere pittance when one considers that in no year were there fewer than 25 million persons in official poverty in the United States. It was the equivalent of spending something like sixty dollars per poor person per year, and much of this money did not even necessarily go to the poor. One might also point to the experience of the politically well-connected Bedford-Stuyvesant Restoration Corporation, the most generously funded CDC in the country. Between 1967 and 1974 Restoration obtained from governmental and foundation sources the seemingly impressive aggregate figure of $50 million. When one disaggregates the total, however, this amounted to an investment of only about $125 per Bedford-Stuyvesant resident over the seven-year period.

Not only were many of these programs underfunded, they were also flawed conceptually. They aimed not to ease the burdens of poverty by providing cash payments, but to remedy the causes of poverty by offering the poor the opportunity to advance themselves. Thus, they emphasized rehabilitation and self-help, manpower training, special education, and day care. Yet the programs generated by the minority component of the Small Business Administration and its successor, the Office of Minority Business Enterprise, were modest in purpose and effect. This segregated form of "candy-store capitalism" never envisaged the development of a black Xerox or General Electric. Most of its creations were small and hence suffered from the normal risks and attrition endemic to all small business enterprises. In addition, they confronted the peculiar problems of location in a generally impoverished neighborhood. Such an approach was designed not so much to fail as not to succeed, which may be a rather fine distinction reminiscent of some arcane theological debate.

Similarly the "human capital" programs, which aimed through manpower training and educational upgrading to raise people's skills and productivity to a level where they would be able to earn an acceptable income, achieved only limited success. Most fundamentally, manpower and education programs dealt only with the supply side of the labor market. In other words, they did not produce or guarantee employment for the poor, and when jobs did not naturally materialize in the economy, they were unable to create them. It is certainly true that some individuals did benefit from one or more of these ghetto economic-betterment models, but such successes were personal and never institutionalized to the general black, ghetto population in need.

Furthermore, the characteristics of the urban crisis that people have most readily perceived and reacted to are not primary in nature. Better mass transit, the restoration of some of the recent reductions in school, police, or social-service personnel, a national welfare system, for example, will affect or ameliorate social conditions in Bedford-Stuyvesant or Brownsville only marginally, but will not interrupt the trends of urban decay and disintegration. The future viability of such neighborhoods, and the cities of which they are a part, depends quite fundamentally and quite simply upon the income of their residents. As long as black median family income in Brooklyn ($6,772 in 1969) remains at only 62 percent of New York City non-Puerto Rican white income ($10,921) or 61 percent of New York State white income ($11,034), that community's blacks will remain significantly disadvantaged for the elementary reason that income is the most consistent and potent predictor of other socioeconomic variables such as educational performance, quality of housing, and personal health.

Thus the black citizens of Brooklyn need above all to be incorporated into the economic mainstream—a solution more easily suggested than implemented or funded. Unemployment in New York City, which had historically been below national levels, has recently risen disastrously to more than 10 percent, to encompass more than 300,000 individuals in 1976. Moreover, this condition is aggravated for Brooklyn, and most other American cities in crisis, by their location in the older northeastern quadrant of the country. If Kirkpatrick Sale's thesis in *Power Shift* is reasonably accurate, political and economic power will continue to drift southward and westward. What can this portend for Bedford-Stuyvesant or New York City but continued deterioration and flight by those able to flee?

In the face of previous program failure and current national trends away from the Northeast generally and its large central cities specifically, the question should certainly be posed and seriously debated whether public policy, especially at likely levels of future funding, can interdict major social and demographic forces. Government programs can assist, guide, mitigate, and encourage such trends, but can they control or stem them? In other words, for example, does it make more sense to encourage internal migration from areas of high unemployment to areas of job growth than to attempt to rebuild the economic base of tired regions; to focus on intelligently guiding and assisting the suburbanization of America than to seek to save and restore the battered remnants of all its older urban areas? What can such a perspective portend for the black residents of Brooklyn?

Ultimately, any decision to do or not do anything to assist blacks and the cities they inhabit will be based not on morality or equity, but on politics. This merely adds to the unlikelihood of any serious effort for a meaningful solution. Most people (that is, voters) do not reside in central cities. Moreover, those who do, blacks especially, are less active participants in the political process. They do not vote with the same regularity as do suburbanites and hence they exert less political leverage. How likely are the voters and representatives of non-central-city areas to countenance the truly massive expenditures necessary to ameliorate significantly urban and/or racial problems?

Moreover, despite the statistically urban character of the United States, it is, paradoxically, peopled by persons of a decidedly antiurban bent. One explanation of this seeming contradiction lies in the official definition of "urban," which encompasses a diversified assortment of living experiences from the small county seat in Kansas to the great metropolis, including that vast amorphous thing called suburbia, in all its own diversity. When one thinks of an urban or racial crisis, however, it is essentially in terms of large central cities like New York and its subcomponent Brooklyn, and not these other patterns of urbanization. It is precisely these major cities that Americans regard with an abiding and pervasive aversion, that have long symbolized for many, from Jefferson to Steffens to Banfield, a broad array of evils. What can such an attitude portend for urban black residents?

Finally, after all the other variables and comments have been considered, one cannot ignore the persistence and virulence of racism in America. To be sure, its more blatant and vicious manifestations have been generally banished, but it remains an undeniable reality, opinion polls and public comments to the contrary notwithstanding. "Clearly, then, there remains a profound discrepancy between, on the one hand, the postwar open-mindedness of a majority of whites toward the principle of integrating blacks into American life and, on the other hand, the transformation of this favorable outlook on racial matters into concrete changes in housing, schools, and jobs." [3] Thus, any public policy or concern that is significantly contaminated by the issue of race is currently and will in the immediate future be destined for acrimonious, spurious debate and probable consignment to the graveyard of controversial ideas. What can such an eventuality portend for cities or boroughs that have become increasingly black and minority in demographic character, as has Brooklyn?

Unless something radically new and different occurs, therefore, the outlook for blacks in Brooklyn and all other large cities is grim. In other words, the relative gap between black and white income, wealth, employment, educational achievement, housing, political representation, and power will persist in the foreseeable future as it has persisted historically. In lapsing into such un-American gloominess, one runs the risk of prophecy and prediction being misconstrued as advocacy, of creating a condition favorable to self-fulfillment. Nonetheless, any unsentimental, honest observer of the present and the past, whatever his values, is moved, if not compelled, in the direction of pessimistic prognostication.

## NOTES

1. Martin Kilson, "Whither Integration?," *The American Scholar* 45 (Summer 1976): 361, 363.

2. A variety of recent writers have expressed concern about the effect of central city ghetto residence upon its occupants. "Young blacks reared and educated in the urban ghettos of the non-South

seem likely to pay a considerable premium for this environment in terms of subsequent earnings," (Bernard Anderson and Phyllis Wallace, "Public Policy and Black Economic Progress," *American Economic Review* 65 [May 1975]: 49). "There is good reason to believe, . . . that, while the averages showed an improvement in the condition of blacks taken as a whole during the 1960's, there was still a deterioration in the economic and social condition of blacks living within the inner city ghettos" (Fusfeld, "Discussion" *American Economic Review* 65 [May 1975]: 61). Moreover, black migrants to the North seemed "less socially disorganized and less prone to deviant behavior and less likely to be poor or on welfare than blacks born in the North" (Larry H. Long, "Poverty Status and Receipt of Welfare Among Migrants and Nonmigrants in Large Cities," *American Sociological Review* 39 [February 1974]: 54). Elsewhere, Long adds, "It is the blacks born and raised in the ghetto-like environment of the North who seem to have the greatest difficulty embarking upon orderly occupational careers" ("The Migration Experience of Blacks," *Integrated Education*, 13 [May/June 1975]: 28-31). "Perhaps because of the prevalence of drugs, crime, and daily violence, the general quality of life in central city ghetto areas may have deteriorated to such a degree that blacks born and raised there experience serious handicaps in planning and pursuing orderly occupational careers." (Larry H. Long and Lynne R. Heltman, "Migration and Income Differences Between Black and White Men in the North," *American Journal of Sociology*, 80 [May 1975]: 1407).

3. Kilson, "Whither Integration?," p. 366.

# Epilogue

While I was reading the galley proofs for this book, there occurred the 1977 New York City blackout with its consequent looting and arson which were so graphically depicted in the national media. How do those events of July 13-14, 1977 relate to the history of blacks in Brooklyn you have just read? It can be argued that this entire book (but especially Chapter 10) represents an explanation, even justification, for the rioting and looting of that night. More seriously, I would suggest, those disorders constituted a manifestation of what I called the "intensifying ghetto." A riot of similar intent by the borough's blacks in the 1940s would have been insignificant because of the size of the black population then. The recent looting once again focused attention upon the rather desperate plight of many urban blacks, upon conditions that seemed to carry the seeds of destruction—destruction of persons, things, and places. It brought to public notice the demise of the Bushwick section of Brooklyn, an old but reasonably sound neighborhood a decade ago, which has subsequently become a component of the geographically expanding and physically devastating "intensifying ghetto." In 1977 Bushwick was on the verge of joining Brownsville and parts of East New York and Bedford-Stuyvesant as a "crisis ghetto" characterized by desolation and abandonment.

Most immediate analyses compared the events of July 13-14, 1977 with those of that November evening in 1965 when the lights went out all across the Northeast and everyone behaved with such civility. A more relevant comparison, however, might have been to the events that had occurred ten years previous, that very July week, when Newark had erupted in violence and destruction. One could point to the racial character of the looting, to the destruction of ghetto property, to the sultry weather, to the underlying socioeconomic ills.

Yet more instructive than these similarities, at least as a measure of changing times, were some rather pointed differences between the two ghetto explosions. There were obvious differences in degree, response, and duration, but more significant were the shifts in tonality. This was evident in the mood of the rioters themselves. Intermixed with mass psychology, hell-raising, and looting for profit in the 1960's was a mood of anger, even righteous indignation, a tone missing from the more recent events. It was evident in the publicly expressed responses to the rioters who were denounced as "animals" and "scum," deserving to be shot, or at least penned. The rioters of the sixties were viewed with hostility and fear to be sure, but any comdemnatory view was substantially mitigated by two countervailing attitudes held by many whites, which are no longer prevalent. First, many whites did feel some sense of guilt and/or responsibility for the plight of blacks in the United States. This attitude produced a certain breast-beating and a search for an understanding and explanation of the rioting. Secondly, and related to the former, was an expressed desire to discover *and* remediate the causes of these urban explosions. This was exemplified nationally in the Kerner Commission and the antipoverty programs. After the recent outburst, the continued, dismal socioeconomic fate of many urban blacks was advanced as a plausible causal explanation, but fewer people seemed willing to accept such reasoning in 1977 than in 1967. While the statistics advanced were indeed deplorable, they were now perceived as excuses that had become tired and lame. As for remedies, they seemed more distant now than a decade ago.

Given the events of July 13-14, 1977, what might we reasonably suggest will be their effects? Persons of a some-

what sanguine nature may foresee a reawakening of awareness of and commitment to the problems and needs of urban
America, which only coincidentally were illustrated in New
York City that night. Given the same circumstances, might
not a similar reaction occur in Chicago or Atlanta or Los
Angeles? Perchance, it might be recognized that the problems
are not specific to New York City but pervade urban America.
Such hopeful persons might also anticipate that the "respectable elements" of the local community itself will band together
with a new mood of purpose and resolve to save their places of
residence and business. All is possible, but I would not wait
breathlessly for such eventualities.

Most definitely the rioting was an occurrence that New
York City could ill afford. It may not constitute the death knell
of the city, but it certainly made New York City a less
attractive place in which to live and do business, and tarnished
further a reputation already besmirched by the city's fiscal
teeter-tottering. How many such tremors can the city survive?
Newark still stands, as will New York City a decade hence, yet
Newark is an economically poorer city now than it was at the
time of its riot. Many non-riot-related factors, of course, have
contributed to Newark's present state, but the riots left their
own real physical and psychological scars.

Moreover, the wanton destruction of property, businesses,
and buildings is bound to leave the black sections of Brooklyn
even more impoverished than they already are. Whatever
comments might be offered about their high prices, shoddy
merchandise, and excessive profits, the businesses looted and/
or burned out did provide essential services and some jobs to
the people of the community. Some will undoubtedly rise from
the ashes, but many owners will decide that the effort is no
longer worth the cost and anxiety. To the extent that this
latter perspective prevails, these sections will become more
deprived and less habitable. Many of the areas devastated in
Newark or Detroit or Washington, D.C. during the ghetto
explosions of the sixties, remain devastated today. May not
this be the fate of Utica Avenue and Broadway and other
streets in Brooklyn?

Finally, it may be argued that the cause of black advancement has been dealt a severe blow, at least for the moment. The gap between lip service to civil rights and meaningful social and economic actions has previously been noted, but it seems inevitable that the happenings of that night will offer legitimacy to those racist views that lie so close to the surface, even in the best of times. They will confirm the bigotted in their attitudes; they will move the indifferent away from disinterest and toward hostility; they will shake the resolve and commitment of those who still espouse the cause of black civil and economic rights.

# Index